Antebellum Culture

BY CARL BODE

Southern Illinois University Press
Carbondale and Edwardsville

Feffer & Simons, Inc.
London and Amsterdam

COPYRIGHT © 1959 by Carl Bode under the title *The Anatomy of American Popular Culture, 1840-1861*
Reprinted by arrangement with Carl Bode
Arcturus Books edition November 1970
This edition printed by offset lithography in the United States of America
ISBN 0-8093-0461-9

Preface to this Edition

In the last few years there has been a livelier interest in popular culture than ever before. The *Journal of Popular Culture* has appeared, along with a national association. Today's culture has attracted all sorts of study, ranging from the feverishly journalistic to the soberly statistical. But little has been done, certainly little in book form, about our earlier culture, especially the culture of the nineteenth century. Nothing has emerged that seems even remotely similar to *The Anatomy of American Popular Culture 1840–1861* which I published a decade ago. Having seen the book go through two editions, I thought this might be a good time to put it in paperback.

I have always considered its title clumsy though exact. The book does anatomize the culture. That is, it treats the fine arts one by one, and then the most popular kinds of works in print. In a sense the book is a piece of analysis rather than synthesis; the result, I hope, is a panorama. The new title, *Antebellum Culture*, has the virtue of brevity and at the same time is literally correct. By "antebellum" I mean simply "before the Civil War." I am concerned with the whole country, not the South alone nor even principally. And, since no one knows how far back "antebellum" reaches, I take the liberty of narrowing it to the two decades prior to the war. They seem to me an organic unit in time.

I want to correct some minor errors for this edition. On page xxi and in an illustration following page 104, "Curtis'" should read "Mitchell's." On page 290 "Quill, Charles" should be noted as the pseudonym of James W. Alexander. There are doubtless other slips that I have missed. In addition, time has occasionally altered circumstance, and so some statements I set down ten years ago are no longer true. For instance, the *Saturday Evening Post* is gone. For instance, the Smithsonian Institution, after exiling Greenough's statue of Washington for decades in a dusty alcove, now displays it for all to see before a blue backcloth. For instance, Grandma Moses is dead. However, I suspect that the reader knows these things too and will be charitable as he reads.

Anyway, in going over the book for minor errors, I have felt again the richness, the color, and the spirit of an era which is to me the most attractive in our cultural history. I hope the reader feels it too.

CARL BODE

University of Maryland
March 23, 1970

꙳꙳ The ground is so fertile that questionless it is capable of producing any grain, fruits, or seeds you will sow or plant. . . . It may not be to that perfection of delicacy because the summer is not so hot and the winter is more cold in those parts we have yet tried . . . than we find in the same height in Europe or Asia. Yet I made a garden upon the top of a rocky isle . . . that grew so well it served us for salads in June and July.

Captain John Smith, *The General History of Virginia, New England, and the Summer Isles* (1624)

An Aside to the Reader

The People's Choice
Culture—that interesting, ambiguous thing—has in recent years been the subject of at least two different kinds of books. One, written by the anthropologist in his Samoan hut, has interpreted it as the sum total of man's learned activities. Here the best-known works are perhaps those of Mead, Kluckhohn, and Benedict. The other kind of book has treated culture as the product of the printed page. In this field, broadly literary, Louis B. Wright's *Middle-Class Culture in Elizabethan England* is the great exemplar.

My own definition lies, at times a little uneasily, between the anthropologist's and the literary historian's, as my aims in this book will show. Those aims are threefold. To paint, in panoramic fashion, a picture of our popular fine arts of the 1840's and 1850's in all their unexpected richness. To try with the eyes of that time to search out, assemble, and display the most prominent varieties of works in print. And to suggest how the American character may have revealed itself through its cultural preferences.

Mass culture rather than high culture has been my concern; and popularity has been my touchstone. Thoreau's *Walden*, published during the years of this study, is my favorite classic. Yet I have ignored it because it had no popular importance at all before the Civil War. This is a book on the people's choice.

❧❧ The Pivotal Period: 1840–1861

It might almost be said that the United States was a simple nation culturally when the 'forties began and a complex one when the 'fifties ended. This was a time of maturing, a time when our culture first assumed its modern shape. The advent of the industrial revolution in the publishing business occurred simultaneously with the advent of popular literacy. The people and the printed word came together. Though the emergence of art was less dramatic the noted lecturer George W. Bethune could write—with truth—in 1852, "Especially within the last ten years, large advances have been made and Art has fairly begun to flourish among us." This was a time, it should be added, of rising prosperity, stopped only briefly by the panic of 1857; this was a time when culture could be expected to grow. To the growing culture of these two decades the onset of the Civil War put a pause and marked the end of the period covered in this book.

❧❧ Act of Faith

The problems involved in determining the nature of the popular book or the popular picture, though stimulating, are apt to be difficult. But they are nothing compared to the problem of inferring American character from cultural preferences. In our sense, character is far more perplexing than culture. Consequently, it might be well, if rather unorthodox, to announce the conclusions about character now, and then to ask the reader to hold them in mind as he goes along, so that he can understand more clearly the evidence for them. Because this book is no murder mystery with a gory riddle to be answered only at the end, no novel with a crashing climax in the last chapter, it should not be improper to give our conclusions first.

Their usefulness, moreover, can be justified, though only with the understanding that the prime concern of the book is with culture rather than character, and culture for its own sake. What this usefulness is, we may at this point profitably remind ourselves.

Today Americans travel abroad more than they ever did before. The interest of others in us is universal though not always kindly. The moment an American steps onto the dock at Amsterdam or the landing field in New Delhi, he is assumed to be an expert on his country. One of the key questions he will be asked has many different guises but can be stated simply enough: What are Americans like? If he were at home, he might throw up his hands in frustration at the complexity of the question. Americans in Vermont are somewhat different from Americans in Mississippi, or Iowa, or Oregon. Rich Americans are not quite the same as poor Americans. Rural Americans are different from urban Americans. Young Americans are different from old Americans. And so on. Or, focusing his attention only on our likenesses, he might smile at the simplicity of the question. Mass media of communication and entertainment have made us more and more nearly uniform in our traits. Already—he might say flatly—we dress alike, talk alike, think alike.

Such are the difficulties. Yet nearly every American will admit that it is wise for his nation to try to understand itself. We need to know what we are, not only to explain ourselves to other nations, other cultures, but also (and this is more significant) to deal effectively with ourselves. "Know thyself" is a cliché we inherited from the ancient Greeks but it still expresses a badly needed imperative.

Two ways of knowing can be particularly worthwhile. One is to compare our present civilization with that of other countries. The other is to study our past civilization in order to compare it with our present. That is what we shall do in this book, moving back a century and more to gain a choice vantage point. From there we shall be able to see certain traits in the American character of that time, traits well evidenced in the flourishing cultural interests of the twenty years before the Civil War. Then we can draw our personal comparisons at leisure.

We shall be able to make out four principal complexes (or clusters) of qualities in that period. Though their outlines are going to be hazy, and may even shift from time to time, we shall be able to discern them nevertheless. Some of them are still here today, and they may seem obvious. But others have altered, often quietly enough. If we mention the family circle, for instance, it is partly because that circle is now apt to be broken up. Here are the complexes, all of them important, in ascending order.

The first will have patriotism at its center. Its everyday symbol will be the flag officially but the American eagle will prove to have a wider cultural appeal—a lifelike object has more artistic personality than a piece of bunting, no matter how sublime its associations. The greatest emotional symbol, however, will be the image of George Washington. We who live in a time of competing heroes, Lincoln above all, cannot realize how completely the figure of Washington dominated the ante-bellum decades. History, biography, belles lettres, drama, and the arts all celebrated him. It would need no psychologizing by Sigmund Freud to show that he fulfilled the father image. The greatest ceremony will be the Fourth of July. It signalized the beginning of national selfhood, the rejection of the "mother country," the deliverance from the womb. And it is important to note that the freeing was made possible, the nation felt, through the help of the father, Washington. This was good history if poor psychology.

Besides patriotism we shall discover in the first complex both chauvinism and its tenacious opposite, the quiet conviction that Europe still maintained a better culture than our own. This conviction would show itself in, for example, the enormous vogue of English novels and would be based on much more than their low price. It would show itself in the enthusiasm a German painting could often evoke over a comparable American one. It would show itself in a clinging to European models in architecture and the corresponding failure of a native architecture to emerge. Chauvinism, on the other hand, would stoutly assert that anything American was better than anything foreign. As Major Pawkins of

Pennsylvania said grandly to Martin Chuzzlewit, fresh from London, "You will see the sun shine *here*."

The second complex of qualities will have aggressiveness as its core. Modern psychologists are modifying the doctrines of Freud by putting more emphasis on aggressiveness instead of sex in the psyche. But even if aggressiveness is considered primary and universal, it cannot be denied that ante-bellum America—with its boundless economic and social opportunities—gave it a scope it had nowhere else. Its most direct manifestation, culturally, will be the literature of success. It will be too early for the Horatio Alger book but the manual of success will be found in many forms, with the *Young Man's Guide* as the most frequent.

Along with aggressiveness in this complex we shall find materialism—not unexpectedly—and also optimism and restlessness. Material things will seldom be omitted from the rewards of virtue in the sentimental novel and never in the manuals of success. The optimism will prove to be both personal and cosmic. Sanctioned by the growth of economic abundance and by a "Manifest Destiny" it will remain unchecked by the panics of 1837 and 1857, and by the gradual approach of the Civil War. In its purest form it will be revealed in the lyceum lectures and essays of Ralph Waldo Emerson. His positive, Transcendental gospel will challenge his hearers, inspiring many of them to face life with a bolder faith than ever before. The restlessness remarked by a number of visitors from abroad will show most clearly in the vogue for travel books. Though a man will not always be able to steam down the Mississippi or up the Rhine, he will certainly be able to read about it. The dashing Bayard Taylor will become the prince of travel writers but he will have many others in his court.

The third complex will be basically religious. Its main cultural reflection will be the Bible's supremacy as the most popular of all books. Under the zealous leadership of the American Bible Society efforts will continue to place a Bible in every home. The American Tract Society will prove equally active. It will labor eagerly at the printing and distribution of its little religious leaflets and bound volumes of works of piety. It will publish all these so frequently and distribute them so lavishly that the total number of copies will run not to the thousands or even hundreds of thousands but to the millions. Religious music will thrive. A multitude of choirs and congregations will rise to sing the tuneful hymns of Lowell Mason and his school.

Several more manifestations of the religious complex will develop. The most immediate will be religiosity: excessive or affected religious feeling. Neopuritanism and humanitarianism will be the others. Religiosity, looking ostentatiously heavenward, will often be discerned. Domestic novels will have many a passage of unctuous meditation, many a pontifical speech. A fair share of the poems composed by the English Mrs. Hemans (highly popular in the United States) and practically all of those by the American Mrs. Sigourney will simply put piety into metrical form. Religiosity will appear in the arts also, in, for example, the ballads of Stephen Foster, the allegorical paintings of Thomas Cole, and the ecclesiastical associations of Gothic architecture (one of its greatest merits will be that it is "heaven-pointing"). The complementary themes of the death of the beloved and the afterlife will be favorites of the period; the Christian consolation, much sentimentalized as a rule, will exist in many aspects of our culture.

Puritanism will revive and then reëstablish itself under the guidance of the code of conduct fashioned by Queen Victoria. Its influence will be felt positively as well as negatively. On the negative side the most notable manifestations will be the dearth of lusty sexual sin in literature and of nudes in art. On the positive side there will be a system of ethics adapted to the most delicate-minded. Virtue will bloom in the soil of every genre.

Much humanitarianism will have religiousness as its source. The two decades before the war will prove to be one of the great reform periods in the United States. In sharp contrast to the cynical postwar era, this will be the heyday of crusades. They will go on for the insane, the poor, the disabled, for women's rights, for the ten-hour day for workmen, and above all for the abolition of Negro slavery. If we had to pick out any single example of a cultural expression of this crusading zeal, it would be Harriet Beecher Stowe's famous, and controversial, *Uncle Tom's Cabin*.

The final complex, and the most important and pervasive culturally, will have as its heart what, for want of a better word, must be called love. This will be an age of the softer emotions; they will provide an offset for our aggressiveness and materialism. When those softer emotions are indulged for their own sake, they will turn into a sentimentalism shedding its rather sickly glow in many a corner. One writer has, in fact, dubbed this period the Sentimental Years. There is going to be some feeling for nature but a great deal more for human relationships. The death of the beloved, mentioned earlier, will be the most sentimentalized of subjects. The dying child and the dying mother will be treated often in everything from chromos and melodramas to ballads. But love will also be shown in its happier forms. The affection of mother and child and, more rarely, of father and child will be described with glowing pen. And the family circle, one of the favorite images of the time, will symbolize the perfected gathering of all such love.

Love between the sexes, though entering with eyes properly downcast, will inevitably play a large role too. Usually it will be shown in its pure, conventional form. After a variety of mild misunderstandings, the breathless maiden will allow herself to be led to the altar by the manly man. Purity will be won by nobility, and the moment of the winning will be memorialized in picture after picture, scene after scene. At rare intervals sinful love will make a furtive appearance. No other novelist will paint its wickedness with such lurid colors as George Lippard, but there will be evidence that ante-bellum culture did not completely ignore the fact that sin existed. The physical side of sex will be dealt with gingerly, so that no lady need feel offended; yet it will manage to make itself felt in spite of the presence of neopuritanism.

Those, then, will be the major traits discernible in the ante-bellum American character. To see them clearly will be, we suggest again, to understand ourselves better today.

But the primary thing to see is the culture itself—surprisingly fertile, bounteous, and exuberant. And it awaits us.

Contents

AN ASIDE TO THE READER, ix

✄ ONE *The Public's Arts*

1   CURTAIN UP, 3
2   MELODY EN MASSE, 19
3   PILLARS, POINTS, AND BRACKETS, 38
4   WHATNOTS IN THE POINTED STYLE, 51
5   PAINT FOR THE PUBLIC EYE, 60
6   HARD LIGHT AND MELLOW MOOD, 80
7   MARBLE MEN AND BRAZEN LADIES, 92

✄ TWO *Interchapter*

8   THE SPREAD OF PRINT, 109

✄ THREE *Popular Print: 1*

9   MANUALS FOR ALL THINGS, 119
10   STEPS TO THE TEMPLE, 132
11   STRONG MEAT, 149
12   THE SCRIBBLING WOMEN, 169
13   THE SENTIMENTAL MUSE, 188
14   PERSON TO PERSON, 201

xvii

❧❧ FOUR *Popular Print: II*

15 FOREIGN PORTS AND EXOTIC PLACES, 221
16 THE STIRRING PAST, 236
17 THE RAMPANT PRESS, 250

❧❧ FIVE *Epilogue*

18 A TRIO FOR COLUMBIA, 269

A NOTE ON THE SOURCES, 277

ACKNOWLEDGMENTS, 283

INDEX, 285

Illustrations

Following page 40

Edwin Forrest caricatured as the hero in Bird's bombastic drama *Spartacus*.

"Old Kentucky Home, Life in the South" as painted by Eastman Johnson and celebrated in song by Stephen Foster.

Jenny Lind, the high points of her tour, and the text of the prize song by Bayard Taylor which she sang.

A home in the Gothic style from Downing's *The Architecture of Country Houses*.

The Italian style of dwelling as envisioned for Americans by Downing in *The Architecture of Country Houses*.

The architect in Thomas Cole's romantic "The Architect's Dream" thinks in terms of Greek, Gothic, and other foreign styles but not American.

Here among the whatnots and gilt the Milligan family in Saratoga Springs received their friends of the 1850's.

Following page 72

The annual lottery through which the American Art-Union distributed its store of paintings and sculpture.

The central, imposing element that Durand learned to paint is here found in "An Oak Tree."

Among the human-interest or genre paintings that made Mount famous was "The Long Story."

Bingham's hard-bitten citizens represent the recurring strain of realism in American painting.

"Shake Hands?" asks the roguish housewife in Lily Spencer's popular genre painting.

Greenough's "Washington" sits today in forgotten grandeur.

In this figurehead of the USB "Massachusetts" can be seen the strength and craftsmanship that American folk art sometimes achieved.

Powers' "The Greek Slave," undoubtedly the cynosure of more eyes than any other statue of its time.

The family circle with the father at its center and love on every side.

A skeleton exclaims about its construction in Alcott's manual of physiology *The House I Live in*.

In this American Tract Society leaflet the results of drunkenness are spelled out.

The first stirrings of love, when the heroine of *The Wide, Wide World* meets the brother of her best friend.

The urgings of lust as limned for Lippard's sensational *The Quaker City*.

The title page of Mrs. Stowe's dynamic volume.

Mrs. Sigourney in her pensive primness.

Following page 104

"Hiawatha's Departure" in Longfellow's phenomenally popular poem.

The essayist and art critic Henry Tuckerman.

xx

Ik Marvel muses by his fire in Curtis' book of sentimental essays *Reveries of a Bachelor*.

The dashing traveler Bayard Taylor in the costume that caused ladies to swoon.

American journalism flourishes in Boston.

The American female, in ideal form, as popularized by *Godey's* to its great profit.

The most famous American example of that favorite subject in ante-bellum literature and art, the death of a little girl.

Part One

THE PUBLIC'S ARTS

1
Curtain up

    ✻   *Beauseant.* Beloved, beautiful Pauline! fly with me—my carriage waits without—I will bear you to a home more meet for your reception. Wealth, luxury, station—all shall yet be yours. I forget your past disdain—I remember only your beauty, and my unconquerable love!

    Pauline. Sir, leave this house—it is humble: but a husband's roof, however lowly, is, in the eyes of God and man, the temple of a wife's honor! Know that I would rather starve. . . . Go!

Edward Lytton Bulwer, *The Lady of Lyons* (American edition, 1844)

If the career of any one man covered the range of American drama during the two decades before the Civil War, it was that of cocky Harry Watkins. In 1845, while still a youth, he started in New Orleans at the very bottom, where he stayed longer than he wanted. Yet when on tour in Galveston, for instance, during

3

this period, he noted his duties cheerfully enough in his diary: "Posted bills before breakfast—spent the morning sweeping out the House, cleaning lamps, and so on. . . . 7 P.M., opened doors, lit up the House, got a person to stay in the box office, hired music to play—all in fine style—and three good pieces to perform." He worked himself up slowly, diligently, until by 1860 he had become a manager (though not always a good one), a star (though with luster a trifle faint), and even a playwright (though not very original).

During the two decades before the war he toured practically everywhere that a theater could be found or improvised. The record of his wanderings, as given in *One Man in His Time*, reveals how our drama spread. It extended itself in forays throughout the nation. New Orleans, Mobile, Louisville, Cincinnati, Baltimore, Philadelphia, Macon, Columbus (Georgia), Montgomery, Newark, St. Louis, Boston, Albany, and New York—of course, New York: these were some of the places, in different parts of the country, that Watkins played.

This is not to say that because theatrical companies played there and elsewhere, they fared well. If one can judge from the journal, the opposite proved more nearly true. Watkins' pages contain many a reference to sparse audiences and meager receipts. "The house was not very good, as might be expected in Louisville, which is one of the worst theatrical towns in the country," he writes crossly at one point. When he is in the South he is apt to blame its one-crop economy: "These small towns pay about once in three years and then only when cotton brings a good price." When he is in the North he blames assorted culprits, ranging from bad weather to competing attractions as diverse as Jenny Lind and a man-monkey.

Nevertheless, the drama managed to stay alive in spite of local reverses. Harry Watkins' own fortunes improved in the long run partly because of better times and partly because he advanced in the profession. At the outset he could report ironically of himself and two others in the company, "Had supper this evening, the finest meal for some time as we have been living on dry bread for a week." When his first turn at a "benefit" came—the device by which on a given evening an actor received half the proceeds—the ticket window took in only $2. "Two men in the boxes, one boy in the pit, and a Nigger woman in the gallery," Watkins complains in his diary that night. Ordinarily the companies he was in broke even, though managers hoped for better than that. By the middle of 1847 we can see clear signs of progress, for he was then offered $12 a week to play supporting roles with a troupe in Boston. In Baltimore the stipend grew to $16. Several years later he was earning considerably more. But then he aspired to be a manager, took his company on a disastrous southern tour, and learned that he too could lose money, as well as make it, with disconcerting swiftness. By 1860, notwithstanding, he had also discovered that managing could be profitable under the right conditions. He hired a charming blonde as his leading lady, took the best male roles himself, and now could boast in his diary, "Our engagement was more successful than anybody anticipated, our income was considerably more than our outlay." He never became a renowned tragedian like Edwin Forrest, earning $40,000 a year; but he made his way.

The plays Harry Watkins taught himself to write enjoyed their share of success also. He gained his first recognition in 1850 through winning the award of $1,000 offered by a New York theater manager for the best native American drama. Watkins submitted *Nature's Nobleman, the Mechanic; or The Ship's Carpenter of New York*. With its proletarian horseplay and melodrama it was his bid for the Bowery audience. And it was spiced with Northern patriotism. The pit cheered when the hero, Herman Gray, pointed to the Stars and Stripes and exclaimed, "Our country's flag! May that traitor stand accursed who from the heavenly blue of its bright firmament would seek to blot a single star or sunder that great eternal chain forged by godlike patriots that binds them into one harmonious whole." In the opening engagement Watkins himself played the lead—and recorded his success.

Once launched as a dramatist, Watkins discovered that he could produce two kinds of plays with a reasonable chance of a good

5

reception. Both represented characteristic forms of current popular drama. The first was the patriotic play based on American history. *The Pioneer Patriot*, for example, dealt with the Revolutionary War. Complete with a Tory spy and a villainous Black, it had repeated runs not only in New York but in other parts of the country. From the day it opened at Barnum's Museum theater, Watkins congratulated himself. "*Pioneer Patriot* all last week to splendid houses. Managers and actors have suddenly thrown off their gloomy looks and are smiling. . . . Everything has been fortunate since we opened with this piece. . . . Barnum . . . is full of enthusiasm." So went typical entries in his journal.

The other kind of play was sentimental melodrama. Here Watkins dispensed entirely with inventing his own plots and relied instead on the feverish, stagy genius of the leading woman novelist of the 'fifties, Mrs. E. D. E. N. Southworth. Near the end of the decade she was grinding out one novel after another for a New York weekly called the *Ledger*, which was owned by the first of the mass-minded publishers, Robert Bonner. Watkins gained Mrs. Southworth's and Bonner's permission to adapt several of these serialized novels; and the closing pages of the diary show that he transformed her *The Bride of an Evening*, complete with its insinuating title, into an acting drama in eight torrid days. Mrs. Southworth in person came to see it shortly after the opening in March 1858. Watkins reported her "highly pleased."

Though Harry Watkins' pen proved as mighty as his actor's sword (one time when the handle broke, he killed the enemy by holding the blade itself), he did not have the good fortune to write the most popular plays of his time. He acted in them, however, and his diary includes references to four out of the five "dramatic best sellers" that best represent this period.

The first was the crudest of melodramas, William Henry Smith's *The Drunkard*. The next was a Britisher's delightful play, Sir Edward Lytton Bulwer's *The Lady of Lyons*. The third was the finest—almost the only—social satire of the middle of the century, Anna Cora Mowatt's *Fashion*. The fourth was a rugged verse tragedy by a Philadelphia author, Dr. R. M. Bird's *The*

Gladiator. These plays, except for *The Drunkard*, which was re-vived in recent years as the butt of self-conscious boos and hisses, have long since passed from the view of the theater-going public. Not so for the fifth "best seller," which was actually a group of plays, the major works of Shakespeare. His splendid tragedies were as much in demand a century ago as today. *Lear, Hamlet, Othello,* and *Macbeth* proved the greatest tragic favorites, with the bloody *Richard III* ranking as the top historical play.

The Drunkard opened during the winter of 1844, in Boston. The published version showed on its cover the figure of Shake-speare smiling modestly and about to be crowned. The preface too made no small claims for the piece. It was "by all acknowl-edged to be the most successful play ever acted in Boston."

This was, as the title page said, "A Moral Domestic Drama." Within its five emotional acts it gathered nearly all of the clichés that the people cherished, and added a moral purpose: to paint the evils of drink. The classic characters and plot situations of folk melodrama as formulated in *The Drunkard* are so numerous that only a few can be given here. The character types include the wicked hypocrite, Lawyer Cribbs; the reckless but basically good young hero, Edward Middleton; the pure, long-suffering heroine, Mary Wilson; the meddling old maid, Miss Spindle; the angelic child, Julia Middleton; and the rich *deus ex machina*, Mr. Arden Rencelaw.

The plot in which the situations are imbedded is likewise classic in its way. Out of vengefulness, Lawyer Cribbs tries to have Mary and her widowed mother evicted from their rural cottage. Mid-dleton, who has inherited the mortgage, upsets Cribbs's plan and marries the girl. They are happy at first and have a child, Julia. Soon, however, Edward is lured into becoming a drunkard and wastrel. After various unsuccessful machinations by Cribbs, Ed-ward is regenerated through the interest of Mr. Rencelaw, Cribbs is foiled and shown to be a criminal, and all ends well for the virtuous.

From its beginning the play is filled with cultural implications. The very first scene, that of the cottage, is described as containing such standard requisites of ante-bellum culture as paintings, flowers, embroidery, and a copy of the Bible. Furthermore, the praise of pastoral simplicity, the detailed depiction of tender love between mother and daughter, and Edward's angry rejection of Cribbs's hint that he seduce Mary are all, in their various ways, parts of the American cultural stereotype appearing in the play.

The first theatrical set piece in *The Drunkard* comes when Edward, having been accosted by Cribbs in the woods with his hint about Mary, turns on the leering villain with:

"Leave me, old man, begone; your hot lascivious breath cannot mingle with the sweet odor of these essenced wild flowers. Your raven-voice will not harmonize with the warblings of these heavenly songsters, pouring forth their praises to that Almighty power who looks with horror on your brutal crime."

And Mary, who has overheard, says gratefully to Edward:

"The blessings of the widow and fatherless be upon thee; may they accompany thy voice to Heaven's tribunal, not to cry for vengeance but plead for pardon on this wretched man."

At this Christian plea Cribbs flees, muttering of revenge. He leaves the stage clear for an elaborately Victorian love scene between Middleton and Mary. It reaches its climax with Edward's ringing affirmation that womanly virtue rather than beauty is what holds "captive the hearts of men."

The next and contrasting scene features the sort of humor that tickled a thigh-slapping American audience. Miss Spindle has just told a forthright yokel named William that he is too shy, and he ripostes with "It's a failing I've got, Miss Spindle. I'm so modest I always go to bed without a candle."

Once Mary and Edward are to wed, Cribbs turns to the audience and promises grimly, "I shall see them begging for their bread yet. The wife on her bended knees to me, praying for a morsel of food for her starving children,—it will be revenge, revenge!" And he nearly succeeds, for it is at this time that Edward begins his swift change into a drunkard. Then Cribbs, seeking out Mary for his own lustful purposes, is repulsed by her. This gives him the chance to make a signal contribution to America's stock

8

sayings: "Nay, then, proud beauty, you shall know my power."

The great scene for Edward occurs at the beginning of Act IV. There he has delirium tremens, and it was a poor player who could not make women shiver and children squeal. Harry Watkins often took the role. He did it first in March 1849 and breathlessly told his diary how it went.

My greatest hope was to get through respectably—applause I did not dream of—I felt nervous—I knew that many in the audience had seen the play and comparisons, I felt, would be made. I heard my cue—went on—no reception—the audience did not expect much and were determined to show it. My first speech received a little applause—my exit a little more—in every scene the applause increased as though the audience were waking from a sleep. At the end of the second act applause grew louder—in the third *I had the audience with me*. The first scene of the fourth act I was discovered lying in the street, a miserable wretch with the delirium tremens. The scene progressed until, through my ravings, I fell upon the stage in convulsions. *Then* —they shouted! At the fall of the curtain, I was called out, received *nine* cheers and made a speech.

The rest of the play is devoted to belaboring liquor and taverns and to winding up the plot. Cribbs has the grace to stay a villain to the end. When Rencelaw suggests, "Repentance may yet avail you?" Cribbs answers stoically, "Nothing. I have lived a villain—a villain let me die."

The Drunkard concludes with a thoroughly appropriate cultural tableau. The scene is the interior of the cottage again, with Edward at the music stand, Julia seated on her little stool, and Mary sewing at the work table. Another table nearby has the Bible on it. Now "Edward plays on flute symphony to *Home, Sweet Home*. Julia sings first verse. Flute solo accompaniment. The burthen is then taken up by chorus of villagers behind.

Orchestral accompaniments, etc. . . . Air repeated slowly. Julia kneels to Edward, who is at table, R. H. seated in prayer. Edward's hand on Bible, and pointing up. Mary standing leaning upon his chair. . . . Music till curtain falls. Picture."

Another of Harry Watkins' favorite roles was that of Claude Melnotte in Bulwer's *The Lady of Lyons*. It was no wonder, for both the part and the play proved an actor's treat.

Set in the post-Revolutionary France of the Directory, it showed that love too should be democratic—a lesson American audiences applauded. Claude, the gifted, self-educated son of a gardener, falls deeply in love with the daughter of a rich Lyons merchant, M. Deschappelles. But Pauline scorns his modest attentions though she also rejects the wealthy and aristocratic M. Beauseant, as well as Beauseant's friend M. Glavis. In their thirst for revenge Beauseant and Glavis seek out Claude. They persuade him to court Pauline in the guise of the "Prince of Como." Claude is successful; the wedding actually takes place. Then, however, his true goodness emerges. He brings her to his mother's cottage, refuses his marriage rights, and returns her untouched the next day to her anxious parents. In expiation for deceiving Pauline, he decides to enlist in the army and shed his blood for France. Two and a half years go by. Now, just when Pauline is about to marry Beauseant to save her father from bankruptcy, Claude returns, a colonel and well-to-do. He tears up the marriage contract with Beauseant, Pauline rushes into his arms, and the play ends with a "picture" of Claude in the center of the stage with Pauline at his one side and her relieved parents at the other.

The play mingles comedy, sentiment, and republicanism. Pauline's mother, a pompous, bustling bourgeoise, holds forth as the leading comic. Her normal reaction to the situations Bulwer sets her in is apoplectic, but at times she is capable of a kind of eighteenth-century wit. For instance, when Pauline has refused Beauseant at the beginning of the play, her mother remarks, "How forward these men are!—I think, child, we kept up our dignity. Any girl, however inexperienced, knows how to accept an offer, but it requires a vast deal of address to refuse one with proper condescension and disdain. I used to practice it at school with the dancing-master!"

Mme Deschappelles' cousin, Colonel Damas, plays the role of the bluff, sensible soldier whose function is to act as an offset to her pretentiousness. He also can give comic relief at a highly sentimental moment. When in Act IV a forgiving Pauline cries out, "Claude, take me; thou canst not give me wealth, titles, station—but thou canst give me a true heart. I will work for thee, tend thee, bear with thee, and never, never shall these lips reproach thee for the past," Damas blurts "I'll be hanged if I am not going to blubber!"

The best of the high comedy comes a little earlier when Pauline, by this time really in love with Melnotte, does not want him to restore her to her parents. This is the time-hallowed dramatic reversal, with the original attitudes of the hero and heroine neatly switched. Pauline says meekly, "You are my husband now, and I have sworn to—to love you, sir." Melnotte answers in all his revived nobility of virtue, "That was under a false belief, madam; heaven and the laws will release you from your vow." At which Pauline sighs to the audience in fond exasperation, "He will drive me mad!"

The themes about which the play's sentiment is wound are not new. Love versus pride is the chief one. Pauline's vain notions get her into trouble; when she subdues them true love becomes hers. Love versus duty is the other important theme. Its high point comes in the last act when Pauline is ready to cancel her marriage to Melnotte and marry Beauseant instead for only one reason, to save her father from financial ruin. All her sobbing done, she says pathetically to her father, "*Now*, call the bride-groom—you see I am prepared—no tears—all calm; But, father [and then came one of her best lines], *talk no more of love!*" Five minutes later, however, Claude enters from the wars to rescue his Pauline.

The republicanism in *The Lady of Lyons* appears in speech after speech. In fact, it represents the basic attitude of the play, that true merit deserves far greater regard than either wealth or noble birth. At the same time audiences, even American ones, were doubtless pleased that humble merit—in the person of Claude—ended by acquiring wealth, honor, and a military title. They probably agreed with Mme Deschappelles, who cheered herself in the final scene with "A colonel and a hero! Well, that's something! He's wondrously improved!"

Republicanism likewise contributed much to the popular success of Mrs. Anna Mowatt's clever comedy *Fashion*. It opened in 1845, the year after *The Drunkard*. Its pretty, talented author turned out to be one of the few women in the American theatrical world who started out at the top and remained there. Her first appearance on the stage (also in 1845) was in a starring role. She played Pauline in *The Lady of Lyons* and played it so well that her fellow actors even applauded her at rehearsal. She managed, in addition, to charm that caustic critic Harry Watkins. He began by calling her mediocre; but after watching her for several years and acting in the same company with her, he said, "It is a pleasure to play with her; a kinder, more agreeable lady I never met with." She enjoyed an English as well as an American triumph, retiring when the Civil War came.

The message in *Fashion* is that foreigners are frauds and wealthy Americans are fools to copy them. Mrs. Tiffany is the rich New Yorker who sets current modes under the influence of her French maid Millinette. As Millinette explains to another servant, "I teach Madame *les modes de Paris*, and Madame set de fashion for all New York." Mrs. Tiffany is also swayed by the French valet who calls himself Count Jolimaitre. She does her best to arrange a marriage between him and her pretty daughter Seraphina. Seraphina herself is taken in; she plans to elope with the count, bringing him her jewels. Her father, a crusty merchant, is not quite so gullible. However, he opposes the marriage to the count for the wrong reason—he wants his daughter to marry his confidential clerk, the evil Snobson, who threatens to expose his forging of endorsements.

Old Mr. Trueman, a farmer from Cattaraugus County and well named, is the person who sets things straight. His blunt common sense sees through European imposture. He exposes the count and copes with native rascality, in the form of Snobson, as well. And his is the last and patriotic word: "We *have* kings, princes, and nobles in abundance—of *Nature's stamp*, if not of Fashion's,—we have honest men, warm hearted and brave, and we have women—gentle, fair, and true, to whom no *title* could add *nobility*."

Supplementing the republicanism, though more diffuse, is a didactic purpose. Mrs. Mowatt showed herself sensitive to that censure of the stage which was an inheritance from puritanism; whenever she could she stressed the morality of drama. In *Fashion* she exalted virtue and humbled vice, although she did it with comic overtones. As she said in her *Autobiography*, "If the acting of a play has been instrumental in causing 'joy among the angels of heaven over one sinner that repenteth,' what stronger proof can there be that the theater is a useful institution?"

In a way the story of *The Gladiator* begins and ends with Edwin Forrest. Probably the greatest tragedian of his time, he was (unlike Harry Watkins, who carped at him) an immediate success. Bull-necked, muscular, handsome, he brought an enormous vitality to his acting. He found from the outset that he had little to fear from native competition. But foreign competition— and that meant English in particular—proved formidable. It was a competition involving not only actors but managers, playwrights, and critics. The English stage had demonstrated its strength in America for generations. English plays, especially those of Shakespeare, were a staple of the American theater; English stars were often given a rousing American welcome; English managers worked their way into the American system; and the critics, even if American, who favored English plays and players constituted an impressive bloc.

Forrest faced this difficult problem intelligently. He soon decided that there was only one satisfactory answer, the establishment of what he called "an American National Drama." The first step was to encourage the writing of actable plays by native playwrights. He began offering prizes for such plays in 1828 when he himself was only twenty-two years of age. And in 1831 his prize of $1,000 was won by the versatile Philadelphia physician, Dr. R. M. Bird, with *The Gladiator*.

Several more prizes were offered and won in later years, but Forrest realized as soon as he read the manuscript that *The Gladiator* was precisely the play for his strenuous talents. It is Bird's recasting of the story of Spartacus and the revolt of the slaves. Crammed with action (one clash follows another), rich in spectacle (the pageantry of ancient Rome), and overflowing with oratorical blank verse (several passages becoming permanent favorites of Forrest and his public), *The Gladiator* created a sensation. A skillful artist, Bird knew quite well what he was doing. Foust's *Life* of Bird quotes him on his theory of drama. "The true secret of effect consists in having everything . . . epigrammatic or climacteric, the story rising to rapidity and closing with power; the chief characters increasing in passion and energy; the events growing in interest, the scenes and acts each accumulating power above their precursors; the strength of a speech augmenting at its close, and the important characters dismissed at each exit with some sort of point and emphasis."

Almost equally important with the play's careful construction was its congenial theme. The rebellion of the oppressed against the tyrant could not help appealing to patriotic American hearts. More surprisingly, part of *The Gladiator*'s popularity came from its being an antislavery play. The South failed to take offense, and the North applauded the abolitionist sentiment smoldering in the author's blank verse.

Bird attended the first Philadelphia performance, at the Arch Street theater, and afterward wrote in his diary, "The jam of visitors was tremendous; hundreds retiring without being able to get seats or stands." He was able to add appreciatively in summing up the situation, "An American feeling was beginning to show itself in the theatrical matters. The managers of the Arch St. theater were Americans, all the chief performers were Americans, and the play was written by an American."

Forrest continued to play Spartacus for years, giving the role hundreds of performances. No new drama in the 'forties or 'fifties

provided quite the same scope, though his repertory shifted somewhat from time to time. Certain speeches, even certain words, in
the piece became so well known that the audiences waited to hear
Forrest deliver them. When, for example, Spartacus' brother reports that the Romans have crucified every captured gladiator,
Spartacus vows to take a terrible revenge. "I swear," he promises,
"For this to make Rome howl"; and when Forrest uttered the
word "howl" in his magnificent, crescendoing voice even wig-
gling youngsters were impressed. Among his long speeches,
audiences knew best the one in which he answered the Roman
envoy's haughty "Men do not war on women" with:

> Men do not war on women! Look you:
> One day I clomb upon the ridgy top
> Of the cloud-piercing Haemus, where, among
> The eagles and the thunders, from that height,
> I look'd upon the world—or, far as where,
> Wrestling with storms, the gloomy Euxine chafed
> On his recoiling shores; and where dim Adria
> In her blue bosom quenched the fiery sphere.
> Between those surges lay a land, might once
> Have served for paradise, but Rome had made it
> A Tartarus.—In my green youth I look'd
> From the same frosty peak, where now I stood,
> And then beheld the glory of those lands,
> Where peace was tinkling on the shepherd's bell
> And singing with the reapers;
> Since that glad day, Rome's conquerors had past
> With withering armies there, and all was changed:
> Peace had departed; howling war was there,
> Cheered on by Roman hunters: then, methought,
> Even as I looked upon the altered scene,
> Groans echoed through the valleys, through which ran
> Rivers of blood, like smoking Phlegethons;
> Fires flashed from burning villages, and famine
> Shriek'd in the empty cornfields. Women and children,
> Robb'd of their sires and husbands, left to starve—

These were the dwellers of the land!—Say'st thou
Rome wars not then on women?

Such sentiments Forrest spoke burningly. His delivery as well
as his whole style of acting had the stamp of excess rather than
restraint. But it developed organically from his own natural
endowment. Here is how his biographer, W. R. Alger, once
described his entrance as Spartacus. "As he stepped upon the stage
in his naked fighting trim, his muscular coating unified all over
him and quivering with vital power, his skin polished by exercise
and friction to a smooth and marble hardness, conscious of his
enormous potency, fearless of anything on the earth, proudly
aware of the impression he knew his mere appearance, backed
by his fame, would make on the audience who impatiently
awaited him,—he used to stand and receive the long, tumultuous
cheering that greeted him, as immovable as a planted statue of
Hercules."

The school of acting Forrest developed was one of heightened
(or according to his critics, exaggerated) naturalism. First of all,
he copied life. Before he played old men to his satisfaction, he
followed them on the street, noting their gait, their gestures, and
their other movements. When he prepared to play a madman, he
went to an asylum to observe the insane. Then, infusing the results of his scrutiny with his exceptional vigor, he would proceed
to tear a passion to tatters but tear it realistically. He set the
American tone, incidentally, and probably influenced more actors
than any other tragedian of his time including his detested English rival, the polished William Macready.

During the first part of the nineteenth century the popularity
of Shakespeare burgeoned until it overshadowed everything.
True, the native drama grew up and also made a handsome place
for itself. Forrest, in the final week of his unusually successful
and extended New York run of 1852, had his printed programs
decorated with the American flag, thereby reminding everyone
of the good fight he had captained. Up to the Civil War, Dr.
Bird's Spartacus of course remained a favorite role for him, and

his curtain speeches on behalf of native drama continued to re-sound. Nevertheless, when it came to Shakespeare, Forrest simply said, "I hold that next to God, Shakespeare comprehended the mind of man." And American audiences apparently agreed.

Of all Shakespearean heroes, Forrest loved Lear the best. He worked on his conception of the titanic king during most of his life. "I have studied the part," he said, "in the closet, in the street, on the stage, in lunatic asylums all over the world." As he grew older and the Civil War neared, audiences found his demon-strative acting rather heavy as a rule but they did not tire of his ever-deepening Lear till after the war.

How did he play it? Alger watched him and in the second volume of his biography described the interpretation in detail. Here is Forrest after Lear has been rebuffed by Goneril:

> A sense of the insulting disrespect and ingratitude of Goneril seemed to break on him afresh, and let loose the whole volcanic flood of his injured self-hood. Anguish, wrath, and helplessness drove him mad. The blood made path from his heart to his brow, and hung there, a red cloud, beneath his crown. His eyes flashed and faded and reflashed. He beat his breast as if not knowing what he did. His hands clutched wildly at the air as though struggling with something invisible. Then, sinking on his knees, with upturned look and hands straight outstretched towards his unnatural daughter, he poured out, in frenzied tones of mingled shriek and sob, his withering curse, half adjuration, half malediction. [Then by] a perfect gradation his protruded and bloodshot eyeballs, his crimsoned and swollen features, and his trembling frame subsided from their convulsive exertion. And with a confidence touching in its groundlessness, he bethought him,—
>> "I have another daughter,
>> Who, I am sure, is kind and comfortable."

One of the standard stories in American theatrical folklore concerns the admirer who complimented Forrest on the way he played King Lear. Glaring back, Forrest retorted, "Played it, sir? *Played* it? By God, I *am* King Lear!"

Such was drama in the decades just before the war. Lusty, many-sided, briskly alive, it and its audiences were both more strenuous than today. No self-respecting audience could be content with watching a single play, five-acter though it usually was. Instead the typical program for a night was made up of at least two plays: the main offering and an afterpiece, usually a farce. Sometimes the bill turned out to be still fuller, with three offerings in all, two plays and the afterpiece.

When audiences found themselves pleased they shouted "hi" as well as applauding. When they became irritated they hissed. Forrest himself while in Britain hissed Macready and then defended his action by pointing out that a hiss was the standard way for a playgoer to register his disapproval. Actors showed themselves as uninhibited as their audiences. Harry Watkins tells about the time when two members of his company had a falling out during rehearsal. When the man involved called the woman "a damned prostitute," she "seized a spear and chased him out of the theater. He returned while she was on the scene rehearsing. When she came off she rushed at him with a large screw driver exclaiming, 'You son of a bitch, die!' He picked up a chair and kept her off until he could make good his retreat."

The plays themselves were full of energy and posturing rhetoric. The language was often lush and the effects broad. The histories of American drama bulge with new plays during this period, as well as with old ones revived or adapted. Many more were probably written, and many more produced, than are now. No great American playwright appeared but lesser men wrote expansively in an expansive time.

2
Melody en Masse

‼ In the two spirited decades before the Civil War, America burst into melody—melody of an unprecedented fullness. Among the people to whom the nation was especially indebted for this, were three men and a plain young woman. The men were deep-eyed Lowell Mason of Boston, the greatly gifted but hapless Stephen Foster, and the towering Norse violinist Ole Bull. The woman was the superb Swedish soprano Jenny Lind.

Mason came first. At the opening of the 1840's he was in the prime of middle life, with a record of remarkable success already to his credit. He became without question the dominating musical figure of the decade. His forte was sacred music, particularly the composing and collecting of hymns. But he also composed, collected, and arranged a host of secular songs. He pioneered in music education for school children, developing a notably superior method. He pioneered too in the establishment of music teachers' institutes, which led ultimately to the music festivals we have today. Through his books as well as his personal prestige he helped to revive—and then extend—choral and family singing throughout New England. In the 1850's, when the modes of mass communication were rapidly improving, his influence spread over the rest of the country. As John Tasker Howard says in his history of American music, few musicians "ever exerted so wide an influence" as Mason.

But Mason's effectiveness, and the effectiveness of the three other people just mentioned, was greatly increased by favorable economic and social factors.

To begin with, it should be recalled that times were good. The twenty years between the panics of 1837 and 1857 saw an unparalleled prosperity. One or two obvious soft spots developed—most notably the wretched condition of unskilled labor and especially of the Irish and German immigrants. But the position of the upper class, the middle class, and the skilled portion of the lower class became steadily better. One result was evident in added attention to the whole cultural side of American life. The same economic conditions that favored better houses and more widely distributed engravings, for instance, allowed more families to buy pianofortes, if not pianofortes then melodeons, if not melodeons then guitars—and if not guitars, then certainly sheet music for singing; since after all, most popular songs could be bought for twenty-five cents a copy.

The sales of these various musical commodities increased, a bit slowly at first in the early 'forties and then sharply in the next decade. Though the exact value of pianofortes made during the year of each decennial census before 1860 cannot be calculated, there is enough data to show the trend. In his lively social history, *Men, Women and Pianos*, Arthur Loesser charts the progress of the piano-manufacturing industry. In 1829, for example, there had been only one new piano for every 4,800 persons. But by the end of the 'forties there was a new piano for every 2,777 and by 1860 there was a new piano for every 1,500 persons.

The census for 1860 offers us the first detailed set of figures. It shows that pianos to a value of over $5,260,000 were being constructed, substantially more than the value of the sewing machines or the straw goods fashioned at the same time and only a little less than the value of all the confectionery that sweet-toothed Americans ate. Piano-making was now a national industry. In the early 'forties, the piano factories had been confined to the East Coast, particularly Boston, New York, and Baltimore. Boston then ranked first, under the aegis of Jonas Chickering, who by 1850 was building almost a thousand pianos a year. By 1860, however, there were piano factories scattered throughout the rest of the country, even in California, though the bulk of them still remained in the East. As the Civil War started, New York was in the process of taking top leadership away from Boston: Chickering was being edged out by the skillful newcomer from Germany, Henry Steinway.

But regardless of who made them, or how economically, pianos continued to be something of a luxury. Even a cheap one, as Loesser points out, could cost $300. That remained more than a good many families would pay and so the melodeon, or reed organ, moved in to satisfy their need. It could do most of the things a piano could, though far less well, and became a growing second choice. Costing perhaps only a third of what a piano cost, the melodeon was to see its most popular days after the Civil War; yet even in 1860 the census shows that melodeons to a value of nearly $650,000 were being made.

The social trends mingled with the economic, and both ran in music's favor. Surprisingly, the most important of the social trends turned out to be the notable increase in Protestant church membership and the changing nature of the Protestant church service.

When the nineteenth century began, the status of religion in America was low. There was probably more open agnosticism at that time than the nation has ever seen since. Though their rigorous theology repelled a good many potential members, the hell-and-damnation sects still set the tone. However, the early decades of the century witnessed the remarkable rise of evangelicalism. It preached a loving rather than a wrathful God. Instead of threatening with eternal fire all but the few elect, it promised bliss to every believer. The heaven it envisioned was a full one, its golden streets joyously crowded.

21

And evangelical religion called for something better, musically, than the old, nasal lining-out of psalms. It called for choirs with some training, supported by instruments. The New England prejudice against the church organ gradually vanished. By 1853 Nathaniel Gould could announce in his *Church Music in America*, without fear of contradiction, "There is a glorious majesty of sound with which an organ fills a house of prayer." Church and church music developed together. Gould himself saw that a connection existed between the two upsurges. "Nor can any close observer have failed to notice a direct relation, both in the individual and the general mind, between the standard of piety and the interest in sacred music. The awakening of the public mind to the subject of music, twenty-five years ago, was nearly coincident with extensive revivals of religion."

Choirs and choirmasters found in Lowell Mason's hymns exactly what they needed. To be sure that everyone got the most out of the hymns, Mason customarily prefaced each of his books with a condensed course in singing. For example, *Carmina Sacra*, which became the most widely used of all his books (it and its supplement had sold half a million copies by 1858), opens with thirty pages on "The Elements of Vocal Music." The hymns that follow are all keyed technically to those thirty pages. They are easy to sing, with a consistently even melodic line. The constructions are ordinarily, to use Mason's own term, primitive. The time is simple: very few smaller-value notes (smaller than eighth notes) make their appearance. The execution is likewise simple, with the melody moving in gentle intervals, in seconds, thirds, and fifths. The net result is that these hymns seem to sing themselves.

If Mason's management of the musical side of his hymn books was ideally suited to current use, his choice of texts proved as timely. For evangelical religion encouraged meaningful song. Though Mason's devotion to music as such was acknowledged by almost everybody, he himself said again and again that the words to be sung were important too. They had to be understood; their message must be plain. A study of the lyrics that Mason selected to go with his music shows how well they went with evangelicalism. Whether he took his texts from others—and he

22

usually did—or whether he wrote his own, their burden is a happy one. "Loud swell the pealing organ's notes, Breathe forth your soul in raptures high." "With one consent, let all the earth To God their cheerful voices raise." "To songs of praise and joy be every Sabbath given."

In full-throated chorus, those sentiments resounded all over America. Every year or two Mason issued a new collection or revised an old one. S. A. Allibone calculated the sales of some of the volumes for his nineteenth-century *Dictionary of British and American Authors*. They were truly impressive, rising with heightened rapidity. It took nearly twenty years for Mason's *The Modern Psalmist* to sell over 50,000—and that was a phenomenal success. But *The National Psalmist* did it in ten. And *The Hallelujah* sold 150,000 in only four!

It is a measure of Mason's greatness that he did not stop with choir music. Even an extraordinary man might have felt that he had accomplished enough. But Mason was deeply committed to spreading the love of music wherever he could, and as widely as he could. That was why, much as he enjoyed fine performance, he eventually decided that whole congregations instead of choirs ought to sing the hymns. In helping to bring this about, he was again successful. He could write happily when he was an old man, "In many places the aristocracy of song is giving way, and the republican or legitimate method is being restored."

Out of Mason's same democratic impulse came his secular music. During his long career he produced half a dozen important "glee books"—books of nonreligious part songs to be sung for pleasure. One of the most often used was *The Boston Glee Book*, first published in 1838. The titles of some of the songs, taken at random, show the amiable nature of this and the other collections: "How Sweet, How Fresh," "Gallant and Gaily," "To All You Ladies," "Land of Our Fathers," "Rise, Cynthia, Rise." In his preface Mason announced that he had gathered "songs cheerful, tender, and patriotic."

He also said two other things in the preface to show how *The Boston Glee Book* was in keeping with the spirit of the times. First of all, he emphasized the pristine purity of his text. The lyrics had all been scrubbed clean so that nothing "impure in sentiment or exceptionable in morals" remained. "Bacchanalian subjects" were specifically excluded. Now Bacchus either put on the white ribbon of temperance or else was barred from the party; and high-bosomed Cynthia cast only the shyest of glances at her timid swain. Secondly, Mason explained that the songs in the collection could be sung without instrumental accompaniment. He was clear-sighted enough to realize that, much as the musical instrument industry had prospered in the preceding years, many a household still had no instrument but the human voice. Consequently, these songs were arranged *a cappella*, with the idea of reaching the largest possible number of people. Moreover, Mason had the collection sell for considerably less than its struggling competitors and predecessors. That too let it reach thousands more.

While the tuneful octavos of Lowell Mason were being carried from the East to the far corners of the country, a young Cincinnati bookkeeper was composing songs that were to make him even more famous than Mason. This was of course Stephen Foster. He became a composer only after his first songs proved popular beyond any imagining. Most of those produced in the middle and late 'forties have long been forgotten, but "There's a Good Time Coming," "Oh! Susanna," and "Nelly Was a Lady" are still being played every now and then. And in the early 'fifties appeared such durable favorites as "Camptown Races," "My Old Kentucky Home," "Old Folks at Home," and "Jeanie with the Light Brown Hair."

By November 1854 Foster's publishers boasted that they had sold 90,000 copies of "My Old Kentucky Home" and more than 130,000 of "Old Folks at Home." Everybody's heart, in fact, seemed to be turning to "de Swanee ribber." "Old Folks at Home," announced a clipping in *Dwight's Journal of Music* for October 2, 1852, "is on everybody's tongue. . . . Pianos and guitars groan with it, night and day; sentimental young ladies sing it; sentimental young gentlemen warble it in midnight serenades; volatile young 'bucks' hum it in the midst of their business and pleasures; . . . all the bands play it; . . . the 'singing stars' carol it on the theatrical boards, and at concerts; the chambermaid sweeps and dusts to the measured cadence of *Old Folks at Home*."

The middle and late 1850's witnessed the decline of Foster's genius. The songs he wrote then, with a few melodious exceptions, are no longer played. But the popularity of his previous work continued and stimulated the market for his new songs. "The Village Maiden" and "Gentle Annie," for example, were warbled and hummed extensively because by this time anything new by Stephen Foster could get an enthusiastic hearing. He did compose a few more songs of permanent interest. In spite of the inroads of drunkenness and irresponsibility, he published "Come Where My Love Lies Dreaming" (1855) and "Old Black Joe" (1860) and thus added to the debt that musical America still owes him.

"Who writes our songs?" asked the New York *Evening Post* in 1859. Its answer was Stephen Foster. Praising him as the most popular living song writer, the *Post* proceeded to list the reasons for his vogue. They were the "easy, flowing melody, the adherence to plain chords in the accompaniments, and the avoidance of intricacy in the harmony or embarrassing accidentals in the melody." The *Post* was correct. But it failed to go quite far enough in analyzing Foster's music, and it ignored the significance of his lyrics.

The winning charm of the music accounts indeed for most of his appeal. The plaintive, simple airs are easy to remember. Their harmonies consist of the most ordinary tonic, dominant, and subdominant chords; their scope stays well within the range of the ordinary human voice. When a high note does occur, Foster smoothes the singer's approach to it by placing it at a point where the breath is full instead of at the end of a long phrase. The beat is firm and regular, designed for amateurs to follow either in group or solo singing. The lyrics too, if we examine them for the moment as units of sound instead of meaning, contribute to Foster's popularity, for the words making them up are often monosyllables. When polysyllables occur, Foster is apt to separate them

25

musically by a deftly spaced sequence of notes. The consequence of all this calculated simplicity is a flow of melody that asked to be sung just as much as Lowell Mason's did.

Yet melody alone was not enough. By itself it could not account for the thousands and thousands of copies of Foster's songs which the American people bought. The lyrics also had their importance. Like those in Lowell Mason's hymns, they were a part of the changing social pattern of their time.

The same rise of evangelical religion which afforded the strongest support for Mason's sacred music helped to assure Foster's popularity if only indirectly so. About religion as such he had little to say in his songs; he was no theologian. The moral and ethical values growing out of evangelical religion, however, were those he advocated in his lyrics. The kindly view of human nature, the emphasis on unselfish love, and the willing obedience to evangelical religion's rules of daily conduct appear and reappear.

The appeal of this side of Foster was powerful. But there was more to him than that. He also offered America escape from its still present puritanism, its materialism, and its aggressive competitive spirit. He did this with a fortunate indirectness, especially where puritanism was concerned.

For he led his hearers away from puritanism only after making his proper bow to it. That is, he offered them a gentle, lively never-never land where the escape was from something rather than to something, from care and stern responsibility rather than to lusty living. The main symbol Foster used in his antipuritanism was the Negro, and he used him well. It is true that this began as an accident, for he was simply writing very catchy minstrel songs. Once having his subject, however, he developed it winningly. He pictured the carefree darky in his prime on the old plantation, cutting up with rousing good spirits. The South was the place the darky loved, and if away from it he longed to return:

> We'll put for de souf
> Ah! dat's the place,
> For the steeple chase and de bully hoss race—

Poker, brag, eucher, seven up and loo,
Den chime in Niggas, won't you come along too.

When he left the South, he also left his joyous childhood: "The young folks roll on the little cabin floor, All merry, all happy and bright." And he left the peace and tranquillity of old age as well.

Often Foster wove together the feelings of childhood and of age for the sake of artistic contrast. He joined the simple, animal joy that the pickaninnies represented with the tender melancholy of "old folks" close to death. But it was death itself that attracted him most. Death on the plantation was always sad but never stark, regardless of what it might be elsewhere. Usually it contained within it the promise of eternal rest, most often shown as sleep. In "Old Black Joe" Foster developed, for his time and place, the perfect popular restatement of an always moving theme, the theme of old age living only for its memories and now ready to make them real again through death.

> Why do I weep when my heart should feel no pain
> Why do I sigh that my friends come not again,
> Grieving for forms
> Now departed long ago?
> I hear their gentle voices calling "Old Black Joe."

When the Civil War began, Foster sided strongly with the North. But before that time, whether he knew it or not, he was making a classic contribution to the myth of the ante-bellum South. The contented darkies, the kind old massa, and the pillared plantation are standard in his songs. Whether the strain be comic or sad, the moral is that the plantation was a pastoral utopia.

The South could justly be gratified. Foster's lyrics assured it that slavery was basically good and did this, doubtless, with more emotional power than any proslavery lectures, tracts, or treatises coming out at the same time. The North, on the other hand, might have been expected to remonstrate. Yet it failed to. Probably it found in his songs simply the reflection of its own minstrel-inspired idea of what the Negro and the South were really like. If any abolitionists had the wit to see the psychological menace to

27

their cause of Foster's conceptions, they never said so effectively. They failed to remark that not till 1852 did Foster travel through the South. And they neglected to observe that his early views were based chiefly on seeing Negro church services and watching minstrel shows.

Foster invited Americans to escape harmlessly from puritanism, but similarly he invited them to escape from the crude materialism that foreign visitors frequently censured. This materialism was accompanied by an emphasis on the competitive spirit, on aggressiveness. Though aggression suited the frontier more than the eastern seaboard, it could be found everywhere in the United States. It had become even then a leading part of what would someday be called the capitalistic ethic. The combination of materialism and the will to win crowded out the softer emotions. If sentiment played any part in prewar business life, it must have been a small one; and Mark Twain was not the only man to point out that in postwar business it never showed itself at all.

Yet the softer emotions still existed. Men might try to dismiss them as fit for women alone but could not suppress them entirely. The anima, the female element in man as defined by the psychologist Jung, was both their source and their haven. In Foster's music these tender feelings found their most popular expression. It is true that some of his best-loved songs are gay but most of them strike a sad note. It is the note of death, of longing, of farewell, or of nostalgia. For every song with the bounce of "There's a Good Time Coming" or "Camptown Races," there are a dozen with the melancholy of "Summer Longings," "Farewell Old Cottage," "My Hopes Have Departed Forever," "Massa's in de Cold Ground," "Old Memories," or "Under the Willow She's Sleeping." The melancholy, however, is always muted. Foster never affects a blatant emotionalism.

Even the love so abundant in his lyrics is not reckless nor extreme—any more than, as we discovered earlier, it was illicit. It is almost always a man's love and so is directed at either his mother or some beautiful girl. If the composer sings to mother, it is the usual paean (still selling widely today) about those dear gray hairs

28

and gentle eyes. Mother stays loyal when all the rest of the world has abandoned us: "Mother, Thou'rt Faithful to Me."

If the composer sings to some other woman, it is to a fragile maiden. She never seems mature nor really nubile, and no hint of sexuality ever lurks in Foster's tender lines about her. Often—and this is the most obvious of retreats from sex but musically quite effective—she is either dead or dying. His favorite metaphor for death, we can recall, is sleep. "Sweetly she sleeps, My Alice fair," Foster will write. One of his favorite devices is to begin the lyrics with the listener thinking that the girl is merely sleeping and then to end by letting him realize that she is really dead. Foster's Annies, his Jeanies, his Lindas turn into lavendered wraiths. And that, it would appear, was the way American men wished them and American women thought they ought to be.

Rich with symbols of escape, Stephen Foster's songs captured the American heart. Turning for a while from the dour trio of puritanism, materialism, and competitiveness, the American listened to Foster's gentle strains. In them the Freudian of today would detect a variety of regressions and projections. He would observe Oedipus complexes, necrophilia, and the "angel theory of childhood," among other things. At the same time even the least speculative among us could notice the escapism represented by distance in time (in three modes: childhood, old age, the "good old days"), distance in space (the South), distance from reality (dreams), and distance from life (death).

"I hear America singing" Walt Whitman could say triumphantly in the years just before the Civil War. He would be right literally as well as figuratively. In this burst of native song Foster would be heard most clearly, his melodies rising above all others. But there were several important aspects of music which he could never represent. The main one was the popularity here of the serious work of the great European composers. The music that the American public played and sang itself was often indigenous but the music it listened to at concerts—then as now—was not. Handel, Haydn, Mozart, Beethoven, and Mendelssohn were played more and more throughout the 'forties and 'fifties. No survey of music during these two decades should overlook them.

Boston had founded its Handel and Haydn Society in 1815, Philadelphia its Musical Fund Society in 1820, and gradually other cities followed. By 1840 European music, both Classical and Romantic in style, had gained an audience in our cities. The main limitations on its spread were primarily mechanical. At the outset there were not enough skilled musicians to play the complicated works of the masters; and so symphonies, in particular, could not get a proper hearing. Instead, solo works, duos, trios, and quartets took the stage. But by the end of the 'forties a substantial immigration of European artists was taking place. They included famous European virtuosi such as Ole Bull, and the first successful orchestra, which arrived in 1848. This ensemble was the Germania Society. According to John Tasker Howard, it toured all the principal cities of this country in the half-dozen years after its arrival.

Its typical program was made up of a brace of overtures, a symphony (in whole or part), two solos, and a semiclassical selection. The overtures it played most often were by Beethoven, Mozart, Mendelssohn, and Weber. The favorite symphonies were Beethoven's nine, the best-known ones by Mozart and Haydn, Mendelssohn's third and fourth, and several by the contemporary German composer Louis Spohr.

Though orchestral music in general now began to prosper, another mechanical limitation still lingered. Because their expenses were high, and trained players still rare, orchestras journeyed only to the places that could afford them—in other words, to the chief cities. Even if a small town or a village wished to hear the Germania or its successors, the chances of being able to were very slight. Anyone who wanted serious music regularly had to live in a cultural center. His opportunities proved fullest if he stayed in Boston, New York, or Philadelphia. The further north, south, or west he went, the rarer the sound of fine orchestral music became.

As a result, the most widely traveled and enjoyed performers were not the orchestral musicians but the solo artists, especially the concert singers or pianists. Their popularity was based, first of all, on their accessibility. Almost any foreign tenor who reached

Sandusky, for instance, would have a grateful welcome from its music lovers. Secondly, audiences have as a rule been drawn more readily to a single personality than to a group. The Germania Society orchestra could not, by its very nature, have a personality distinct enough to win attention. But the individual magnetism of Ole Bull was so strong that everyone felt it.

The nineteenth-century musical critic George Ferris felt impelled to compare him to a Viking. He added admiringly: "The great stature, the massive, stalwart form, as upright as a pine, the white floating locks framing the ruddy face, full of strength and genial humor, lit up by keen blue eyes—all these things made Ole Bull the most striking man in *personnel* among all the artists who have been familiar to our public." Bull's playing created just as dramatic an impression as his appearance. His art was full of romantic showmanship; the tone poem was his forte. The average American no doubt marveled at the way the music of Bull's violin could speed from a whisper to a tumult. Through his touring he developed into almost a folklore figure, able (it was said) to use his colossal strength to play all four strings of his fiddle at once or else, when he wanted, to play so delicately that his bow just breathed on the strings.

His playing and his programs were one. Whatever composition he chose he made his own by the robust individuality of his technique. He liked Paganini's lush pieces but gave them his personal stamp. As time went on, he himself composed works for the violin. They became the heart of many of his programs. Two compositions among those he wrote before reaching this country turned out to be great favorites here. One, which he had produced at the request of some Italian friars, was his melancholy "Adagio Religioso." When these same friars asked for something more stirring, he wrote his "Polacca Guerrieria." Audiences everywhere loved the facile, emotional quality of both.

Arriving in New York in 1843, Bull achieved an instant success. James Gordon Bennett's *Herald* greeted his first concert with "We cannot describe Ole Bull's playing—it is beyond the power of language. . . . Some of his unearthly—his heavenly—passages work on the feelings and the heart till the very tears flow. Others it makes vociferous, mad, and terrible in their applauses. At the close of some of his wonderful cadences, the very musicians in the orchestra flung down their instruments, and stamped and applauded like madmen." Early in 1844 he began his tour of the rest of the United States. He got as far south as New Orleans (where he gave seven concerts), as far north as Boston (which he reached later than Boston liked), and as far west as the Mississippi. A modern biographer, Mortimer Smith, says that he played his violin in every city of any size east of the great river.

The same devotion to his native Norway which moved Bull to compose many pieces relating to the Norwegian past and its traditions helped him to understand America's patriotic impulse. He sympathized with our desire for native program music. So he wrote and played such pieces as "Niagara," "Prairie Solitude," and "To the Memory of Washington," the last being a musical goulash that included everything from the sounds of battle to the strains of "Yankee Doodle." It was a dull audience that failed to pound its palms on hearing it.

He thoroughly enjoyed America and America enjoyed him. To Bull the American crudities that antagonized a Mrs. Trollope or a Dickens meant nothing. His own vigor, force, and native democracy met and mingled with those of this country. He could throw a Kentuck over his back if need be, and the Kentuck would come with sheepish enthusiasm to hear him play the next evening. When Ole Bull sailed for Europe in December 1845 he had traveled a hundred thousand miles and given more than 200 concerts. Clearly he and America were in rapport; he was to return four more times.

It would be hard to believe that anyone could have been received by the American public with more ardor than Ole Bull. Yet the arrival of Jenny Lind in the summer of 1850 kindled an excitement beside which his reception seemed cool. The next year Charles Rosenberg, a gossipy and cosmopolitan music critic, wrote a book on her American tour which remains the most detailed account. According to Rosenberg, the Sunday afternoon that Jenny's ship reached New York Harbor, thirty or forty thousand people were gathered at the piers and vessels near where she was to dock. "The spars and rigging . . . , the bulkheads along the wharves, and the very fenders of the Hoboken Ferry House were covered with eager gazers; while from every quarter of the city crowds might be seen hurrying toward the dock . . . , and increasing the thronging and almost countless multitude already waiting there." Dressed demurely in gray and blue, she disembarked under the guidance of top-hatted P. T. Barnum, who had captured her for the panting public. She had scarcely been put into her carriage and started on the drive through the triumphal arches of evergreens and flowers, when the members of the mob snapped the planking that was supposed to fence them off and surged upon her. After the police repelled them, the carriage proceeded slowly while the people who lined the streets threw flowers at it.

This enormous enthusiasm continued with only slight fluctuations during Jenny's nine-month tour. Barnum, anxious to be respectable now that he had made a fortune exploiting the public's credulity, had offered her the magnificent sum of $1,000 a concert for 150 concerts. After accepting, Jenny decided that she should have even more; Barnum yielded without a murmur and gave her half of the net profits in addition. As became his practice, he had the first tickets for the first concert auctioned off. In New York the first ticket brought $225 but other cities were easily to surpass that later on. At any rate, the total paid for all admissions to the opening New York concert on September 11 reached nearly $25,000—a monument to Barnum's shrewdness as well as Jenny's fame.

This concert set the pattern for those to follow. The audience overflowed; the voice of the Swedish Songstress, the Northern Nightingale, or the Scandinavian Swan (she answered to all those appellations) won her hearers completely; bouquets from every quarter of the house were tossed at her on the stage, and she had to give encore after encore and make bow after bow.

Though from the beginning the audience had ears for Jenny alone, she made her tour as a star with supporting performers. She took along a versatile young director, composer, and pianist named Julius Benedict, who was to conduct the orchestra recruited at each stopping place, and Signor Giovanni Belletti, an admirable baritone. Benedict and Belletti were both old European friends of hers; on entering this country she added a crisply precocious Anglo-American pianist, Richard Hoffman, to her party.

The first concert opened with the overture from Weber's *Oberon* played by Benedict and his orchestra. It received an applause that was obviously less for the orchestra than in anticipation of Jenny's song. She came out overwhelmed by the audience and sang the "Casta Diva" from Bellini's *Norma* so surely and finely that the audience "drowned the last portion of the air in a perfect tempest of acclamation."

Benedict and Hoffman appeared next, playing a two-pianoforte duet composed by Benedict himself. Mildly applauded, it served as a preface to a stirring vocal duet between Jenny and Signor Belletti, from Rossini's *The Turk in Italy*. Then came an intermission during which the artists rested, the audience marveled to one another about Jenny's voice, and the police outside continued to fight off several hundred river roustabouts who were trying to smash their way into the concert hall.

Part II opened with the playing of another composition of Benedict's, the overture to his now forgotten opera *The Crusaders*. Then came a trio for voice and two flutes. Written by Meyerbeer expressly for Jenny, in an opera called *The Camp in Silesia*, it offered her voice a setting of superb delicacy. For contrast Belletti followed with the rousing "Largo al Factotum" from *The Barber of Seville*. Next came a selection that the audience had been awaiting with especial anticipation, "The Echo Song." "This song she sings in her own native language," Rosenberg explained, "accompanying her voice, at the piano, with her own fingers. In it she imitates the herdsman calling his cattle, and the echoes of his voice, which are heard among the mountains." Singing it, added Rosenberg, "completely and irrevocably sealed her triumph." Jenny's last song was "The Welcome to America," for which the widely known hack poet Bayard Taylor had written the lyrics. It began "I greet with full heart, the Land of the West, Whose Banner of Stars o'er the world is unrolled" and continued in the same vein. The audience wore out its gloves, when it had them, with clapping and would not stop till exhausted. Finally it called for Barnum, with "a loud cry." He marched out to announce that Mademoiselle Lind was giving her part of the evening's profits, which had leapt to the astonishing high (under her new, liberalized contract) of $10,000, to New York charities. After this everything else was anticlimax and the audience straggled home.

As she and her entourage traveled over the rest of the country her triumphs were repeated. She made the American equivalent of the Grand Circle; Rosenberg's chapter headings indicate its extent. They name New York, Boston, Philadelphia, Baltimore, Washington, Richmond, Charleston, Havana (she sang in Cuba too), New Orleans, Natchez, Memphis, St. Louis, Nashville, Louisville, Cincinnati, Wheeling, and Pittsburgh.

With good sense, she gave the audiences everywhere a mixture of two kinds of music: airs mainly from Italian and German operas, such as those from *Norma* and *La Sonnambula*, and lieder such as "The Echo Song," "The Last Rose of Summer," and "The Bird Song." Her voice proved consistently bright and thrilling. The upper part of her register was much more effective than the lower and so lent a somewhat false glitter to her tone; her audiences were, typically, more impressed by high notes than low ones. Her singing possessed one other characteristic that Americans in general marveled at. It was her ability to sustain a note for an amazing length of time. In addition to those characteristics that would appeal to mass audiences, she had qualities of true musicianship. The best critics of the day agreed on her adroit execution, her brilliant technique. Composers of the rank of Mendelssohn praised her. She had, in a musical sense, something for every level of listener.

But it was more than her music which accounted for her great acclaim in the United States. Not only was Jenny a superb singer, she was also a pious and generous young woman. She fulfilled the "daughter image." Her personal life had escaped the scandal that smirched so many a European artist in American eyes. She had not been given to high—or low—living. Furthermore, the stamp

35

of moral approval in this Victorian age had been put on her by a command performance before the English queen herself.

Coupled with Jenny's good conduct was her generosity. Charity after charity received hundreds or even thousands of dollars from her. She gave gladly, and more often than not secretly. On her American tour Barnum was the one who publicized her gifts to many and various organizations, and he let out that she made frequent gifts to individuals as well. The shares of the $10,000 she gave away after her first New York concert went to everything from the Fire Department Fund to the Protestant Half Orphan Asylum. Her rooms were besieged by cadgers who got money from her, often no doubt by fraud. In its public figures America liked the open, generous hand (few performers with a reputation for stinginess did well), and in Jenny Lind it found everything it could ask. She left in 1852, but she is still remembered today.

Yet even a century ago there must have been millions of Americans for whom Jenny Lind or Ole Bull were no more than names —and these were Americans who enjoyed music, moreover. In the farmland and on the frontier a different kind of music was flourishing, a kind much closer to Lowell Mason's and Foster's. Hymns rang out robustly in the camp meetings and revivals of the South and the West. Some of them were spirituals, which had been kept alive just by singing them. Others were adaptations of tunes in print. The songbooks used at the meetings testified to the musical simplicity of the singers, for the melodies were usually set down in the already old-fashioned "shape notes" invented in New England about 1800. With this system *fa* was as a rule a triangle, *sol* a circle, *la* a square, and *mi* a diamond; and there were only four notes to bother with. Something else that appealed to the people was the thumping refrain often printed after each verse. It might merely be a hallelujah or perhaps a phrase such as "Roll, Jordan, Roll," but whatever it was, the country folk obviously relished it. It helped to make the camp-meeting hymn their favorite musical expression.

A good deal of secular singing too could be heard. If not religious, it was nonetheless moral, and often sad and sentimental as well. It was taught to the people by that valuable supplement to the choirmaster, the itinerant singing teacher. He was apt to organize a one-month singing school where the unsophisticated lovers of song, the "fasola folk" as Gilbert Chase calls them in *America's Music*, learned the rudiments. Under his tutelage they began by sounding the simplest of scales, went on to learn of staffs and signatures, and ended by doing part singing with considerable vigor if not subtlety. According to Chase the main path of the singing-school movement appeared to have been from New England to Pennsylvania and then to the South and the West. The movement, since it was at the folk level, has left few artifacts; among those William Walker's *Southern Harmony and Musical Companion* is outstanding. First published in 1835, it had four more editions by 1854. Walker himself asserted that 600,000 copies of it were sold in all. Although printed in the North, it became particularly popular in the very region, the South, where orchestras and concert artists most seldom penetrated. As its title page announced, it contained "Tunes, Hymns, Psalms, Odes, and Anthems," all set in shape notes. Singing societies and singing schools, and choirs in addition, found much to use in Walker's rousing volume.

Scattered records show that other songbooks, likewise combining religious with sentimental secular music, also attained popularity in rural regions. Especially for the South and the frontier these were the books that best represented the music of the time. They too contributed to our musical culture.

37

3

Pillars, Points, and Brackets

❧❧ To the many of us who live in cramped little dwellings, the housing situation of a century ago can easily look utopian. A seven-room residence with some pretensions to style could be built for $2,000, and you could be in step with current fashions. In the 'forties you could have Greek pillars for your porch or a touch of pointed Gothic, with its curlicued barge-boards, for your roof. In the 'fifties you could have a mildly Italian house, with its characteristic consoles. Even when we allow that a dollar then bought much more than it does now, $2,000 remains a modest price. The result was the biggest building boom in the history of this country. From 1840 to 1860 our population came close to doubling. Most people had, during those two decades, money in their pockets and big families to house. The combination proved irresistible. Ax, hammer, and saw sounded in a loud and universal symphony.

Cheap materials and cheap unskilled labor played their vital parts. There was a wealth of wood to be had almost for the taking. In most localities it grew within easy reach; where it did not, water or wagon transportation made it accessible. Moreover, by the 1840's wood went further than it had before, since the so-called balloon frame—a light frame of studs and plates nailed together—had come into general use. It took less wood than the old, jointed frame; it took less time to erect; and it lent itself to more flexible building plans.

That the balloon frame saved time for the builder was not important so far as the wretchedly paid unskilled help was concerned, but it did mean something for the skilled workman. His wage represented the one substantial exception to the general cheapness of construction. The craftsman in the building trades—the carpenter, the bricklayer, the plumber, the plasterer—was even then an aristocrat among laboring men. In 1851 when Horace Greeley campaigned for a decent living wage for workers, he suggested a minimum of $11 a week as the proper sum; this was an amount, as F. R. Dulles has remarked in *Labor in America*, that only the craftsman in the building trades usually carried home. True, the panic of 1837 had hit his struggling young unions a blow that took them some time to recover from, but he knew prosperity anyway.

Some people felt that the craftsman's quarters themselves could testify how well he lived. When kindly Francis Grund toured this country, he for one was much impressed by the dwellings of skilled labor in general. "On entering the house of a respectable mechanic in any one of the large cities of the United States," he remarked, "one cannot but be astonished at the apparent neatness and comfort of the apartments, the large airy parlors, the nice carpets and mahogany furniture." He concluded that "the laboring classes in America are really less removed from the wealthy merchants and professional men than they are in any part of Europe." Greeley would have groaned at this, but he was concentrating on the plight of the unskilled workers.

They were the ones who inadvertently helped to keep building costs down. The surge of immigration from Europe provided an enormous quantity of manpower, of cheap, ready labor. Furthermore, it did so at just the right time from the builder's point of view. In, roughly, the first half century of our nation's existence

39

about a quarter of a million immigrants entered the United States; in the single decade beginning with 1846 more than triple that number, on the average, landed every year. From the ranks of these newcomers, especially the Irish, came the unskilled labor that the journeymen carpenters needed to assist them. And the master carpenters rubbed their calloused hands together as they put the Irish on their payroll at a pittance.

The structures erected during the years from 1840 to 1861 varied from stately capitols to the rudest of log cabins. A pompous public building could cost hundreds of thousands of dollars. Domestic dwellings could range from the cheapest of hovels, such as the one Charles Quill described in his little book, *The Working Man:* "barrel chimneys, floors without boards, windows without glass, and a dunghill at the entrance," to the stately Lanier mansion in Madison, Indiana, which cost $50,000.

For the way that fashions spread, both in public and in private architecture, the image of the ripples made by dropping a stone into a pool is a good one. The center for American architectural thought was the part of the eastern seaboard between Boston and Philadelphia. The innovations adopted there gradually made their way throughout the rest of the country. Even before the 1840's opened, the Greek Revival was already dead according to the eastern leaders of American architecture. Gothic was now the mode. A fine church in Boston, a group of college buildings in New York, a massive prison in Philadelphia—these went up to prove the leaders right. But in the meantime, out in Ohio, down in South Carolina, or up in Wisconsin, the master carpenters were still buying copy after copy, edition after edition, of such manuals of the Greek Revival as Minard Lafever's *The Beauties of Modern Architecture* or old Asher Benjamin's *The Practical House Carpenter*. Those books had their pages crammed with drawings and diagrams of fluted columns, Ionic porticoes, and so forth. Only in the unusual elaborateness of some of Lafever's designs was there a foretaste of the Gothic style that later conquered the architectural hinterlands. When the Italian style, especially in domestic architecture, later replaced the Gothic itself along the seaboard,

Edwin Forrest caricatured as the hero in Bird's bombastic drama Spartacus. (*Museum of the City of New York.*)

"Old Kentucky Home, Life in the South" as painted by Eastman Johnson and celebrated in song by Stephen Foster. (New-York Historical Society.)

Jenny Lind, the high points of her tour, and the text of the prize song by Bayard Taylor which she sang. (Lithograph by Nagel & Weingaertner.)

A home in the Gothic style from Downing's The Architecture of Country Houses.

The Italian style of dwelling as envisioned for Americans by Downing in The Architecture of Country Houses.

The architect in Thomas Cole's romantic "The Architect's Dream" thinks in terms of Greek, Gothic, and other foreign styles but not American. (Toledo Museum of Art.)

Here among the whatnots and gilt the Milligan family in Saratoga Springs received their friends of the 1850's. (Brooklyn Museum.)

it took years to reach the towns of the Midwest, upper New England, and the South. The ripples widened outward slowly.

During the twenty years before the Civil War, fashions in public building changed less than in private building. The trend in domestic construction, slow but definite, was from Greek to Gothic to Italian. In public architecture, though, the Grecian style would lose favor only slightly to Gothic. The main reason lay no doubt in the aesthetic conservatism of the legislators who ordered the public buildings constructed.

All the essentials of the then-prevailing taste in public architecture can without undue difficulty be discovered in one building, the capitol of Tennessee, located on the highest ground in the city of Nashville. Designed by William Strickland, an adopted Tennessean who had been a pupil of the great Greek Revivalist Benjamin Latrobe, it took a decade to erect. It was finished in 1855, having cost—thanks to some political high finance—more than $1,500,000. A massive stone structure, 232 by 124 feet, it drew its main model (as Nashville historians never tired of mentioning) from an actual Ionic temple. The great central block of the building is Doric, but decorated with an Ionic porch on each of its four sides. The two porches at the ends of the long axis (the floor plan is rectangular) each cover one side of the structure. The other two porches are smaller, with one placed in the middle of each façade. Crowning the long gable of the roof is a Corinthian tower copied after a monument in Athens.

If the capitol errs, it errs on the side of simplicity despite its mingling of Classic styles; and that seems to be the kind of error that wears well in architecture. The main lines of the building are regular and severe, devoid of fussy ornament. The proportions of the four porches harmonize well with the main mass of the building; the proportions of the stately windows harmonize with those of the porches. Only the Corinthian tower, which is perhaps too large, detracts from the general impressiveness.

From the beginning the people of the state felt proud of their capitol. Sheer size accounted in part for the effect it had. For many a red-faced farmer it represented the biggest building he had ever gawked at. And it was not only big, it was rock solid. He sensed in its stone walls, its heavy blocks, more than a physical firmness; it had psychological stability. To the more educated citizen, classic Greece continued to make a deep appeal, and this was an instance of Greek art at its most imposing. He could note the Greek orders, along with the copying—under republican modifications—of Greek originals. Here he saw the concreted symbol of Jeffersonian learning and federal grace. The most thoughtful men who stopped and stood before the capitol no doubt felt satisfied by its mass and balanced proportions, by its aesthetic tradition, and by its symbolizing of the public virtues of America. They would have known what the American art critic James Jackson Jarves meant in saying, "Grecian architecture not only elates the mind from the consciousness of its intellectual greatness, but gives it repose from the purity of its material, the perfect correspondence of its spirit and form, and the harmony between its principles and uses."

At exactly the same time that the essentials of the old order were being preserved in the West in the form of the Tennessee state capitol, the new order was consolidating its hard-won victories in the East. The most striking monument of the Gothic style in public buildings was going up in the early 1850's in Washington, D.C. It was the Smithsonian Institution.

A precocious young aristocrat, James Renwick, Jr., won the commission to design it in 1846. He had already planned one of the finest Gothic churches in New York City. Combined with his other successes, this attracted enough attention so that the Smithsonian's Board of Regents laid aside its normal official conservatism and stood ready to consider something new. It is doubtful, though, that it really foresaw the tremendous pink Gothic pile whose design it approved.

Actually, the Smithsonian building represented, upon its completion in 1852, the spirit rather than the letter of the Gothic law. Gothic had already become known as the "pointed" architecture and was recognized as being the most appropriate for churches, college buildings (perhaps because of their early ecclesiastical connection), and certain institutions. Its steeples, its buttresses, its arches, its groined vaultings had rich religious connotations. The main lines of its buildings were—as an even more influential young architect than Renwick, Andrew Jackson Downing, recognized —"all vertical." ("Aspiring, tending upward," he explained.) To a nation as marked by piety and religiosity as the United States, any architecture known to point toward heaven was bound to have a psychological appeal.

But the Gothic style was also interpreted more widely, to stand for many of the things that Romanticism stood for. The irregular instead of the regular, the unique instead of the common, the rough instead of the smooth, the medieval instead of the modern, the aspiration instead of the reality: these were characteristics that Gothic and the Romantic movement shared. Indeed, ante-bellum Gothic was largely a part of Romanticism.

This larger interpretation of the Gothic style made it attractive to several other elements in the American temper besides the religious. Robert Dale Owen, studying public architecture as both a utopian liberal and an active politician, saw that plainly. He was convinced that his fellow citizens would value Gothic for its flexibility, for the fact that it lent itself to additions and modifications much more than Greek ever would. Gothic allowed for change, and change was progress. Furthermore, being interested in natural beauty, Americans would soon learn to love "the irregular variety of Gothic . . . far beyond the rigidly formal" Greek Revival style. Its boldness and loftiness likewise made Gothic appeal to Americans, Owen asserted. It truly harmonized, he felt, with the spirit of their age.

If, then, we conceive of American Gothic as more than pointed arches, the Smithsonian building can be its perfect public representative. Some historians see a Lombard or a Norman influence in it; others suggest that it bears traces of Renwick's interest in Oriental architecture; still others simply throw up their hands. But they need not. In its grotesque variety—it has, for example, nine various and assorted towers—lies an abundant American strength. It is eclectic architecture but not without congruity. Today the cloisters, the crenellations, the cruciform slits in the

43

walls, and the smudgy pink freestone repel the observer. But accounts in the 'fifties show that the public though amazed was not displeased. In this sprawling combination of cathedral and castle (the façade is over a block long), it had bought something that would confound Europe and show what young America could do.

In the meantime American domestic architecture was busily running its gamut from the hovel to the mansion. The log cabin was still being raised on the frontier. Its logs were apt to be dressed flat, their corners interlocked, and their chinks filled in with chips and mud. The fireplace was stone, if stone was handy; otherwise logs would have to do. The slanted roof was covered with hand-split shingles held down by weight poles. When the sawmill came to the frontier, the cabin walls could be covered with siding; later and better houses would have it from the start. More variety and more artistry could be attempted with the passing of each year. Yet over all, the most frequent style of home—if any one could be proposed for this entire period and for the whole country— would be the square two-story wooden box. It gave its owner the most for his money. In addition, it had some artistic potentialities —potentialities that Greek Revival architecture was particularly well fitted to realize. It satisfied the wish for regularity and proportion that most houseowners cherished before the advent of Gothic. When Charles Quill wrote about the kind of dwelling the laboring man ought to have, he advocated a classical design even if he refrained from calling it that. "Symmetry is as cheap as disproportion," he advised his humble readers and warned them that "the eye is shocked when, in a clever building, the door has three windows on one side and five on the other."

By their precept as well as their example, the writers of builders' manuals such as Benjamin and Lafever aided the Greek Revival. The basic box was easiest for the carpenters to construct and its ornamentation, though restrained, could be as elegant as the owner wished. The best places for ornament were gables, porticoes, and doors. The gable facing the street often projected; on it and on the entablature beneath, the carpenter could put decorous embellishments for the passerby to see. The gable might have a fan light in its center. The entablature might be pierced with circular windows, as was done for the Lanier house mentioned earlier. And below the entablature, holding it up with stately grace, would stand the white columns. They might be Doric, Ionic, or Corinthian but their presence was inevitable. In many a community they became the hallmark of the best house.

Looking back after the Civil War, even Mark Twain acknowledged this fact in *Life on the Mississippi*. A little sourly, he described the typical southern village mansion in its setting: "large grassy yard, with paling fence painted white—in fair repair; brick walk from gate to door; big, square, two-story 'frame' house, painted white and porticoed like a Grecian temple—with this difference, that the imposing fluted columns and Corinthian capitals were a pathetic sham, being made of white pine, and painted." If he expected many stone columns, he would have been disappointed not merely along the Mississippi but everywhere else in the country. In the South itself, only a sprinkling of the wealthiest of planters, building what came to be called "Plantation Greek," would indulge themselves by using stone.

But regardless of whether the pillars were stone or pine, the South continued to cherish the Greek Revival—and for more than utilitarian reasons. With the tensions over slavery mounting year after year, the South sought every psychological aid it could find. Not the least of these was the conception of itself as a Greek democracy: a democracy of gentlemen if not of philosophers, flourishing on a foundation of helots or slaves. And the pillared houses of the Greek Revival were one of the main symbols of the South's attachment to the Greek idea.

For the well-to-do American anywhere who wanted the "best" house or for the average American who wanted the most housing for his money, the Greek Revival had much to offer. If thrifty common sense was an American characteristic, then Gothic architecture (in spite of its flexibility) was doomed from the start. For it was not functional; it was decorative, and expensively so. Yet we Americans have proved that bare functionalism seldom appeals

45

to us. Anyone who has studied the design of the contemporary American automobile, for example, knows that it has but the faintest of connections with utility.

The elaborately fretted or curlicued bargeboards, which protected the gable ends of the Gothic house, cost time and money to carve. The bay windows were often topped with expensive crenellations; for that matter the bay window itself was a luxury. Windows had expensive "labels" over the top of their frames. Even the chimneys rising above the steep roofs were embossed with patterns of serpentine-work, lattice-work, or some other decoration. All this meant that a Gothic house would cost substantially more than a comparable Greek Revival house. Yet Gothic crowded the Greek Revival despite the continued popularity of handbooks like Lafever's. It became, in our period, the best-liked building style for the middle class. In northern New England, in the Midwest, and in the South it began competing with the Greek in the late 'forties. By the late 'fifties the Italian style was coming in. But during the years between, Gothic had a genuine heyday. Even afterward it retained enough vitality to influence Victorian architecture of the post–Civil War period and so stayed alive until the twentieth century started.

For a picture of the most tasteful among representative Gothic houses, there is no better place to go than to the plans of the widely respected Downing. In *The Architecture of Country Houses*, first published in 1850, he pictures a two-story villa which, with two or three minor modifications, might well serve as the "ideal type" of Gothic house both in town and country. He designed it to be built of brick but in many parts of the United States wood had to be used instead, either because it ordinarily cost as much as 50 per cent less or because of local fashion.

It was a handsome house that Downing drew. Its proportions were good and the roofs steeply yet nicely pitched, so that the beholder had the feeling that the house grew out of the ground instead of being planted insecurely atop it. The floor plan was irregular, as we would expect. Primarily it remained a rectangle but a rectangle extended by adding a small greenhouse on one side and a kitchen wing on the other. Moreover, two protrusions broke the façade, lending additional interest to it. One was the bay window, the other the small enclosed front porch. Each had a gable above, complete with bargeboards and breaking into the main gable. On the rooftop stood two clusters of chimney pipes. Because this was supposedly a country residence the long veranda lay at the rear, for the best view. No doubt, though, Downing knew enough about the American character to realize that when his plan was adopted in town, the veranda would be switched to the front of the house. There it would make a perfect vantage point for watching neighbors and rocking comfortably in warm weather.

The entire outside, whether brick or wood, was to be painted. Over brick Downing merely proposed some "agreeable" color but obviously he did not mean white. White was thoroughly unfashionable for Gothic, brown or gray being preferred, with colored glass in an occasional windowpane to add an accent.

Inside were four rooms on the first floor in the main rectangle. The drawing room (the least used in the house as a rule—it later became the formidable Victorian parlor) and the dining room occupied the rear half of the block, the dining room being close to the kitchen wing. In the front half were the library (so attractive with its bay that Downing predicted it would become the family gathering place), a large entrance hall, and a powder room (or "boudoir"). The boudoir could be turned into a den if desired. The second floor contained five bedrooms of various sizes, a bathroom, and two little utility or dressing rooms.

Here was an ample house for a sizable middle-class family. It was not a home that a poor man could afford, nor even the industrious mechanic Grund mentioned. But shorn of its greenhouse and some of the Gothic decorations, it became a home that many another American might build. He would do so in towns as far apart as Bangor, Maine, and Dubuque, Iowa. With good fortune it would last for three generations or more. Even now we can see it on an old street, probably with its bargeboards removed or its window decorations trimmed off but basically the same house that Downing deftly designed.

The last of the architectural fashions of pre–Civil War days was the Italian. Examples of it are harder to find in our time, for it never gained quite the popularity that Gothic did. For most Americans it was a bit too staid, too formal. They would find an outlet for their aggressiveness, showiness, and individuality in the Gothic rather than the Italian mode. In addition, the Italian house, much more than either the Greek or the Gothic one, lost its character when reduced in size. The moment it had to be built small, for whatever reason, it became a cluttered cube. Built large, it had a restrained dignity—a dignity especially suitable for the home of a man of blunt decisions, a man who was all business, an architectural conservative in other words. Fifteen years earlier he could have unbent enough to enjoy the Greek Revival since its buildings were basically conservative too. But never for him at any rate the cobweb intricacies of Gothic; he valued the soundness of the simple line and the smooth curve.

Downing listed the characteristics of Italian in *The Architecture of Country Houses*. "Roofs rather flat, and projecting upon brackets or cantilevers," he began. The brackets—or consoles—gave the style its characteristic nickname. As the Gothic had become the "pointed" style, similarly the Italian became the "bracketed" style. "Windows of various forms, but with massive dressings, frequently running into the round arch when the opening is an important one (and always permitting the use of the outside Venetian blinds)," he went on. The round arch was, in fact, one of the main marks of the Italian mode; and the long wooden shutters can still be found today on a few of the bracketed houses. "Arcades supported on arches, or verandas with simple columns." The arches repeated the smooth roundness of the window tops. "Chimney tops of characteristic and tasteful forms." By that Downing meant simple columnar or roofed chimneys instead of the elaborate stacks of the Gothic style.

Dominating the house was the square, hooded tower. As Downing observed, "Above all . . . rises the *campanile* or Italian tower, bringing all into unity and giving picturesqueness, or an expression of power and elevation, to the whole composition." He judged the effect of the tower shrewdly; if any one element symbolized the Italian style, that was it.

For his conservative reader Downing thoughtfully provided

the plans for an Italian house. More spacious than his Gothic villa, it nevertheless cost less. He proposed that it be built of wood, and if this was done in one of the "cheap lumber" districts, the house could be finished for under $4,000. It had a good many things that would appeal to modern eyes as well as to modern pocketbooks. Its volumes were solid but not dull. It had two full stories: four large rooms on the first floor and four ample bedrooms on the second. The floor plan was L-shaped, with the tower rising within the angle of the L and standing in the center of the façade. To the right of the tower was the drawing room, whose bay window Downing treated in the Italian manner by squaring it and rounding the window arches. Behind the drawing room lay the library. It connected with the dining room. To cut off cooking odors Downing separated the kitchen from the dining room by a hall. There were also a scullery, a pantry, and a kitchen porch. The front entry was through a porch door at the base of the campanile. The only mark of the unusual in his plan was his treatment of the veranda. He made it small and semicircular and put it at the opposite end of the house from the kitchen porch. Normally, the same neighborliness that made the Gothic veranda an indispensable part of American social life also caused the Italian veranda to be lengthened and set in front of the house.

The attractions of this Italian house to the man who purchased it would be of two sorts. First of all, he would have bought sensible, functional housing, with a minimum of waste space and frippery. Secondly, he would have a home of quietly distinguished design. Its main masses are simply those of three child's building blocks pushed together. The tall thin block is the tower; the large rectangular box is the foot of the L; and the smaller box is its stem. But Downing has arranged those three solids in such a way that their disposition could not be improved. They now constitute a unit; aesthetically, the whole has become greater than the sum of its parts.

The Greek, the Gothic, the Italian: we have mentioned all those styles without saying a word about the American. The reason is, frankly, that aside from the log cabin there was no embodiment of an American style during these decades. More-over, nobody seemed to care. Emerson would call stirringly for a new national literature; the American Art-Union, for native paint-ings of native scenes; William Henry Fry, for native music; and the American public would demand native statues of native he-roes. But Andrew Downing—the outstanding architect of the time—placidly offered Greek, Gothic, and Italian houses to the acquiescent public. Anglophile that he was, he looked to England for guidance and got it: each style of house was popular in Eng-land before being introduced over here. The work not only of Downing but of practically all ante-bellum architects was con-sistently cast in the English mold. For any notable native develop-ment, the American people would have to wait for the skyscraper and the end of the nineteenth century.

So far we have been looking at houses from the outside. Now it is time to go in and see how they were furnished and what they might suggest about the nature of the people who furnished them. We can view them through the sharp eyes of such observers as Mark Twain and Downing.

4

Whatnots in the Pointed Style

≫≪ Now the parlor was still. The afternoon's guest from Long Island had gone, leaving not even an echo behind her. The heavy room settled back into a static symbol of respectability and middle-class taste.

With its flowered diamonds of pink and yellow against a deep green background, the carpet stretched from one imposing wall to the other. The wallpaper had a curved figure on it, in gray against a rose background. The heavy drapes around the two tall windows hung in folds of yellow. And the furniture, spaced evenly around the walls, appeared to be an overripe elaboration of some French style—it was hard to decide which one. The sofa, the two armchairs, and the pair of straight chairs were all tightly padded in green. A confusion of carved tracery covered their black walnut tops. The three marble-covered tables (actually, two were half tables or "pier tables") were similarly elaborated with carving and tracery work, except that here it was on the curved legs and stretchers instead of the backs. The round table, of rosewood, stood next to one of the armchairs; the two pier tables guarded each side of the big square doorway with its pair of sliding doors. Above each of the pier tables hung a round gilt mirror—the pier glass—with its entire frame covered by tracery work as full as that on the tops of the chairs and settee.

On the other side of the room, facing the open door, hung a fine square mirror above the marble mantelpiece. On each side of that mirror was a round-framed portrait. The last important article of furniture in the room occupied the space between the two windows. It was a tall bookcase, with an intricate triangular top. Likewise of black walnut, it had five shelves, with the bottom two enclosed by cupboard doors.

Those were the main pieces in the parlor. Since the room was sizable, they alone did not account for its feeling of fullness. That was partly caused by the multitude of little things, from beaded flower baskets to china bric-a-brac. There was something laid on every horizontal surface in the room.

Mark Twain had a Southern rather than a New York parlor particularly in mind when he compiled his wonderful, jeering catalogue of its contents for *Life on the Mississippi*; but with allowance for his exaggeration, this clutter would have been just as easy to find in any other part of the country:

> A parlor, fifteen feet by fifteen—in some instances five or ten feet larger; ingrain carpet; mahogany center-table; lamp on it, with green-paper shade—standing on a gridiron, so to speak, made of high-colored yarns, by the young ladies of the house, and called a lamp-mat; several books, piled and disposed, with cast-iron exactness, according to an inherited and unchangeable plan; among them, Tupper, much pencilled; also, "Friendship's Offering," and "Affection's Wreath," with their sappy inanities illustrated in die-away mezzotints; also, Ossian; "Alonzo and Melissa"; maybe "Ivanhoe"; also "Album," full of original "poetry" of the Thou-hast-wounded-the-spirit-that-loved-thee breed; two or three goody-goody works—"Shepherd of Salisbury

Plain," etc.; current number of the chaste and innocuous Godey's "Lady's Book," with painted fashionplate of wax-figure women with mouths all alike—lips and eyelids the same size—each five-foot woman with a two-inch wedge sticking from under her dress and letting-on to be half of her foot. Polished air-tight stove (new and deadly invention), with pipe passing through a board which closes up the discarded good old fireplace. On each end of the wooden mantel, over the fireplace, a large basket of peaches and other fruits, natural size, all done in plaster, rudely, or in wax, and painted to resemble the originals—which they don't. Over middle of mantel, engraving—Washington Crossing the Delaware; on the wall by the door, copy of it done in thunder-and-lightning crewels by one of of the young ladies—work of art which would have made Washington hesitate about crossing, if he could have foreseen what advantage was going to be taken of it. Piano—kettle in disguise—with music, bound and unbound, piled on it, and on a stand near by: Battle of Prague; Bird Waltz; Arkansas Traveller; Rosin the Bow; Marseilles Hymn; On a Lone Barren Isle (St. Helena); The Last Link is Broken; She wore a Wreath of Roses the Night when last we met; Go, forget me, Why should Sorrow o'er that Brow a Shadow fling; Hours there were to Memory Dearer; Long, Long Ago; Days of Absence; A Life on the Ocean Wave, a Home on the Rolling Deep; Bird at Sea; and spread open on the rack, where the plaintive singer has left it, *Ro*-holl on, silver *moo*-hoon, guide the *trav*-el-ler his *way*, etc. Tilted pensively against the piano, a guitar—guitar capable of playing the Spanish Fandango by itself, if you give it a start. Frantic work of art on the wall—pious motto, done on the premises, sometimes in colored yarns, sometimes in faded grasses: progenitor of the "God Bless Our Home" of modern commerce. Framed in black moldings on the wall, other works of art, conceived and committed on the premises, by the young ladies; being grim black-and-white crayons; landscapes, mostly: lake, solitary sail-boat, petrified clouds, pre-geological trees on shore, anthracite precipice; name of criminal conspicuous in the corner. Lithograph, Napoleon Crossing the Alps. Lithograph, The Grave of St. Helena. Steel-plates, Trumbull's Battle of Bunker Hill, and the Sally from Gibraltar. Copper-plates, Moses Smiting the Rock, and Return of the Prodigal Son. In big gilt frame, slander of the family in oil: papa holding a book ("Constitution of the United States"); guitar leaning against mamma, blue ribbons fluttering from its neck; the young ladies, as children, in slippers and scalloped pantelettes, one embracing toy horse, the other beguiling kitten with ball of yarn, and both simpering up at mamma, who simpers back. These persons all fresh, raw, and red—apparently skinned. Opposite, in gilt frame, grandpa and grandma, at thirty and twenty-two, stiff, old-fashioned, high-collared, puff-sleeved, glaring pallidly out from a background of solid Egyptian night. Under a glass French clock dome, large bouquet of stiff flowers done in corpsy white wax. Pyramidal what-not in the corner, the shelves occupied chiefly with bric-a-brac of the period, disposed with an eye to best effect: shell, with the Lord's Prayer carved on it; another shell—of the long-oval sort, narrow, straight orifice, three inches long, running from end to end—portrait of Washington carved on it; not well done; the shell had Washington's mouth, originally—artist should have built to that. These two are memorials of the long-ago bridal trip to New Orleans and the French Market. Other bric-a-brac: Californian "specimens"—quartz, with gold wart adhering; old Guinea-gold locket, with circlet of ancestral hair in it; Indian arrow-heads, of flint; pair of bead moccasins, from uncle who crossed the Plains;

three "alum" baskets of various colors—being skeleton-frame of wire, clothed-on with cubes of crystallized alum in the rockcandy style—works of art which were achieved by the young ladies; their doubles and duplicates to be found upon all what-nots in the land; convention of desiccated bugs and butterflies pinned to a card; painted toy-dog, seated upon bellows-attachment —drops its under jaw and squeaks when pressed upon; sugar-candy rabbit—limbs and features merged together, not strongly defined; pewter presidential-campaign medal; miniature card-board wood-sawyer, to be attached to the stove-pipe and operated by the heat; small Napoleon, done in wax; spread-open daguerreotypes of dim children, parents, cousins, aunts, and friends, in all attitudes but customary ones; no templed portico at back, and manufactured landscape stretching away in the distance—that came in later, with the photograph; all these vague figures lavishly chained and ringed—metal indicated and secured from doubt by stripes and splashes of vivid gold bronze; all of them too much combed, too much fixed up; and all of them uncomfortable in inflexible Sunday-clothes of a pattern which the spectator cannot realize could ever have been in fashion; husband and wife generally grouped together—husband sitting, wife standing, with hand on his shoulder—and both preserving, all these fading years, some traceable effect of the daguerreotypist's brisk "Now smile, if you please!" Bracketed over what-not—place of special sacredness—an outrage in water-color, done by the young niece that came on a visit long ago, and died. Pity, too; for she might have repented of this in time. Horse-hair chairs, horse-hair sofa which keeps sliding from under you. Window shades, of oil stuff, with milk-maids and ruined castles stencilled on them in fierce colors. Lambrequins dependent from gaudy boxings of beaten tin, gilded.

Anyone who considers Mark Twain's exaggeration gross should remember that this was the age of the coyly elaborate. When, for example, the popular Florence Hartley told readers of her *Ladies' Hand Book of Fancy and Ornamental Work* how to cover a lampshade, the materials she recommended were: much rose-colored silk, a wealth of artificial flowers to sew on the silk, a supply of overlapping artificial leaves for the border of the shade, and several trailing vines (artificial of course) to hang down from the edge of the shade! Against this kind of thing men of taste campaigned tirelessly but not very effectively.

In beginning the several chapters on proper furnishings in *The Architecture of Country Houses*, Andrew Downing himself warned against "elaborate exhibition of style." He seemed almost as sensitive to it as Mark Twain. All the pictures of sample interiors, even of the popular Gothic parlor, which Downing printed in his book show a definite degree of restraint.

He proved himself a realist as well as a man of conservative taste. He recommended that the cottager make a plain box or bench out of boards, cover it with canvas stuffed with cornhusks or something similar, and then turn it over to his wife to cover with chintz. She also could add square pillows and so have a simple yet useful couch or sofa. To go with the sofa Downing proposed several kinds of homemade barrel chairs. Unlike their present-day descendants, these were literally to be made from barrels. The back was to be cut with a hand saw into the usual high-curved shape, boards were to be nailed in for the seat, and then the chair too was to be covered with chintz. One of the "cheapest and simplest seats," was his opinion.

But Downing suggested that his cottager buy a set of chamber furniture rather than make it. Here Downing was ahead of his time; though prices were settling, they would not go down to where a cottager could pay them until after the Civil War. However, the middle class provided the furniture industry with a better market every year. The industry grew during the 'forties and 'fifties from an economy of small shops and individual artisans to one of moderate-sized factories with at least rudimentary power tools. And the value of factory-built furniture and up-

holstery soared from an estimated $7,000,000 in 1840 to $28,000,-
000 in 1860. Factories sprang up not only on the East Coast but
also in the Midwest, where they could be near all the lumber they
needed. The invention of the jig saw and carving machines allowed the middle-class customer to indulge his love of ornateness
fully. Only at the two economic extremes would simplicity be
found—and there it would be for opposite reasons.

The cottager's furniture was simple because he could afford
nothing else. The rich man's was likely to be simple—compared
with that of the middle class—primarily, perhaps, because of
better taste. This is not to deny that the parlor of a man of
means could be a wilderness of bad taste, especially in the Gothic
mode. But as a rule contemporary pictures of homes of the rich
are more attractive than those of homes of the middle class. Two
factors besides taste help to explain that. One is that the spacious-
ness of a rich man's rooms lessened the impression of crowded
furnishings. The other is that the rich, more than the middle class,
had all three major styles of architecture to choose from; and only
one of those, the Gothic, customarily invited an excess of furniture. The fittings of an Italian-style parlor, for example, tended
to be heavy but not profuse. And the interior of a Greek Revival
parlor, as Downing and others conceived it, was formal in its
restraint.

For the Grecian mode Downing pictured a large room, as usual,
and one made strikingly cold and classical by the elimination of
any carpeting. In its place he put a kind of parquet floor. The
simplest of paper covered the walls, which were hung with a
number of large pictures. The fireplace, with the usual mirror
above it, was quasi-classical in design. The few pieces of furniture
—the two long sofas, the pianoforte, the center table, and the two
chairs—were quasi-classical in decoration as well. Surveying the
whole room, Downing accurately termed it "very plain but characteristic" of the Greek Revival.

So much for the parlors. They are revealing, aesthetically, but
we must admit that the American people did not live in them
much; they preferred the sitting room and kitchen. We should
never overlook the center table of the sitting room, one of the

most significant pieces of everyday American furniture. It had genuine social importance, for the family gathered around it every night. Downing himself called it "the emblem of the family circle." The furniture in the rest of the house, aside from the parlor, was apt to be a catch-all of inheritances and incidentals: it would not show trends in cultural taste to nearly the same extent as parlor furnishings. The parlor was the barometer. On the other hand, we should not try to exaggerate the trends either. They were there, they can still be seen; yet it must be allowed that their development was limited. For every parlor fitted out with new furniture, there must have been several which made out as best they could with only one or two new pieces to dress up a room.

Granting, then, that the nation's homes were filled more with old furniture than new, we can still ask if the new fashions revealed anything about the American character of a century ago.

They did, in various degrees. Perhaps most notable was the quiet abandoning of the symbols of nationalism, with the American eagle most prominent among them, and the lack of a national style in interior decorating. That eagle, heavily gilt and with claws clutching a bundle of arrows, had been carved onto many a mirror or mantelpiece of the Federal and Jacksonian periods. It had been the most characteristic single decoration of the generation before the 1840's; now it disappeared. Nothing else especially reminiscent of the American past remained either. The fashion for colonial furniture had not yet been revived. Even the popularity of the Empire style, which the country had adopted from France during the early days of the new century and had associated with Jeffersonian republicanism, was now on the wane.

Although in most of the arts the demand for nationalism was strong, in interior decorating as in architecture this country appeared content to borrow from one European fashion after another. Andrew Downing, having offered Greek, Gothic, and Italian houses to his public, further proposed that if money were available they be furnished in Grecian, French (ranging from Francis I down to the last of the Louis'), Elizabethan, Gothic, Romanesque, or even Flemish. Everything but American. His complacent borrowing was typical. No new American furniture appeared during the entire fifty years in the middle of the nine-teenth century; nor did any demand for it develop.

This absence of cultural nationalism is unexpected, but side-lights that furnishings give on this country are less of a surprise. For one thing, they illustrate the acquisitiveness of the American character. These crowded rooms indicate an interest in material things, and an interest that a productive nation could satisfy. The parlors, in particular, were not for the poor nor for philosophers. They were for the middle-class, and upper-class, American. In them he demonstrated something else too, a corollary to his ac-quisitiveness: his almost childlike desire to show everybody what he had acquired. American braggadocio glittered brightly in the kind of parlor that became most popular. Here was a parlor to display proudly to visitors (except such as Mark Twain). It put the host, he doubtless thought, in the most impressive possible light. The well-furnished home had one other function, thor-oughly Victorian: it was supposed to improve the character of the persons in it. The beautiful would be conducive to the good. As one author put it in 1859, with emphasis on woman's role, the housewife "refines and purifies the hearts and desires of her house-hold by surrounding them with things of beauty."

5

Paint for the Public Eye:

CANVAS AND CULTURE IN THE 'FORTIES

The spread of art among the American people during the twenty years before Fort Sumter fell was truly remarkable. Today its extent has only begun to be recognized. For stimulating this renaissance in art the greatest credit must go to two ably managed societies, the American Art-Union, which existed from 1839 to 1853, and the Cosmopolitan Art Association, which was founded in 1854 and carried on to the outbreak of the Civil War. They bought modern paintings generously and then raffled them off while the nation watched with lively interest; they sent their steel engravings everywhere, as far as Bangor, New Orleans, and San Francisco; they published art magazines for their members (and the magazines grew increasingly good); and they opened their galleries wide. In describing the public response to one of these activities, the one last named, the historian of the American Art-Union, C. E. Baker, has declared that "the fact stands striking and unshaken that the Art-Union galleries elicited a keener interest among a greater proportion of the population than has any other museum or gallery of art over an equal period at any time before or since, anywhere in America." He could have added that for its time the Cosmopolitan would do almost as well.

The trouble with such prosperity was that it invited competition. The American Art-Union ran into it headlong in the late 1840's when its market was threatened for a time by the aggressive French art house of Goupil, Vibert & Co., which had just invaded New York. As a front for its selling of prints and paintings, the French firm had set up something it called the International Art-Union. It lured subscribers by offering them the chance to own foreign works of art rather than the native art that the American Art-Union fostered. The hereditary prestige of European art still prevailed, and many an American felt that a painting or print was the better for having crossed the ocean to reach him. Moreover, the partners in Goupil showed an astute sense of public relations by offering to award fellowships for foreign study to promising American artists. This idea had never been suggested by the American Art-Union in spite of its announced intention to encourage native art, and the result was at least a minor victory for Goupil. *Goupil* was French for *fox*, supporters of the American society noted acidly.

An innocent query from an art lover in Vermont touched off the American Art-Union's angry defense. "Which of your two art-unions would you advise me to patronize this year?" he asked in a letter to New York's *Morning Courier and Enquirer* of October 1, 1849. "The International is making strenuous efforts to procure subscribers and represents its advantages as far superior to those of the other establishment. Can you give me any reliable information on the subject?"

The outraged American Art-Union reprinted the letter in its October *Bulletin* in order to answer it. "There is but one art-union in this city," the *Bulletin* asserted and left no doubt about that one's identity. Strictly speaking, the *Bulletin* was right, for the American Art-Union constituted a legitimate union of subscribers, not a profit-making enterprise. Its history proved the point.

It was organized in New York in 1839. First called the Apollo

Association, it acted as a subscription lottery to stimulate the sale of American art. The idea came from England, where the London Art-Union had been successfully established two years earlier. According to the American Art-Union's plan, each subscriber paid dues of five dollars annually. Out of the year's dues the union bought a collection of current art. Then at the end of the year (or, strictly speaking, at the beginning of the next one) the works of art bought during the previous twelvemonth were raffled off. For the most part these were paintings but some pieces of statuary were often included too. There were two other inducements. Each year (after the first year) the union ordered an engraving made up for distribution to all its members. And the union promptly started some publications and gave them to each subscriber. In the early days all he received were the little pamphlets of the *Transactions* and then the *Bulletin;* but as the union grew, the publications burgeoned and by 1850 the modest *Bulletin* had turned into a handsome monthly folio on contemporary art.

Since this was a period when America would gamble on anything from a horse race to the number of peas in a pod, the appeal of the art lottery proved powerful. Even if the subscriber failed to win an art original he could count on the other perquisites of membership; but the chief attraction lay in the lottery. Eloquent testimony to that fact could be found in the subscribers' habit of waiting till near the end of the year to see what their potential winnings might be. Not until most of the paintings and statuary had been bought by the union—and the subscribers could know what they might win and what the odds were—did the bulk of their subscriptions pour in.

Generally the odds were not impossible. One year, 1841, turned out badly. At that time there were 937 members and only seven works of art to be awarded to the lucky numbers. But for the first year, 1839, the odds were only twenty-two to one against the subscriber—not an unsatisfactory ratio in the eyes of chance-loving Americans—and a decade later, at nineteen to one, they were even better.

And the cause was good. The expenses of running the union stayed small, while the amount of money devoted to the purchase of contemporary native art climbed impressively. The country clearly demonstrated its interest. With only a single dip during the first decade, the membership rose from 814 in 1839 to 18,960 in 1849. Subscriptions began coming in from all parts of the United States. Though New York continued to dominate, the total number of members from distant parts rose with satisfying steadiness. For instance, there were some 250 members enrolled from New England in 1842; by 1849 there were over 3,000. In 1842 the Midwest had less than a score of members; in 1849 it had more than 1,600. Over the nation the receipts mounted from $4,200 in 1839 to nearly $100,000 in 1849. No wonder Goupil, Vibert & Co. licked their lips.

Behind the imposing statistics lay a story of genuine cultural service to the American people. This story the managers of the union proceeded to tell in an article, in the October 1849 *Bulletin*, headed "What Has the American Art-Union Accomplished?"

The managers dwelt on two points: the service to the professional artist and the service to the public. First, they listed their achievements in helping artists. The union had, they asserted, raised the fees paid American artists to the European level and was "always a ready and willing customer for [works of merit] at the advanced prices." The union had encouraged the execution of more varied subjects as well as more painstaking workmanship. And the union had brought to public attention "a considerable number of men of decided ability" who would otherwise have been forced to struggle for recognition. Here the union could be specific; here it could name names.

From the vantage point of today the artists that the American Art-Union thought it helped were a mixed group indeed. The first it named was Emanuel Leutze, the German-American historical painter and star of the Düsseldorf school. The union conceded that Leutze's "distinguished talent" (best evidenced to nineteenth-century eyes by his pompous "Washington Crossing the Delaware") would have gained him recognition anyway but declared that the union had speeded the process. The next names cited were those of Deas and Bingham. Charles Deas, a Philadelphia-born painter of Indian subjects, is relatively ignored today while

63

George Caleb Bingham, the brilliant Missouri realist, constitutes a contemporary vogue. The next three singled out were Baker, Church, and Kensett—each now somewhat better known than Deas but without any measure of Bingham's current popularity. Charles Baker liked to paint landscapes of the Hudson and other rivers and of upstate New York mountain scenes. By 1849 the union had bought a round dozen of his works, paying well for them. John Kensett's forte too was painting woods and mountains; he also sold many a work to the union. Frederic Church learned to paint in a variety of manners but did best perhaps in literal renderings of out-size American scenery. In *The Art-Idea* the American critic Jarves stigmatized Church as either the prime leader or the misleader of the whole school of landscape painters. By 1849 the union had taken sixteen of his canvases.

Last of all, the union listed a group of since-forgotten artists whose fortunes "had been rapidly advanced" by its assistance. Tactfully, it arranged them in alphabetical order: Cropsey, Glass, Grunewald, Hinckley, Inness, Matteson, May, Peele, Stearns, Wenzler, "and others."

Next, the managers expatiated on the services to the populace which the union performed. To prove the extent of its usefulness the managers printed a set of salient figures in the *Bulletin*. These showed that during the first decade of existence the society had distributed throughout the nation nearly 1,300 paintings, 700 medals, more than 50,000 single engravings (about 12,000 in mezzotint, the rest in line engraving), nearly 20,000 sets of outline engravings, over 55,000 copies of the *Transactions*, and over 67,000 copies of the *Bulletin* itself!

The result, averred the union, had been "to elevate popular taste and increase the knowledge of the people in matters of art." Admittedly, other things had contributed to the current wave of excitement about art, but the society believed that its role had been the major one. Although its own prosperity offered the most obvious index, it added that there were many other evidences of growing interest.

The *Bulletin* listed the main ones. Drawing was beginning to be taught in the public schools. More and better illustrated books were being published and purchased. Books on art itself were increasingly popular. Art exhibitions were now more frequent as well as better attended. The market for prints was much improved. Better taste was being shown in both public and domestic architecture, in household furniture, and in interior decoration.

Such was the argument of the American Art-Union, with considerable justification. It became the leader of the people during the richest period American art had so far known. The cautious nature of the leadership testified to the acumen of the society's managers. They were careful to stay ahead of the parade but only a short distance, never losing sight of those mass attitudes that influence taste. The things they felt were right, artistically, proved to be the ones the public wanted. What they did in large measure was to make explicit the code of ethics in art which the American people had adopted implicitly.

This is not to say that the managers were Machiavellian manipulators. They were able, honest men, as far as we know, who induced some of the best minds in the nation to work with them. Among the union's officers the most distinguished was William Cullen Bryant, but a dozen others were not far below him in stature. The point is simply that the managers, like some politicians, were men of uncommon ability and common—that is, popular—attitudes.

A useful, if overlapping, synthesis of the managers' code has been made by Baker in his historical sketch of the American Art-Union. He finds ten operating principles, a kind of artistic decalogue: 1) Break the shackles of the past. (The study and imitation of Old Masters will result in artistic sterility.) 2) Renounce subservience to Europe. (It is almost as bad to imitate modern European art as to copy the classics of the past; the palpitating voluptuousness of some French painting is especially reprehensible.) 3) Develop individuality. (Variety, originality, and a wider range of subjects go hand in hand with resistance to foreign authority.) 4) Paint native subject matter. (Illustrate the "national character, or history, or scenery" and make a prime appeal to the "national feeling.") 5) Attempt the higher branches of art. (Paint more than portraits and landscapes; paint the ideal.) 6) Take as your

65

motto "Truth and Purity." (Never offend the moral sense of the most refined.) 7) Cherish American simplicity and freshness. (Work from unspoiled nature.) 8) Think out your pictures in advance. (Fine execution is the result of study.) 9) Strive for fuller realization, higher finish, more accurate drawing. (Avoid the sketchy and incomplete.) 10) Maintain native superiority while emulating the excellencies of foreign schools. (That is, steer a middle course between aversion toward and imitation of foreign art.)

This code has three high points. The first and most important is its pronounced, assertive, almost arrogant nationalism. The next is the stress on propriety. As the managers chorused at their most rhapsodic in the report for 1849, "Let this ever be the motto of American art, inscribed in golden characters upon a snow-white scroll, 'Truth and Purity.' " The last is the urgent plea for better (and usually more realistic) workmanship.

The clearest illustrations of the code—and in turn the most representative examples of popular taste—can be found in the pictures that the managers chose for nationwide distribution in the form of the annual engravings and, still more, in the host of pictures the union bought for its annual lotteries. The managers agreed heartily with the noted lay critic G. W. Bethune when he remarked, in a lecture on the prospects of art, that "a good engraving of a good picture, in its effect upon the mind, is incomparably superior to a painting of ordinary merit." In addition, the union tried manfully to buy as many good pictures as it could find.

The trend in subject matter in the hundreds of originals that the union bought reveals a quiet revolution in American taste. Clearly, the American public had rediscovered nature, for the most popular kind of canvas by far was the landscape. But it was nature of a particularly significant kind: nature in its kinder aspects, tame, gentle, and no longer a primeval, frontier foe. One canvas may have depicted a placid pool and another revealed a noble mountain, but regardless of whether the landscape was "beautiful" or "sublime," it never menaced man. It was not even allowed during most of this period to make him feel uncomfortable. Chill winter landscapes would not begin to be bought until the late 1850's when George Durrie pioneered in painting them.

In the exhibition records of the American Art-Union, landscapes outnumbered other subjects by about four to one. The proportion was to prove nearly the same in the next decade for the Cosmopolitan Art Association. In 1864, J. J. Jarves could look back and rightly call landscape art the "thoroughly American branch of painting, based upon the facts and tastes of the country and people," and surpassing "all others in popular favor."

Because the throng of artists who made landscape painting their specialty grew so great, all we can do is pick out a few of the union's most interesting favorites—for example, John Kensett, Asher Durand, and Thomas Cole—for closer examination.

When the union proclaimed that it had furthered the career of Kensett, it was demonstrably correct. It had started buying his compositions before he was thirty, and from 1845 on, it purchased from him as generously as any reasonable artist could wish. When in 1852 the Union's holdings had to be auctioned off, nine Kensetts were among them—and one, "Mount Washington from the Valley oi Conway," had already had the prestige of nationwide distribution in its engraved form.

Although he began well and continued to develop during his career, this friendly wanderer can represent—in kind if not degree of excellence—the average landscape artist who was active when the union flourished. Having spent his middle and late twenties painting in Europe, he returned to the United States to find his reputation already made by the tasteful canvases he had sent ahead of him. Two samples of his subjects are "Landscape Composition," which is briefly described in the American Art-Union catalogue of 1850, and "Holiday in the Woods," one of the nine pictures sold when the union closed its doors in 1852. "A river, beside which are lofty trees. In the distance are mountains," says the catalogue about the first painting. And "Holiday in the Woods" is described as having "a forest with lofty trees, through

67

which the sun falls, checkering the grass. An opening shows an extensive view of hills and stream. A party are enjoying a picnic in the glades of the wood."

In *The Art-Idea* Jarves laid aside his usually caustic pen and praised Kensett's landscapes for their lyricism. "He is the Bryant of our painters," Jarves decided, ". . . a little sad and monotonous, but sweet, artistic, and unaffected," with an "exquisite delicacy of pencil." Henry Tuckerman, the other leading American critic of the period, came to much the same pleasant conclusion.

By the time the American Art-Union reached its peak, Asher Durand was already a nationally known painter. Born twenty years before Kensett, he traveled a long road before reaching prominence, however. The main progress in his art was away from literal reality to selective realism. He started out by doing engraving—then the most feasible work for someone with talent in art. He carefully copied the portraits and other paintings assigned him. But after a time, dropping his burin in boredom despite his skill with it, he turned to landscape painting. In teaching himself, he did something unusual for the 1830's. He went outdoors with his palette and easel to paint nature direct. Gradually he learned not to paint everything in the scene before him. His pictures became more selective, far better composed.

Besides buying many of his pictures—mainly landscapes but also a few historical canvases—the union chose his "Dover Plains" as one of the engravings for distribution in 1850. Today copies of it are hard to find, but we have enough other examples from Durand's brush to give a clear idea of the sort of painting he ably produced.

One example is a "Landscape," which the union admired enough to engrave for the frontispiece of its November 1851 *Bulletin*. Here readers of the magazine saw an interesting piece of his transitional work. The faithful copyist of nature had disappeared but the mature artist had not yet entirely shown himself. The incompleteness of Durand's growth is best revealed by the awkward boldness of the composition. The picture is practically divided into halves up and down. On the right-hand side, a row of the usual lofty trees stretches almost straight away from the viewer and separates a road from the margin of the picture. The shadow of those trees lies across the road and marks off the distance. In contrast to the subdivided, darkened space of the right-hand half of the canvas, the left-hand side extends levelly in two low planes to the low horizon. The expanse of late afternoon sky, its many clouds edged with sunshine, sets off the dark leafy mass of the row of trees to the right. In the foreground, which attempts without success to tie together the halves of the painting, a few sheep and cows move slowly, while a farmer idles the oars of a rowboat on a patch of water. The total effect, even in black and white, is striking if disorganized. This is no ordinary painting.

Durand continued to heighten the quality of his work after the closing of the union. Owing in part to foreign competition, particularly that of the Düsseldorf school and the French romanticists, his popularity declined. But the high esteem his fellow artists always accorded him was demonstrated by their electing him president of the National Academy of Design in 1845 and regularly reëlecting him until the Civil War.

An example of his maturest creativity is the canvas called "An Oak Tree." A single splendid bole dominates this picture. Everything about it shows the painter's ultimate artistic method in operation, which was, as his son recalled, "while faithfully painting what he saw, not to paint all that he saw. Finding trees in groups, he selected one that seemed to him, in age, color, or form, to be the most characteristic of its species, or, in other words, the most beautiful. . . . Every outdoor study, as well as every pictorial composition, was regarded as a sort of dramatic scene in which a particular tree or aspect of nature may be called the principal figure; other trees . . . being subordinate and of relative value in giving the most interesting object strong relief."

While Asher Durand advanced from engraving to landscape painting, Thomas Cole progressed from finely emotionalized landscapes—in which he maintained that nature expressed sentiment—to romanticized nature allegories. Born a few years after Durand, he ended his life as an artist much earlier, dying in 1848. With Durand and one other man he established what has since been called the Hudson River school of painting. Its earliest adherents, among them Kensett, found in the vistas of the Hudson, as well as in the mountain country of New York and New England, noble subjects for their brush. Proud that they were painting American subjects—and developing an American school—they copied what they saw with loving care. They loved largeness (an American characteristic), and therefore their early canvases were apt to be panoramic. But as time went on, the best members of the school found themselves dissatisfied, in varying degrees, with their original conceptions. Now literalness and largeness looked to them a little naïve. Of the three men we have been discussing, Kensett matured the least, Durand experienced a genuine ripening, and Cole grew imposingly from an intellectual point of view but found himself unable to make his painter's imagination deepen as much as did his mind.

The result for Cole was that he could never finish his final symbolic series, "The Cross and the World." And his landscapes proved far better than his allegories. From a strictly aesthetic point of view the height of his attainment can be found in the warm, lazy magnificence of "The Oxbow." Pitching his easel on Mt. Holyoke, Cole looked down on the broad Connecticut scene and painted it affectionately. A stunted mountain tree and a rich triangle of greenery occupy the lower left-hand quarter of the canvas. Above, an approaching storm shrouds the sky in contrast to the flooding light of the heavens on the other side. On that side, the light streams down mellowly over the blue oxbow of the Connecticut River. Yellowish green fields are in the foreground and low, gray-blue mountains in the distance. Color and composition are both remarkably handsome. Here is the strength of the school he helped to found; here is his permanent contribution to American painting.

Not quite so, however, to the public of a century ago. It liked a savor of morality and therefore found Cole's early series of moral allegories, "The Course of Empire" and "The Voyage of Life" (which he did finish), even more to its taste. In the five huge canvases of "The Course of Empire," Cole described the rise and fall of an Augustan civilization. The empire in question appeared a pagan, materialistic one and the moral derived from its fall was obvious to any beholder. In this series "Consummation" shows the empire at its summit. Its richness outrivals Rome's; but the gorgeous buildings grouped around the blue water, the colorful crowds, and the imperial glitter all betoken an empire too much like the Caesars'. The next canvas shows the ruthless pillage of the city by the barbarians; the last one shows the scene reduced to the vacant quietness of pastoral nature.

"The Course of Empire" was extraordinarily popular yet its vogue paled beside that of "The Voyage of Life." It has been estimated that half a million people saw this set of four pictures when they were exhibited by the American Art-Union. And the union chose "Youth," the most famous of the four, to distribute as the engraving of the year for 1849.

When the subscribers unrolled "Youth" from its mailing tube, they saw a composition whose two main masses were divided obliquely. Elaborate trees, their reflections on one side of a stream, and the vegetation on the other side, constituted the lower mass. Haze-covered mountain tops, a light-filled sky, and the vague outlines of a heavenly castle set in the center of the sky constituted the upper one. Along the stream glided a little boat with the youth himself at the tiller and a figurehead angel at the prow. On the bank stood an actual angel—white, shining, and hopeful—ready to direct the youth.

This was an allegory that could be comprehended at a glance, and the American people at once took "Youth" and its companion pictures to their heart. Painting as painting—art for art's sake —they could enjoy; but painting as the vehicle for a "message" they could enjoy still more.

In that fact lies the reason not only for the universal esteem for Cole's allegories but also for the favor that genre painting now found. It too had a message. It told a story, one that could likewise be seized at a glance, and if it was a kindly or humorous story all the better.

Thus it was that genre painting, with its hearty emphasis on the anecdotal and human-interest elements, came to rank second only

71

to landscape painting both in the purchases of the American Art-Union and in the public's affection.

The pioneer and leader in American genre painting was handsome, kindly William Sidney Mount. He made his living by portraiture but his heart was always in the scenes of what a contemporary critic called "domestic, comic, or rural" life. To him the nation owed the discovery of the American people as a subject for the painter's art. The people repaid him by their unstinted enthusiasm for his genre work. The point when Mount attained success could be fixed at 1843, the year his "Farmers Nooning" was picked by the union as its engraving for mass distribution. Before selecting it, the society had chosen examples of derivative, Europeanized art; but in Mount it took pure American—of the rural Long Island variety. The shade of a tree and its lower branches frame the indolent figures of the farm hands who are resting from their harvest. Behind them lies the sunny, late-summer field they will shortly labor in again. On a little pile of hay a Negro sprawls asleep while a mischievous boy tickles him with a straw. The colors are warm, the painting meticulous, the tone gentle. The figures appear well composed, and the total effect is a winning one. Because America still loved the country more than the town, the picture took on an added attraction.

Mount's creative powers rose and fell, it happened, with the American Art-Union. The 1840's proved to be his ripest period, with "The Power of Music" (1847) ranking as his finest work. During the 1850's his vitality slackened. In 1851 the union picked "Bargaining for a Horse" as one of a group of five small engravings to distribute to the nation along with the usual single large one, but Mount had painted that particular canvas years before. By the time of the Civil War his artistic fire was dead.

"The Power of Music" indicates the twofold nature of his appeal. Consciously or not, Mount selected a subject thoroughly flattering to the American ego. Here three men listen at a barn while a fourth plays his fiddle. Two of the listeners, one a Negro farm hand, stand with heads bent reflectively as they follow the music's strains. The third, an older man, sits facing the viewer. His

The annual lottery through which the American Art-Union distributed its store of paintings and sculpture. (Lithograph by Sarony & Major.)

The central, imposing element that Durand learned to paint is here found in "An Oak Tree." (John Durand, The Life and Times of A. B. Durand.*)*

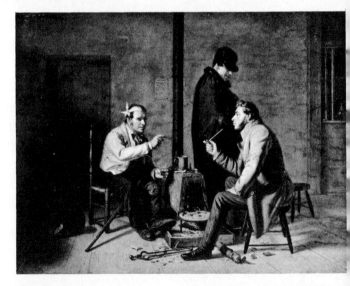

Among the human-interest or genre paintings that made Mount famous was "The Long Story." (The Corcoran Gallery of Art.)

Bingham's hard-bitten citizens represent the recurring strain of realism in American painting. (St. Louis Mercantile Library and John F. McDermott.)

"Shake Hands?" asks the roguish housewife in Lily Spencer's popular genre painting. (Cosmopolitan Art Journal, December 1857.)

Greenough's "Washington" sits today in forgotten grandeur. (Smithsonian Institution.)

In this figurehead of the USB "Massachusetts" can be seen the strength and craftsmanship that American folk art sometimes achieved. (Pinckney, American Figureheads.)

Powers' "The Greek Slave," *undoubtedly the cynosure of more eyes than any other statue of its time.* (Cosmopolitan Art Journal, *December 1857.*)

The family circle with the father at its center and love on every side. (Library of Congress.)

A skeleton exclaims about its construction in Alcott's manual of physiology The House I Live in.

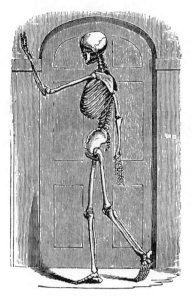

"I am fearfully and wonderfully made!"

THE

REWARDS

OF

DRUNKENNESS.

IF you wish to be always thirsty, be a *Drunkard*; for the oftener and more you drink, the oftener and more thirsty you will be.

If you seek to prevent your friends raising you in the world, be a *Drunkard*; for that will defeat all their efforts.

If you would effectually counteract your own attempts to do well, be a *Drunkard*; and you will not be disappointed.

If you wish to repel the endeavors of the whole human race to raise you to character, credit, and prosperity, be a *Drunkard*; and you will most assuredly triumph.

If you are determined to be poor, be a *Drunkard*; and you will soon be ragged and pennyless.

If you would wish to starve your family, be a *Drunkard*; for that will consume the means of their support.

If you would be imposed on by knaves, be a *Drunkard*; for that will make their task easy.

Vol. 6.   B

this American Tract Society leaflet ...e results of drunkenness are spelled ...t. (Library of Congress.)

...he first stirrings of love, when the heroine ... The Wide, Wide World meets the ...other of her best friend.

The urgings of lust as limned for Lippard's sensational The Quaker City.

THE PERILOUS SITUATION OF MABEL WITH PARSON PYNE.

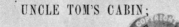

The title page of Mrs. Stowe's dynamic volume.

Mrs. Sigourney in her pensive primness. (*Duyckinck*, National Portrait Gallery of Eminent Americans.)

head is lifted slightly; on his face is an expression of genuine sweetness. To every hostile foreign critic, this picture said that Americans were not uncultured, avaricious braggarts. Right here, in point, were several of them—farmer folk at that—who could stop toward the end of an afternoon and give their souls to the enjoyment of art. Evidently love of art, and the ability to create it, did not belong purely to the upper classes; in America everyone could claim it as his own. This, said the painting, was the land of universal democratic culture.

Matched with the psychological appeal of the subject was the excellence of the technique. The rectangles of the main composition are masterfully interrelated. Mount has posed the figures of the four men with a seeming inevitability that actually testifies to long labor on his part. His brushwork is meticulous without looking finicky. Here is the appearance of reality for those who could appreciate it; and here is imaginativeness of a reasonably high order for the critics of his time and ours. He once admonished himself in his journal by saying, "Paint pictures that will take with the public—never paint for the few, but the many." But his sound, honest technique and his artist's imagination allowed him to transcend that advice.

Four years after honoring Mount by making his "Farmers Nooning" their engraving of the year, the managers of the union similarly honored a Western painter-politician. They took the very first genre painting, in fact, that he had finished. The artist was George Caleb Bingham. The picture was "The Jolly Flatboatmen," which the union also printed as a frontispiece to its *Transactions* for 1846. It was a subject that Bingham painted at least twice more, with considerable improvement each time. Though the version mailed to members of the union in 1847 received widespread praise, today it is hard to tell why. The merits of "Farmers Nooning," for instance, remain clear; but the awkward, pyramidal composition of "The Jolly Flatboatmen" is only partly balanced by the lively drawing and the humor and verve of the style. The initial impression the picture makes is amateurish—no doubt one reason Bingham later reworked it.

But to judge Bingham or even his popularity by this one canvas

73

would be unfair. He made it his purpose, he said, to record the social and political characteristics of the American people; and he proceeded to do this for the West in particular with a growing sureness of line and composition that ultimately allowed him to rank above Mount himself.

"County Election," painted during the winter of 1851-52, shows Bingham at his virile best. Over sixty figures are so shrewdly placed on the canvas and drawn with so incisive a stroke that each one of them is individualized. Several of the artist's preliminary sketches have survived. They reveal the care as well as the engaging naturalness that characterized Bingham's drawing. In them everything is rendered with striking effect, from the figure of the drinker at the far left, lolling back in a chair while his glass is being filled, to the massive official at the other end of the canvas who is swearing in a voter and by his porcine bulk epitomizes all politicians who have fed fat at the public trough. Of all the elements of "County Election," only the coloring is poor. The paints on Bingham's palette were simple hues and strong ones; the gradations, the varying textures were missing.

Bingham personally had "County Election" engraved, then put it on tour to advertise the engravings, and sold those by subscription. Lacking the country-wide machinery of an art union, he failed to sell as many copies as he might have wanted but still sold enough to prove the popularity of his work.

The public enjoyed him and Mount almost equally well. Yet the appeal the two painters made, though they became the leading genre artists in the United States, was not the same. Mount cast over his canvases a gentle glow that showed the American people at their best. Nothing crude or uncomplimentary mars his mellow Long Island scenes. He reminds us of the men (though clearly their superior in both technique and conception) who paint *Saturday Evening Post* covers today. Not so Bingham. He paints America with its wart. His strong-jawed, toothless rivermen brim with gusty life; no one would ever accuse them of looking noble or even gentle. The drunken, argumentative voters and politicians in his political scenes show democracy "as is." The appeal of Bingham's unflattering pictures was to another side of the American character, the side that guffawed at the tall tales of the South-west, snorted at vitriolic caricatures of political leaders, and slyly pulled the chair away from a neighbor just as he sat down. The public could slap its thigh and admit the truth of Bingham's earthy scenes at the same time that it sensed the amiable beauty of Mount's compositions.

A panoramic view of popular American painting in the 'forties needs one more thing to complete it. That is the kind of crafts-manship exemplified by the Düsseldorf school and its leading ex-ponent in America, Emanuel Leutze.

Born in Germany, Leutze grew up in the United States and passed his apprenticeship as an artist here. By 1841 he had enough commissions to finance a trip to Europe, where he went to study at the celebrated academy in Düsseldorf. He swiftly mastered its main characteristics. They were, as Alan Burroughs points out in *Limners and Likenesses*, much careful preparatory drawing, an even finish to the brushwork, minute depiction of detail, and exact if superficial realism. In Düsseldorf fashion Leutze painted a long series of historical and dramatic pictures. His primary interest lay in the past. This interest joined with his interest in America to lead to his first success, "Columbus before the Council of Sala-manca," which the art union at Düsseldorf itself proceeded to buy.

Though Leutze stayed in Europe nearly twenty years, the United States became his most lucrative market and he returned here in 1859. Finding his pompous paintings much to its taste, the federal government commissioned Leutze in 1861 to help decorate the Capitol. The result was six hundred square feet of wall space covered with the dull immensities of "Westward the Course of Empire Takes Its Way." But the painting for which Leutze at once became celebrated is still widely, and incorrectly, admired as the noblest example of American historical art. It is "Washing-ton Crossing the Delaware." It must be true that every American child has sometime seen a copy of it. Standing resolute in the bow of his boat, the heroic general fixes his eyes on the opposite shore of the river while his men row with difficulty through the glassy blocks of ice. This is the image of Washington enshrined in American hearts. Despite the technical shortcomings of the picture its popularity remains unabated, fed now as it was a century ago from two sources. The first is the love for the absolutely literal that marks American taste in historical pictures. The second is the interest in the anecdotal, which accounts for so much of the popularity of genre painting. This, then, is a notable historical scene, believed by nearly all beholders to be painted with utmost fidelity, which also tells a human-interest story. Such a combination is hard to surpass.

Just as pleasant and profitable as Leutze's connection with the federal government was his connection with the American Art-Union. Made early in his career, it was highlighted by the use of his "Sir Walter Raleigh Parting with His Wife" as the engraving for 1846 and further by the choice of his "Image Breaker" as the subject for one of the five small engravings sent to the membership for 1850.

The subscribers to the American Art-Union could easily have felt the double pull of the "Raleigh," for it was another specimen both of historical and genre painting. Sir Walter, about to leave the cell for his execution, is shown standing in the right center of the scene. He comforts his wife, who clings to him in sorrow. Behind her and to her left, the turnkey stands at the open cell door; he gazes at the halberded guards coming down the corridor for the condemned man. The play of light and shade is strong. The lightened area of the opened door is repeated by the light of Raleigh's lamp against the groined wall of his cell. Leutze makes the spacing of the figures simple yet effective. The drawing of the wife's down-turned face is clumsy but other errors of draughtsmanship are few. The picture constitutes a fair sample of his much applauded work. Jarves conceded, "Leutze is the representative painter of the American branch of [the Düsseldorf] school and stands the highest in popular esteem." But the reasons for that standing were not, at least to Jarves, the most praiseworthy. He frankly felt that Leutze had become popular because of his "bias to the exaggerated and sensational" and his cultivation of "the

76

forcible, common, and striking, at the expense of the higher qualities of art."

In summary, the extremes of popular taste for the 'forties reveal themselves on the one hand in Leutze's bombastic panoramas and on the other in the sensitive woodland scenes of Kensett, the first painter we discussed. Yet the range is actually much narrower than we should normally expect. The main reason beyond a doubt is the leadership of the American Art-Union. The existence of that leadership cannot be denied, although admittedly we cannot pinpoint its degree. How much it formed public opinion and how much it merely expressed it are questions no one can answer precisely. Nor can we tell how far the union influenced American artists in their choice of subject or, to a lesser extent, of technique. But that there was a close harmony between the union's critical principles, the critical principles (felt if not formulated) of the public, and the kinds of pictures which the most popular artists of the time painted is not to be denied.

True, most artists took certain of the union's dicta more seriously than others but all received at least some attention. Though the union aroused anger at times, its views could not be ignored. To the proposal that the native artist break with the past and renounce subservience to Europe, the artists we have looked at, as well as their compatriots, gave varying degrees of assent. Few would go as far as Mount, who simply refused to study in Europe or to stare at Old Masters; but many served an apprenticeship abroad and then readily returned to this country. The one foreign influence that affected some of them substantially was that of the Düsseldorf school, whose characteristics clearly appealed to American mass taste. To the proposal that the American artist paint American scenes, the assent was enthusiastic. The multitude of landscapes painted were nearly all of native woods and meadows. The genre subjects were likewise almost entirely indigenous ones. To the proposal that the artist attempt the "higher branches" of art there was, on the other hand, relatively little acquiescence. Most painters persisted in painting what they saw. Only Thomas

77

Cole, in his much admired allegories, painted the "ideal" that the union hoped for rather than the real.

To the exhortation to take as a motto "Truth and Purity," the artists listened with proper approval. Not a licentious, not a sensual picture reached the gallery of the union. Such paintings as could arouse the libido were quickly hidden away by their private buyers. In spite of the eternal appeal of the feminine form, only a few nudes appear to have been painted; and those, maidenly ones. To the exhortation to better their workmanship, lastly, most artists paid some heed. On the technical side, American painting improved perceptibly throughout the decade. Though we have few records of revision as striking as those for Bingham, it is a safe assumption that many of his co-workers strove just as long and earnestly.

The life of the American Art-Union ended, for most practical purposes, with the end of the year 1852. The competition from the French firm of Goupil, Vibert & Co., which had aroused great apprehension, turned out not to be very important. But three other things were. The first was an almost inexplicable drop in enrollment in 1851. Right up to November, subscriptions came in well. However, in December—the time when last-minute memberships usually poured in—the managers found to their dismay that subscriptions for that month were 5,000 under those for the previous December. They admitted themselves at loss to explain the shattering decline. Their lieutenants, the faithful honorary secretaries scattered throughout the nation, reported a stringency of money and a surplus of competing attractions.

The membership rolls did not have a chance to recover, for by the spring of 1852 the union was in enough legal trouble to deter any prospective member. The reason lay in some public opposition to the union's most famous feature, the annual lottery. On moral grounds certain people opposed any lottery, even for a good cause, and dubbed this particular one a prostitution of art. On behalf of that point of view a suit calling the lottery unconstitutional was now entered. Bitterly waged, the suit worked its way up to the highest court in the state of New York. There the union lost decisively.

A final factor that must be taken into account was the ill will of the professional artists' guild, the National Academy of Design. Although its members had sold the union a host of pictures over the years, the academy charged it with being merely an opinionated merchandiser of art. In the last year or two of the union's existence the relationship between the two societies improved; however, the damage was already done.

After the court's decision the American Art-Union struggled fitfully but it was no use. The managers sold the large art collection still on hand, the auction taking place within a few weeks after the legal judgment was announced. Early in 1853 the managers allowed the mortgage on the gallery and lot to be foreclosed. For several years afterward they tried to do something for American art, but finally in 1858 they transferred the remnant of their collection to the New-York Historical Society and so wound up the union's affairs.

However, the virtual dissolution of the union in the early 1850's did not mean the end of its influence. In the first place, a kind of cultural momentum carried the union's principles well through the 'fifties. In the second, the individual painters it had encouraged during the 'forties continued in most cases to paint during the next decade. They did so, moreover, without major changes in either matter or manner. True, certain painters (for example, Durand) developed while others (for example, Mount) deteriorated. But neither the development nor the deterioration turned out to be startling. After the Civil War fresh talent would be discovered. New influences, especially French impressionism, would arise. Yet it should be added that the story of the 'fifties is by no means a simple repetition of that of the previous decade. The 'fifties have an interest of their own.

6

Hard Light and Mellow Mood:

Painting in the 'Fifties

The death of the American Art-Union proved premature, for interest in art continued to well up. By the time the 'fifties began there were at least four other unions in operation, with headquarters in Cincinnati, Philadelphia, Boston, and Newark respectively. None, however, could approach the scope of the American; and when that was cut down, its place was soon taken by a remarkably energetic newcomer. This was the Cosmopolitan Art Association, established in June of 1854. It made its headquarters in Sandusky and two years later opened an increasingly important New York office. A sagacious businessman named C. L. Derby provided the guiding hand. Although in effect the director of the association's entire financial affairs, he assumed the neutral title of Actuary of the Association. And he ran both the midwestern and the eastern offices.

The psychology behind the speedy success of the Cosmopolitan Art Association was explained by its *Art Journal* in November

1856. Previous art unions, it said, failed because they did not realize that the American people valued literature even more highly than art. Art required a kind of static contemplation that the people, because of their "exciting and 'fast' character," were not ready to give; but reading, being quick-paced, suited them nicely. The solution the directors of the Cosmopolitan hit upon was to offer for each $3 membership one share in the usual art lottery plus one year's subscription to any of the $3 current magazines. These included the best in the field, among them *Harper's*, *Graham's*, *Putnam's*, *Godey's*, and the *Knickerbocker*. Obviously, it was the sort of bargain no shrewd lover of the arts could afford to miss.

Mindful of how the American Art-Union was forced to end its raffles in New York by court decision, the directors of the Cosmopolitan conducted theirs in the safety of Sandusky. Their very first lottery included as the main prize a replica of the most exciting work of art in this country, Hiram Powers' "The Greek Slave." Pandemonium must have ruled in Sandusky when the beruffled little girl whose job it was to pull out the lucky numbers reached the one for this celebrated statue.

To the query about where the money came from to buy a $4,000 statue and other prizes, the Cosmopolitan Art Association had a logical answer. By agreement with the publishers of the coöperating magazines, it had to give them only three-fifths of the money collected for subscriptions (the publishers were more interested in the added circulation) and could use the remaining two-fifths to buy its art and meet its administrative overhead. Its overhead was low, incidentally, because the association borrowed from the American Art-Union the idea of appointing a network of "honorary secretaries" throughout the nation. These faithful servants to the cause of art accepted subscriptions to the association in their locality at only a nominal profit to themselves.

Soon the Cosmopolitan expanded its services. It initiated the publication of its handsome journal with the number for July 1856. This was a wise move, for relationships with the $3 magazines were already beginning to be unsatisfactory and would become worse. Subscriptions were getting lost, members of the association were not being served promptly, and one or two of the magazines were undercutting it. When the association decided to stop taking magazine subscriptions, it could do so readily because it now had a journal of its own to offer its members. The next year it took another step forward. It revived the American Art-Union's noteworthy plan for nationwide distribution, each year, of an engraving. The first was John Faed's genre "Saturday Night," based on Robert Burns's famous poem "The Cotter's Saturday Night"; the last, offered for 1861, was Adolf Schroedter's frisky "Falstaff Mustering His Recruits."

Further expansion of the Cosmopolitan's services came with the bold purchase, for $180,000, of the famous Düsseldorf gallery in New York in June 1857. By buying this center of popular German art, the Cosmopolitan both removed a competitor and secured a showing place in the art center of the nation. As the *Journal* later observed, "New York is fast becoming the metropolis in art as well as in commerce and money-power." Aware too, no doubt, of the attention Goupil, Vibert & Co. had secured by offering fellowships for foreign study to a few fortunate American artists, the Cosmopolitan as one of its latest actions adopted a similar plan. The June 1860 *Journal* announced the "Cosmopolitan Gold Medal and Artists' Prize Fund." The idea was to offer a prize of $2,000 and a medal to the painter, under forty, of the best picture entered in an annual show to be sponsored by the society. The money was to finance two years of European experience for the winner.

The Cosmopolitan Art Association's resourcefulness and vigor brought prosperity with them. It was a prosperity substantial enough to need a national panic to dent it and a war to destroy it. In the supplement to the *Journal* for 1858, the association printed some figures on its growth. Rightly headed "Extraordinary Statistics," the report revealed a steady rise from 1854, the excellent first year, through 1857, the year when the panic started. Memberships climbed from 22,000 to 24,000 to 33,000 to 38,000. Had the report waited one more year, however, it would have been forced to include the dismal figures for 1858. That was when the effects of the panic were really being felt everywhere, and there must have been little surprise in Mr. Derby's office when the total reached only 18,600. Considerable though the decline was, it failed to discourage the Cosmopolitan. It went ahead vigorously, with the result that it enrolled 27,700 members in 1859 and regained half of its lost ground. Exact figures for 1860 are lacking; to all indications this was an even better year. Apparently the prospects for 1861 looked exceptionally promising, but the directors of the association had not anticipated actual civil war. When Fort Sumter fell, the association split in two and soon died struggling. One of its prime assets had always been that its membership was spread throughout the nation far more than that of any other art union. When war came this asset was turned into the association's greatest liability, for the South vanished from the membership rolls. Like many another cultural enterprise, the Cosmopolitan found that war tolerated no competitors.

While the Cosmopolitan Art Association did not hesitate to adopt any of the devices of its predecessors, it also learned from some of their mistakes. Most important, probably, was that it took a much less positive tone when talking about what American art ought to be. The strident insistence on middle-of-the-road native art and on pure, native subjects which had marked the American Art-Union's principles did not appeal to the directors of the Cosmopolitan, especially when they recalled how it had aroused the anger of the National Academy of Design. This is not to say that the Cosmopolitan neglected to have critical principles. It did and they were like those of the American Art-Union, but it never rubbed the professional artists raw with them.

The Cosmopolitan announced its critical platform in an article in the first volume of the *Journal*. Though the details are vague, the main ideas are clear. The article is essentially a plea for a national art. This is an art that would glorify our golden historical past ("inexhaustibly rich in incident and adventure"). It would not be an art for art's sake alone; it would be art designed for use, and the use would be to inspire Americans to be proud of their country. "To be merely decorative, art fails of its object in invention; for it possesses a nobler purpose, . . . the conservation of patriotism." In place of this exalted kind of painting, American artists have so far been guilty as a group of providing little but humdrum realism. Only for the good landscape painter has realism proved fruitful. But even he, while copying nature, has missed the spiritual element. As for most painters, their work is marked by "monotonous placidity and deleterious inertness."

Here, then, is a repetition for the most part of the principles of the Amercian Art-Union. It becomes more noticeable in the next two years. The nationalism continues to dominate; the eagle continues to scream until at least 1860. The plea for painting the "ideal" reappears; so does the plea for better workmanship. So, by implication, does the plea for purity; for if art is to teach, it must of course teach what is good and pure. But the tone is always less positive.

Since the two societies agreed (despite some differences of stress) in principle, we should expect them to agree in practice. In the American Art-Union we have seen that theory and practice complemented each other. In the Cosmopolitan Art Association this was something less than true. Although it showed a consistent preference for native art in the pictures it bought for the annual lotteries, it ignored American artists when it came to choosing the annual engravings for mass distribution. Every year, during the five years that the distributions took place, the association settled on both a foreign artist and a foreign scene.

It twice honored the Scottish painter Faed, in 1857 by using his "Saturday Night" and in 1860 by using his "Shakespeare and His Friends." A family at prayer is seated around the cottage table in the first picture, with the devotions being led by the local curate on behalf of the father and son, who are evidently both away at sea. The association told its readers what it found in the picture: an "air of repose and innocence," "pastoral surroundings," "peasant beauty"—and an uplifting lesson for every heart. Specifically, this was a picture that would arouse "gentle and ennobling thoughts." One other factor probably helped persuade the association to pick out Faed. It was his early training as a miniaturist, which had given him a command of fine detail and careful finish, thereby making his work more suitable for engraving. The same training shows in the second picture, though it differs in every other way. In this one, Shakespeare is seated at a table surrounded by fourteen of his most noted contemporaries, including Bacon, Jonson, Donne, Raleigh, Beaumont, and Fletcher. "The grouping," the Philadelphia *Press* thought, was "admirable, wholly free from stiffness, and the likenesses are from the most authentic contemporary portraits." So they doubtless were, but the picture strayed far from the standard of a national art based on native scenes which the association advocated officially. On the other hand, the cottage scene was both "pure" and "ideal" if not American. The point was not that these paintings failed to conform to any of the association's tenets; it was that they failed to conform to most of them.

The remaining pictures underline the point. The one for 1858 received a punning American title from the association, "Manifest Destiny," but its painter originally entitled it "The Favors of Fortune." The work of a rising Englishman named Abraham Solomon, it shows one elegant lady telling the fortunes, by cards, of two others. Its subject, an aristocratic anecdote, was palpably not American and far from "ideal." John Herring painted the next year's picture. English too, he specialized in immortalizing race horses. His work was "The Village Blacksmith" but the scene pictured was English, not American, and apparently had nothing to do with Longfellow's poem. The last annual engraving once again had a Shakespearean subject. Painted by the Düsseldorf artist, Schroedter, who specialized in literary scenes, it shows Falstaff calling up his mangy crew to inspect them. It was, according to the *Cosmopolitan Art Journal* for June 1860, a superb work of art, with "one grand effect" of humor. In addition, the *Journal* noted that this picture made an ideal companion piece for the Shakespeare engraving of the previous year. Yet it was hardly American art.

When it came to buying art for the annual lotteries, however, consistency returned to the association. It stocked up on native paintings of native scenery, and it bought a fair number of genre paintings that also dealt with American subjects. Its purchases, moreover, were characterized by "purity" if not often by "ideality." If allegory, for example, was lacking so was nudity. For these canvases the association patronized some of the best established artists of the preceding decade as well as a number of newer ones.

As a matter of fact, the association became particularly interested in the work of a group of younger artists, men mainly in their early thirties. It bestowed its favor on such painters as Albert Bellows, James Thom, A. F. Tait, C. W. Knapp, Alfred Copestick, Marinus Harting, W. L. Sonntag, and George Durrie. And it also fancied at least one lively woman, Mrs. Lily Spencer. If some of the painters approved by the American Art-Union in the 'forties now seem rather neglected, these Cosmopolitan artists of the 'fifties are, in most cases, totally ignored. Through some historical accident, their work has proved devoid of permanent interest. Yet their times thought them adequate and sought their canvases.

To understand popular taste during the later 1850's, we might select from the annual catalogues of the Cosmopolitan Art Association several well-liked painters whose work would represent the prevailing fashions.

Landscape and genre painters continued to dominate (with the concocters of sentimentalized animal paintings as the most promising newcomers). The amiable Mrs. Spencer was a noteworthy representative of the genre school. She grew up on an Ohio farm, a homely child who was always drawing. Her talent soon attracted attention and she went to study art in Cincinnati. ("The field of art in Cincinnati is perfectly unbounded," *Cincinnati in 1841* bragged.) There the Western Art-Union bought several of her paintings. Then she moved to New York, sold eight canvases to the American Art-Union during its last years, and ultimately became one of the most pleasing artists in the Cosmopolitan's sphere. The *Cosmopolitan Art Journal* praised her "fresh, finely-colored, delightful designs" and suggested that they showed "something merry and genial in the soul of their author."

The titles of her paintings indicate her forte: "The Jolly Washerwoman," "The Little Navigator," "Don't Touch," and "Kiss Me, and You'll Kiss the 'Lasses," for instance. "Shake

86

Hands?"—which the Cosmopolitan ran as the frontispiece of its December 1857 *Journal*—shows her art at its cheerfulest. A house-wife, sleeves rolled up, stands at her kitchen table preparing din-ner. At the moment she is mixing dough. With a broad smile, every tooth gleaming, she turns to the beholder and offers him her flour-covered hand. Here were a scene and an action of universal appeal to the American middle class, and the picture-buying upper class could appreciate the painting too. The roguish warmth of the housewife's expression, the naturalness of the kitchen setting, and the boldness of the design make an appealing combination. The woman's figure is highlighted in the foreground of the pic-ture; the background is darkened almost to obscurity. Anyone who saw the picture would be likely to remember it, and most people probably would have enjoyed owning it.

Among the landscape painters, Sonntag and Durrie typify the artists whom the association helped early in their careers and who then consolidated their professional standing by election to the National Academy of Design and their sources of income by painting for the newly flourishing firm of Currier & Ives.

Sonntag was born in Pittsburgh in 1822 and like Mrs. Spencer soon went to study in cultured Cincinnati. He gradually worked his way upward, opened a studio, and found a sympathetic patron. Then for several years he wandered through Kentucky and Vir-ginia, painting their rugged scenery on the spot. Next he gravi-tated to New York, where he made his home except during two trips abroad. The second of these, in the mid-'fifties, included a full year in Florence, from which he derived "great profit, pecu-niarily and artistically." The National Academy of Design elected him an associate in 1860, after his return, and a full member the following year.

The Miami Valley, the Wyoming Valley in Pennsylvania, and the headwaters of the Licking River in Kentucky were among the subjects he showed at the academy just before the Civil War. Starting out with rather brittle drawing and harsh colors, he de-veloped into a painter who was, in the opinion of the art historian Wolfgang Born, "competent, neat, and easy to understand." The people liked him more than the critics did, Born adds. Among his favorite subjects was "the warm glow of an evening sky stretched out over hills and valleys from which rose the bluish smoke of bonfires."

The Cosmopolitan listed among its purchases during 1857 only one Sonntag, a landscape, with a routine road, river, and trees; but by the end of 1859 things had improved greatly. That year saw the society buy no fewer than fourteen of his vigorously colored canvases, mostly of Ohio and Virginia scenes but with a few foreign ones resulting from his European sojourn. What the Cosmopolitan found to praise was what its customers doubtless also liked: Sonntag's "strong palette," bold chiaroscuro, "forcible rendering," "purity of tone," and close study of nature. Actually, these and the other laudatory phrases from the 1859 catalogue indicate that the association was impressed by his striking colors and by his painstaking fidelity to nature.

We know little about his work for Currier & Ives later on, yet it is clear from what we shall see about the concern that it wanted just the kind of painting Sonntag did. But his reputation received no great fillip from the firm. It remained for George Durrie to have his fame consolidated by Currier & Ives.

Ironically enough, Durrie's widest recognition did not come till after the end of his short life. As an artist he followed in part the pattern of his contemporaries. Beginning as a portrait painter in New Haven, he dallied briefly with genre painting (possibly showing the influence of Mount), and then reached fullest development as a landscape painter. He was able to show a few pictures at the National Academy of Design but his first popular recognition came in the enthusiastic purchase of his work by the Cosmopolitan. Thereafter Currier & Ives took him up. They lithographed a pair of folio prints of his paintings in 1861, two years before his death at the age of forty-three, and went on to publish his work increasingly. In his "Home to Thanksgiving" the firm printed perhaps the most widely enjoyed picture of American life for the nineteenth century.

Durrie's landscapes of New England winter became the major

source of his renown. Before him, the winter scene was an un-popular subject. The artists of the Hudson River school and their inheritors loved to paint the three remaining seasons, and summer in particular, but shivered at snow even on canvas. Durrie proved to be a genuine pioneer, starting a new trend if a minor one. When the 1859 *Art Journal Supplement* appeared, it revealed him in his prime, doing the kind of painting he loved best. In the course of the year the Cosmopolitan acquired a dozen of his pictures. Every one of them portrayed snowbound scenery. "Winter Scene in New Hampshire," "Getting Ice," "Winter in the Country," "Farm Life in Winter"—so the titles ran.

Oliver Larkin has called Durrie the John Greenleaf Whittier of American painting. In his characteristic farm scene, Larkin sees simple and steady relationships of "cottage, barn, fence, and trees, making much of repeated horizontals." On the outer branches of the oaks or elms are the crisply painted little pockets of snow which Durrie made his trademark. His favorite colors are "quiet browns, cool grays, and near whites." He carefully studied his chilly fields and farmyards, noticing how the color of the snow changed with the time of the day. In their appealing austerity Durrie's pictures brought a new note to popular American painting.

COLORED ENGRAVINGS FOR THE PEOPLE read one of the ornate display cards that Currier & Ives distributed to their dealers. Up to now we have been talking about individual artists and their popularity, artists of some responsibility. A few of them, such as Durrie, proved able to retain their professional standing and at the same time produce work that gladdened the heart of Nathaniel Currier and his brisk partner, James Ives. But the demands of the firm became too urgent for most professionals; accordingly, many a hack artist was hired to paint pictures to order. A high propor-tion of the total number of prints that the firm issued were litho-graphed from the work of artists so obscure that they never signed their names to their paintings. This kind of situation made for anything but great art—but it did secure uniform art, for the partners knew what they wanted: art *en bloc*. Like the astute managers of the art unions, they both gauged and shaped the public's taste.

Nathaniel Currier's first popular success came in 1840 with the publication of his lithograph of a current tragedy, the sinking of the steamboat "Lexington." Over a hundred persons perished when the paddle-wheeler burned in Long Island Sound. Since Currier's shop was in New York, the lithograph enjoyed a heavy and immediate local sale. This kind of print, illustrating a newsworthy current event, soon established itself in popular favor. It was not long before the firm issued prints of other kinds. Widely varied in subject, they provided something for nearly everybody. What they provided most of, pragmatically, was what most persons wanted.

Landscapes and genre paintings proved the most popular subjects for Currier & Ives as they had for the art unions. But the firm knew it had to depend on a broader and less sophisticated market than theirs. Consequently, the landscapes were apt to be literal paintings of actual scenery, and the views were usually labeled: "Sunrise on Lake Saranac," "Moosehead Lake," "California Yosemite Falls," and so on. Many a city scene was likewise lithographed faithfully. As to the genre paintings, if they were humorous, their humor was apt to be exaggerated or loud in comparison with Mount's gentleness or Bingham's sharpness. If they were sentimental, they were mawkishly so. Later on, after the Civil War, sunsets or waterfalls would give way to roaring trains or clipper ships. And a genre painting of a husking bee in a barn would be overwhelmed by a flood of Darktown comic scenes.

In his book on the firm, Harry Peters has a check list of the subjects lithographed throughout its existence. Some of the categories had not been much built up by the end of our period, but the variety is nevertheless remarkable. One section of the check list can offer an idea of the rest: Circus, Comics, Dance, Drama, Drink, Fire, Flowers, Freaks, Fruits. Also, there were sizable groups of historical prints, marine prints, hunting prints, political prints, rural prints, animal prints, sporting prints, and—not the least significant—"sentimental" prints. There were even the pin-up prints of a century ago, portraits of pretty girls in what Currier & Ives called its Gallery of Beauty.

That here was a thriving business is shown by more than check lists and catalogues. Probably about 5,000 different pictures were lithographed. How many copies of each were printed and how many sold, no one today can tell. One of the postwar "Darky" prints supposedly sold 73,000 copies but whether that was an unusually large number is not clear—probably, though, it was. Unquestionably, one reason for the vast popularity of the prints is that the smaller ones sold, wholesale, for a mere six cents apiece. Art had never before been so cheap. The retail prices varied from seller to seller, yet even their range was a modest one: from fifteen to twenty-five cents a picture. The pictures were sold by peddlers with pushcarts, first in New York City and then elsewhere; by traveling agents; and of course by a great many dealers scattered throughout the nation. Currier & Ives furnished the dealers with catalogues and display matter. The pleasant result of using these varied media was that a traveler could go to any frontier village with some chance of seeing a bright Currier & Ives print staring at him from the wall.

All this, as Larkin has intimated, was art for the people. Art by the people, in spite of its random character and primitive crudity, deserves at least to be mentioned. In the theorem paintings, especially of still life, which were stencils filled in with oil or water color; in the wall paintings; in the clumsy landscapes painted on wood panels as often as on canvas; and in the artless portraits by local amateurs—the impulse toward creative art in America continued to find an outlet. Gradually, homemade art would be driven out by lithos, chromos, and their successors, but the years before the Civil War were a period when folk art still found a satisfactory expression. Today a Grandma Moses earns rich honors; a century ago she would have been less esteemed because her peers could have been found in a fair number of little towns.

7
Marble Men and Brazen Ladies

The best time—almost the only time—to be a sculptor in America, whether native-born or foreign, was a hundred years ago. The two decades before the Civil War saw public interest at its peak. Never before and never afterward would the people of the United States see, talk about, and in fact buy as many statues, statuettes, or busts. Here is the way the pattern developed.

The art-conscious American tourist who happened to be staying in Florence at the opening of the 1840's could count himself fortunate. To him was given the chance to see, in process, the two most discussed statues of the mid-nineteenth century in America. They would become major landmarks of our sculpture. One, first shown in the United States in the spring of 1842, would reveal national taste by the scorn and hostility it aroused. The other, shown in England in 1845 and then exhibited in America from 1847 on, would through its various and searching appeals to American psychology become the most popular statue of its generation. The first was Horatio Greenough's "George Washington," the second Hiram Powers' "The Greek Slave."

The man who created the "Washington" looked the spitting image of a rustic Yankee stonecutter—lanky, sharp-featured, taciturn—and so he dubbed himself. Actually, however, Greenough was a Harvard graduate of the class of 1825, drawn to sculpture from his early youth. In Massachusetts he received encouragement as ample as he would have received anywhere in the United States. The doors of the austere Boston Athenaeum, the private library of the city's men of means and letters, opened easily for him, and he was allowed to copy the plaster casts of classical sculpture which the Athenaeum owned. He trained his fingers by cutting the copies from chalk, first being careful to put a patch of carpet (provided by the Athenaeum) before him so that the polished floor would not be soiled. Harvard was merely an interlude, and soon after graduation he went to Italy, the home of sculpture for all the western world. He worked with ardor but contracted malaria, and he had to come back to the United States for rest. He recovered quickly and by the winter of 1828 was in Washington making a bust of President John Quincy Adams. Though other commissions followed, he longed to return to Italy. Arriving there with relief in 1829, he took up his work again.

In 1832, when only twenty-seven, he received a commission that any sculptor could have counted the crowning recognition of his art. Mainly through the efforts of his long-time sponsor, the kindly littérateur Washington Allston, Greenough was chosen to prepare what had every possibility of becoming the nation's outstanding sculptural monument. Congress itself directed him to carve a statue of the nation's greatest hero, to be set in the rotunda of the Capitol. Greenough's elation is easy to imagine.

He could not foresee the mischances lying in wait for him. At first he worked uneventfully enough throughout the pleasant days and evenings in his Florentine studio; and the small clay model took shape. But he soon encountered the problem, not a small one to him, of finding the right chair for his seated Washington. Also, he wanted to model the head after the French

93

sculptor Houdon's noble creation but had trouble in securing a cast of the Houdon "Washington" to copy. And the workmen he hired to help with the routine of his sculpture proved to be ignorant or dishonest almost beyond belief. Nevertheless, the work went on. He made a full-scale copy in clay of the model and then the plaster cast. Finally the marble copy was carved. The finished monument arrived in the United States in 1841 and by the end of May 1842, resting uneasily on the overburdened rotunda floor, it was unveiled to the curious public.

"What will be its reception as a work of art I know not," Greenough had confessed before the completed statue arrived. Once the American public saw it, however, his doubts were swiftly and bitterly resolved. A tumult of indignation arose. Here was a matter about which people found themselves united. The tobacco-chewing congressman from Tennessee guffawed in contempt at this half-undressed Washington and so did his drawling colleague from Maine. The senators from the North concurred with the senators from the South. The statue outraged the rich citizen as well as the poor one. The opinionated patrician Philip Hone, for example, wrote scornfully, "It looks like a great Herculean, warrior-like *Venus of the bath;* . . . undressed, with a huge napkin lying in his lap and covering his lower extremities, and he, preparing to perform his ablutions, is in the act of consigning his sword to the care of the attendant." The man in the street was equally waspish.

Greenough thereafter met scorn with scorn, complaint with complaint. What he failed to comprehend was that a revolution in American taste was taking place within his own lifetime, indeed since his chalk-cutting boyhood. Typically, it began from below. It began when the legislators—municipal, state, and national— and the most vocal of their constituents became the arbiters of national taste, thereby replacing the occasional gentleman patron. Moved by patriotism, lawmaking bodies throughout the young nation started to commission statues or busts of many a military or political hero and thus became the best if not the only customers of the ambitious sculptor. Many a state capitol is still decorated with the elaborately detailed, stone-cold result. A new, democratic

94

tradition was being established. The older, aristocratic one it demolished was substantially different.

Thomas Jefferson summed up the tenets of that earlier classical taste in a letter of 1816. It was addressed to a North Carolina legislator but the fact is incidental: the standards Jefferson sets are aristocratic, not popular. Asked for counsel about a statue of Washington to be commissioned for the state capitol, he numbers the parts of his answer in orderly fashion. First, to the query, could the statue be made in the United States, he replies firmly, "Certainly it cannot." He explains that we have neither the men nor the marble. Second, who should do it? The answer is, the prince of European sculptors, the Italian Antonio Canova. Third, size and style? Larger than life and Roman rather than realistic ("Our boots and regimentals have a very puny effect"). And from what model? The finest of antiquity.

But Jefferson's was the voice of the eighteenth not the nineteenth century. And the legislators—it can be inferred—felt that they had to be practical men. After all, the money they must appropriate was not unlimited. Though they might realize the superior reputation of a European sculptor, they were ready to compromise on an American stonecutter. Though they might wish expensive Carrara marble, they would accept American stone. And about design and technique they were practical too. They were not buying abstractions either for themselves or for the voters.

They all seemed to want, and enjoy, a nearly photographic realism. Even Greenough's "Washington" had touches of it with its carefully cut hands, every finger nail carved, and its minutely modeled chair. But the people, through their elected representatives, obviously asked for more. They wished a realism of wrinkles, lines, boots and regimental clothing. They cared little for togas and nothing at all for nudity; and even a half-clothed hero, such as Washington, annoyed them. Congress recognized a mandate when it saw one. Greenough's massive statue was moved laboriously from the inside of the Capitol to the outside, to a place where it would attract little attention. Today it sits dust-stained and fly-specked in a far corner of the Smithsonian Institution.

In testimony to the triumph of the people's taste a statuary of fully-dressed heroes on horseback obediently appeared. Perhaps the most admired of such equestrian statues was unveiled a decade after Greenough's thankless work. Only a few blocks from the neglected "Washington," Clark Mills's statue of General Andrew Jackson can still be seen in Lafayette Square, surrounded by streams of motor traffic. Born in 1810, Mills started out as a common laborer. He developed in the tradition of the shrewd mechanic who is unusually good with his hands. After he had picked up the elements of carving and casting, he received a variety of portrait commissions. His leap to fame occurred when he submitted the best design for an equestrian statue of Jackson to the Jackson monument committee in Washington. The committee accepted the bronze model with enthusiasm and paid him $12,000 to do the statue itself. Overcoming a good many vexing problems, he finally finished his work in 1852 and the public found it good.

He made the statue everything that Congress—and the electorate—could have wished. The grim-lipped old general sits nearly bolt upright in the saddle, his cocked hat raised politely and his sword hanging down beside him. Every line in his wrinkled face is shown, and every seam and frog of his uniform. This is the hero of New Orleans as the people wished to view him. Even more impressive and remarkable than the general—we know from contemporary accounts—was the posture of his horse. Most other creators of equestrian statues had at best allowed the horse to raise one foot. But General Jackson's mount, through a triumph of Mills's ingenuity, reared high in the air with both forefeet off the ground. To bring this about, Mills had cleverly balanced the statue's mass with internal weights. The effect in the eyes of the public was spirited indeed.

The popularity of Mills's "Jackson" was great. Yet it could never compare with the renown of Powers' "Greek Slave." That had every appeal the "Washington" lacked.

Luck and planning combined to create the tremendous popularity of this shapely nude. A remarkable public-relations job was done for the statue, through Powers' business agent Miner Kellogg, before it was presented to the American gaze. Powers himself, more acute in his knowledge of the American character than Greenough, realized that the prime obstacle to his statue's acceptance was its nudity. Therefore he elaborately explained that it was "not her person but her spirit" that stood exposed. When the first marble replica of the statue was shown in London—two years before another of several replicas was shipped to America—he found with delight that English critics and English clergymen agreed with him and said so. Thus it was with the added cachet of foreign approval that the "Slave" reached the United States. Upon its arrival many more clergymen and critics saw it and were likewise impressed. As one minister was moved to remark (taking Powers' explanation a step further), she was not unclothed, she was clothed in holiness.

With the proprieties satisfied, the curious came by thousands and tens of thousands to eye her. She was shown in New York, in Cincinnati, in Boston, in New Orleans. What the crowds saw was a life-size marble figure of a supposedly Greek maiden. Her "slippery and boneless body," to use Oliver Larkin's phrase, rests its weight on the left foot. The right foot is slightly bent, to balance the left arm, which is placed slightly across her body. Her hands are chained, and the right one rests on a post over which her clothing is draped. Her head is turned down and away, in the classic pose of modesty and shame. Her face and form are idealized but the clothing—the tasseled robe, the embroidered Greek cap resting on it, as well as the manacles and the prominently displayed Christian cross and locket—is realistically wrought down to the smallest detail.

The many thousands were impressed by what they saw. Perhaps Mrs. Caroline Kirkland, then well known as the author of frontier sketches, best described the proper reaction on beholding the statue. "Men take off their hats," she wrote, "ladies seat themselves silently, and almost unconsciously; and usually it is minutes before a word is uttered. All conversation is carried on in a hushed tone, and everybody looks serious on departing." For many no doubt she was right: the impact of beauty on the beholder is at

97

times almost a religious one. But for many more among the thousands there was surely something besides that.

As a matter of fact, it was a curious mingling of social and psychological reasons that accounted for the nearly universal popularity of "The Greek Slave." To begin with, the subject was still topical. The Greek struggle against the heathen Turks for independence was only ten years past when the statue was unveiled. The image of Lord Byron dying for the cause, the crusade-like nature of the struggle between Christian and infidel, the feeling that this had been the "right" kind of revolution—all that aided in the statue's acceptance. And how fortunate the choice of revolutions was can be seen at a glance if we compare the Grecian with the French one. To a substantial segment of the middle- and upper-class mind the French Revolution stood for atheism, bloody excesses, and mob rule; whatever the actuality, the Greek Rebellion connoted none of these. Furthermore, it was reported that the Turks, when temporarily triumphant, had sold Greek women into slavery. Here was an additional tie with reality for a generation that esteemed it: this could have happened to the model for the statue and—it was assumed—doubtless did.

A certain sanction for the nudity was afforded because cultured people knew—and the uncultured ones were likely to be at least dimly aware—that ancient Greek and Roman sculpture often showed the human figure more or less undraped. In that sculpture, nudity was acceptable both because it was ancient and because it was Art. Labeling the statue Greek made the most of this.

Beneath such a sanction were more fundamental and physical reasons for seeing the statue. Those reasons cannot be proved but may be suggested. First of all, at the most basic level, here was a handsome girl with nothing on. To overlook this attraction to men would be less than realistic. To women, it afforded a chance to display themselves, by projection, without any social stigma. Certainly the slave is unclothed—her garments are draped over the post she leans on. But it is not her fault. True Christian that she is (and the viewers saw the conspicuous cross hanging over her clothing), the Turks made her disrobe. The psychological result of seeing the clothing was certainly more powerful than if none had been shown at all. This was not the nudity of an antique Age of Innocence; this was the nakedness of being undressed here and now.

Particularly for the male part of the audience there were other titillations. The graceful Greek they viewed was a slave. That meant that she was at the mercy of anyone who bought her. As a somber background to this, there was the realization that Negro slave women in the United States were at times as much at the mercy of their owners. Here again the statue revealed a tie with reality. And, lastly, over and above sexual possession by the male, the statue stood as the marble image of the domination of woman by man. To men this domination provided a primitive satisfaction hard to exhaust. To some women, perhaps to most women who saw the statue, it represented their wish to be helpless, to be possessed.

The satisfactions from seeing "The Greek Slave" were, therefore, many-sided. The official reasons for prizing the statue were not. In fact, they sum up in two: the statue conveyed a moral message (as Powers himself had asserted) and it presented an artistic picture to the beholder. In that connection, the same Philip Hone who sneered at Greenough's "Washington" found himself so moved by "The Greek Slave" that he compared Powers favorably with Praxiteles. "I certainly never saw anything more lovely," Hone added about the statue with emphasis. Right up to and past the Civil War, "The Greek Slave" stood for the height of artistry in sculpture to the American people.

The vogue of "The Greek Slave" on the one hand and Mills's "Jackson" on the other can give us one perspective on pre–Civil War sculpture in its relation to the American people. The swift rise and remarkable success of two art societies can give us another. For in sculpture, as in painting, much of the burst of interest that marked the 'forties and 'fifties could be traced—directly or indirectly—to the American Art-Union and its principal successor, the Cosmopolitan Art Association. They brought sculpture, of the private, domestic kind, before the public for the first time.

They wrote about it in their bulletins and journals, reproducing examples of it in their pages. They purchased it both from native and from European artists. They included it among the awards at the annual lotteries. Yet because it was both expensive and hard to ship, sculpture never became the favorite of the art unions that painting and engraving did. The engravings that every member received offered no trouble either in reproduction or in mailing. Even the original paintings did not prove too great a problem to send across the country. But statues and busts were notoriously heavy and clumsy to crate.

Nevertheless, during the late 1850's the Cosmopolitan Art Association gave sculpture the widest circulation it has ever had in the United States. This is not to say that the practical difficulties, which had hampered sculpture in the art unions, did not continue. They did, and so paintings and engravings maintained their priority. But the degree of attention paid to sculpture grew much greater than before.

The first year's Cosmopolitan lottery illustrates the fact well. A replica of "The Greek Slave" became the most prominent prize, and in addition five other statues and fifteen fine statuettes were awarded, along with about a hundred and fifty paintings. Throughout the rest of the decade pieces of sculpture continued to be offered as prizes.

The Cosmopolitan's distribution of original art in January 1858 shows the trends in taste for the last years before the Civil War. The prize of prizes was the same replica of "The Greek Slave" which the shrewd managers of the Cosmopolitan had bought back after their first winner, a Mrs. Kate Gillespie, had decided to sell it. They paid her $6,000 for it. (The replicas originally cost about $4,000.) Along with "The Greek Slave" there were four more statues of the same general sort—topical or pseudoclassical in subject, smooth and generalized in treatment, and sentimentalized in tone.

The statue of Psyche, for instance, by the Florentine Eumone Baratta (most of this year's sculpture, and a good deal to come, was now the work of Italians) shows her seated and thoughtful, with draperies laid across her lap. "The pose," said the catalogue, "the air of repose, the voluptuous beauty of figure, all are in keeping with the Greek conception of the goddess." Just as "Psyche" illustrated the classical subject, Baratta's "Fidelity" illustrated the modern subject given a pseudoclassical treatment. "Fidelity" is a marble group of a little boy and his dog gazing at each other in great devotion—a subject beloved of Americans and used again and again in painting and poetry. But the treatment is not American. The boy is nude, his head is crowned with Grecian curls, he has a pair of wings attached to his stocky little body, and both his face and figure are idealized.

Three intelligently chosen bronze portrait busts were included in the list of sculptural offerings of the year. Instead of a single original in each case, the Cosmopolitan had fifty-one duplicates cast and thereby stood ready to distribute a total of over 150 bronze busts among its prizes. That meant that sculpture bulked large in the number of prize offerings, for the catalogue listed in all only 345 pieces of art as prizes. As faithful to life in their style as they could be, and clothed realistically as well, these busts forecast the increased interest in realistic as opposed to pseudoclassical sculpture on the private as well as the public level.

The Cosmopolitan knew popular taste and demonstrated this in its selection of subjects for the busts: Shakespeare, Byron, and Scott. The regard for Shakespeare mounted throughout the middle decades of the nineteenth century until he became the one universally esteemed literary figure. Many a middle- and upper-class home, in addition to practically every academy and public school, would contain a likeness of his smooth, graceful features. Byron too appealed to the lovers of literature but to a narrower range among them. To compensate for this, however, there was his lingering fame as a symbol. By the middle of the century Byronism as a personal cult had pretty well died out but the renown —and the notoriety—of its source lived on. He stood for the elegant, wicked, reckless yet somehow dedicated spirit, in opposition to the smug Victorian Age. And the appeal of doughty Sir Walter Scott was still wide, though strongest in the South.

The last year or two before the Civil War saw a lessened emphasis on sculpture in the Cosmopolitan prizes. Yet, as the prizes for 1860 show, the interest was diverted rather than dead. Although only three marble statues were listed, thirty-eight pressings of a pair of copper medallions of Henry Clay and Daniel Webster were offered in the lottery. So were seventy-five photographs of two sets of basso relievos by the famous Danish sculptor Bertel Thorwaldsen. Taking advantage of this new technique of reproduction, photography, the managers of the Cosmopolitan had the reliefs photographed, reduced to one-third their original size, and then attractively mounted. One set was called "The Seasons," the other "Night and Morning." The catalogue descriptions suggest the treatment as well as giving the subjects. "*Night* is represented by the messenger-angel bearing away a child to sleep. An owl, as typical of darkness, floats in the ether. *Morning* is the angel bearing in the child, in whose hand is the torch of day, and joy upon its features."

Similarly, the titles of the three statues, "Maternal Affection," "Repose of Innocence," and "The Truant," throw light on how their subjects were handled. Each statue is thoroughly sentimental but the sentiment still has a pseudoclassical touch to it. It is a sentiment with Grecian folds draped across its modest nudity.

That kind of topic and treatment would always have some hold on the American public. But the new trend toward domestic realism could also be detected at least briefly in other prize offerings of the Cosmopolitan. The group of bronze statuettes awarded in January 1859, a year before the medallions, provide a good example. Of the eight pieces, four are specimens of the pseudoclassical, two are realistic in subject but partly classical in treatment, and the remaining two are realistic in both. Among the first four, the pieces entitled "History" and "Poetry" are companions. Each is an image of a pained-looking woman amply attired in the usual Attic costume. The other two pseudoclassical works are Roman in dress and feeling. One is "The Roman Senator" ("the dignity of the office is clearly written in the embodiment"); the other is "Fabius" ("the great Roman in his thoughtful mood before the hour of battle"). "The Fisherman" and "The Hunter" represent the compromise, for they are somewhat classical in drapery and posture but their accouterments are not. The fisherman has a net. The hunter has a wolf's scalp for a crown on his head and carries a bird and rabbit thrown over his shoulder. Lastly, the two pieces called "The Reaper" and "Returning from the Vines" represent the artistic innovation, for they are realistic. The pose of both figures is free, informal. The woman vintager balances the basket of grapes on her head and curves her body almost into an *S* to do it. One hand steadies the basket, the other is placed naturally on her out-thrust hip. The reaper, with the full sheaves of grain over his shoulder, appears equally lithe. The hair of both figures is modeled in realistically untidy detail; the facial expressions look natural. But the clothing is not yet everyday American, seeming instead to be continental European, perhaps of the Renaissance period. Probably the Cosmopolitan's managers thought that the American public was not ready to go any further toward contemporary realism at the moment.

Nevertheless, the shape of the future could be detected. In the meantime, the young Yankee who would mold it—in his fresh way, as much as Powers had in his traditional manner—was returning discouraged from Europe. Like his most noted predecessors, John Rogers had made the European pilgrimage. He had spent eight months in Florence, Rome, and Paris studying to become a sculptor in the accepted fashion. Now he was back in the United States, in that most American of cities, Chicago. Though he supported himself as a draughtsman, his heart was in the clay figures he constantly modeled. To a charity bazaar held in 1859 he offered one of his first little groups, which he marked "The Checker Players." Success was instant for the work. "All day long admiring crowds surrounded it," his biographers say, "praising the accuracy of the little figures' anatomy and the delightfully simple delineation of their humorous feelings." Unfortunately no picture of this group remains; but we can gain a clear idea of the nature of his achievement through the three groups he next composed.

These were "The Slave Auction" (December 1859), "Checker Players" (1860; a reworking of his first success), and "The Village Schoolmaster" (September 1860). "The Slave Auction" obviously anticipated his famous Civil War groups. Three main figures are set around its central mass, which is an auctioneer's post. The auctioneer himself leans forward over it, smirking. He holds his gavel as he pricks his ears for a bid. A Negro family constitutes the merchandise for sale. The father, a full-blooded black, stands defiantly erect with arms folded across his chest. The mother, a quadroon according to Rogers, stands on the other side of the auctioneer. Her head is bowed in grief and touches the face of the baby she cradles in her arms. Half concealed, another child tries to hide behind her skirt. Every detail is modeled painstakingly although the whole group is only nine inches long and thirteen inches high. In spite of its small size, "The Slave Auction" conveys the feeling of a highly emotional scene on a scale as large as life.

This was the very first of Rogers' so-called published groups. "Publishing" meant that the original became the source of many plaster copies, painted gray, as it happened, and sold commercially. The "Auction" group proved to be timely, and Northern propagandists for abolition helped sell it as an excellent symbol of their cause. Among the works unconnected with the current crisis, "Checker Players" clearly reveals the reasons for their country-wide popularity. Here the two seated figures, both men, have the board set between them. One leans back in laughing triumph, his body modeled in an easy sprawl. The other leans forward over the board, chin on fist. His body is tight and concentrated. Between them they form a composition with a pronounced, pleasing rhythm. The eye takes a circular path as it follows the structure of the group. Yet the broad, solid mass of the bench where the players sit keeps the composition from becoming uneasily orbitical, and its over-all effectiveness is attested by the many plaster copies soon sold.

Though Rogers' greatest fame would not arrive until the war's end, the prompt popularity of his earliest efforts showed that the American public liked realistic detail and fidelity to nature as much in private sculpture as in public. Just as they wanted a Clark Mills to carve or cast their presidents for the city square, they wanted a Rogers group for the family circle.

Of professional sculpture other than that already described the country saw little. In every sizable cemetery there were likely to be a few angels and some smoothly cut urns but little more. Wash-

"Hiawatha's Departure" in Longfellow's phenomenally popular poem. (Lithograph by Currier & Ives.)

The essayist and art critic Henry Tuckerman. (The Knickerbocker Gallery: a Testimonial.)

Ik Marvel muses by his fire in Curtis' book of sentimental essays Reveries of a Bachelor.

The dashing traveler Bayard Taylor in the costume that caused ladies to swoon. (Beatty, Bayard Taylor, Laureate of the Gilded Age.)

American journalism flourishes in Boston. (*Gleason's* Pictorial Drawing-Room Companion, *July 31, 1852.*)

The American female, in ideal form, as popularized by Godey's to its great profit.

The most famous American example of that favorite subject in ante-bellum literature and art, the death of a little girl. (Library of Congress.)

"I AM GOING THERE",
OR THE
Death of little Eva.

Dep. Aug 17. 1852
Sec Vol. 27. Pag. 367
Oliver Ditson prop'r

"UNCLE TOM'S CABIN."
JOHN S. ADAMS.

OLIVER DITSON,

ington's Rock Creek cemetery contains a typical angel, having the date 1851 on it. With its heavy features raised to heaven, it looks beyond the beholder, trying no doubt to communicate the hope its commissioner assuaged his grief with. The treatment of the figure is broad and formalized. The carving, barely competent, bespeaks the simple stonecutter more than the sculptor.

Sculpture on the folk level was fairly popular. Demonstrating that a feeling for form and volume was not exclusively the possession of the professional, every so often a workman whittled a little statue out of pine or a housewife bought a cheap chalk-ware figurine. Weather vanes, children's toys, and cigar-store Indians were frequently carved out of wood. All showed a primitive love for strong color and simple mass. The best of such products were the ships' figureheads. Ordinarily, those windswept ladies looked far too stiff to divide the breezes coming toward them. Yet they were marked at times by genuine sweep and grace. Perhaps the median in artistic quality could be found in a "Columbia" that was carved from wood and then polychromed in 1858 for a Great Lakes schooner. She stands gracefully enough. The many folds of her drapery are cut with care and her expression is lively, rather pleasant, and alert. Perhaps she represents—as much as any work we have considered—the broad average of American sculpture.

Such, then, was the pattern of popularity for sculpture in the United States during the two decades before the Civil War. Through its irritation at Greenough's "Washington," its enjoyment of Clark Mills's shrewdly contrived "Jackson," and its fascination with Powers' "Greek Slave," the American public marked the bounds of its taste. Through its gradually growing indifference toward the imitations of "The Greek Slave" (if not the "Slave" itself) and its increasing enthusiasm for the more everyday subjects of the kind that John Rogers perfected, the public explicitly defined the major change in its taste. After the war still other changes would come, but the wide interest in sculpture which the 1840's and 1850's showed would never be duplicated. Those were the heydays of the men in marble and the women in bronze.

Part Two

INTERCHAPTER

Part Two

INTERACTION

8
The Spread of Print

⚘ Cultural arithmetic seldom yields exact answers. Yet we need to know something about quantities. In the study of mass culture a book, for instance, is obviously more meaningful if ten thousand people have read it instead of ten. Ideally we ought to have an accurate account of the number sold—and read—of every popular book. What do we find in its place? Either publishers' boasts or grandiose statements such as "Carleton & Co. have published for Mrs. Holmes twenty-two different works, the aggregate sales of which have been something immense"! Furthermore, we ought to have polls furnishing properly weighted answers to these questions to the reading public of the 'forties and 'fifties: Why did you pick this particular book; and What did you get out of reading it?

But we have neither exact figures nor century-old opinion polls. That means that any generalizations about the place of the printed word in ante-bellum culture must be risky. But some will be less so than others—and that will include the most important one, that reading increased vastly during the two decades before the Civil War. Though this too is a grandiose statement, the supporting evidence is solid and specific enough.

The increase accompanied the general economic and social expansion of the period. Those were good times, we remember, with only the depression years of 1857–58 as an exception. The population nearly doubled; the national income more than doubled. The book business benefited of course—the value of books manufactured annually more than tripled! By 1840, publishing finished its striking change from a scattering of small local printing shops into a centralized industry with distribution facilities that covered the nation. It was now concentrated mainly in New York (which would never lose its eminence as the country's publishing center), Philadelphia, and Boston. Baltimore, Cincinnati, and Charleston, South Carolina, also had a certain importance, the last two acting as publishing centers for their respective regions.

The mechanical improvements in printing matched those of many other industries, for publishers had at their command the expanding resources of the machine age. They exploited them ably. As a matter of fact, the first half of the nineteenth century has been pointed out as one of the two greatest periods in the entire development of typography. In the most productive printing houses the hand press gave way to the flat-bed press and the flat-bed press to the cylinder press. Type-casting and composing machines also gained acceptance, though more slowly. Paper-making machinery improved, with both rag and wood-pulp paper being made more cheaply as well as more swiftly than ever before.

For the publishing industry, production turned out to be less of a problem than distribution. A publisher still had to sell his books. The market was there—indeed, it was growing all the time—but the question was how to reach it expeditiously. As the 'forties opened, selling by book agents in the glib tradition of Parson Weems was on the wane. So was selling by subscription. Too often a customer had put down his name for a book only to refuse it when it appeared. After the Civil War both the book agent and the subscription seller would again have their day, but in the meantime the bookstore became the prime channel for selling books. And it held its place throughout our period; in 1859 the bibliographer Orville Roorbach could publish a substantial volume listing more than 2,000 booksellers scattered about the United States.

W. S. Tryon has examined the business records of the Boston publishers Ticknor & Fields, and he finds that they supplied booksellers in most of the population centers of the United States. Northern New England bought its Ticknor volumes through booksellers in Bangor, Portland, Portsmouth, and Keene. In Massachusetts, Boston stores were supplemented by those of Worcester and Springfield. Southern New England bought in New Bedford, New Haven, and Hartford. The system worked the same way in the rest of the country. As Tryon observes, "In New York State, the great volume of Ticknor books flowed through the bookstores of Albany, Auburn, Rochester, and Buffalo; in the South, from Baltimore, Washington, Richmond, Raleigh, Charleston, and New Orleans; in the West, first, through the river towns of the Ohio valley, Louisville, St. Louis, and especially Cincinnati; later, more directly westward, through Detroit, Cleveland, and Chicago."

In shipping their books to these bookstores, Ticknor & Fields and their competitors customarily chose rail transportation. True, most major cities could be reached by water but "the cars" carried the books more swiftly and safely. Throughout the Midwest trackage grew with vigor; so did the sales of Ticknor imprints. In the South trackage grew more slowly at first, and unevenly; and book sales suffered there. Actually, the connection of the railroads with the spread of books was a matter both of cause and effect. Railroads were built because the cities needed them, and the cities expanded because the busy railroads fed them. Bookstores could prosper in the cities but seldom in the country: an urban culture was more hospitable toward reading than a rural one. Perhaps the most vivid illustration in the Ticknor records of all this is that the entire South in its best year before the war bought only $400 more of books than the main Midwestern city, Cincinnati, in its best year.

In a survey of the Midwest, including the cities of Cincinnati, Louisville, St. Louis, Cleveland, Columbus, Detroit, Chicago, and Milwaukee, Tryon emerges with grand totals for the firm's sales of $70 for 1843 (the first year of record), $2,098 for 1850, $22,203 for the boom year of 1856, and $10,890 for 1859 (a reduction due to the panic of 1857).

In a parallel study of Ticknor & Fields in the South, Tryon again gives specific figures. He tabulates the annual sales for the chief bookstore centers, Baltimore, Washington, Richmond, Charleston, Savannah, and New Orleans, as well as for the entire region below the Mason-Dixon line. In 1844 (here his figures start a year later) the grand total was $49 worth. In 1850 it was $992. The sum crept up steadily during the 'fifties, for the agrarian South withstood the panic of 1857 better than the much more industrial North. By 1859 the peak was reached, $10,462. Here was a noteworthy gain over the figures of the 'forties, yet only a little more than Cincinnati bought in 1856.

Regardless of the region of the country, however, the town bookseller became the chief customer for the publishing houses. And the relationship, once established, proved enduring. It had its complications of course. The publisher soon found out that he needed to make things as attractive for the bookseller as possible. The discount system and the "trade sale" became his favorite devices. When the 'forties opened, many books were still shipped on consignment; that meant that they could be returned for credit by the bookseller. On such books the discount allowed him ran as a rule to 25 per cent. As the years passed, publishers tried to modify this part of the system because it made them bear so much of the risk. They attempted various schemes and succeeded to a limited extent. Gradually both sides compromised. By the time of the war 33⅓ per cent was about the normal discount rate though it held mainly for books that were not returnable. In spite of tensions the system worked and millions of books were distributed under it.

The trade sales were a different sort of device. They were held regularly in Philadelphia, New York, and Boston. According to Tryon, the Philadelphia sales were most important during the 'forties; after that those in New York dominated. The prime purpose was simply to sell publishers' books to retail booksellers. Catalogues were printed, samples sometimes sent out, and then the book went in lots under the auctioneer's hammer. Though most booksellers could not attend, enough did to make the occasions significant. In an article on the New York sales of 1856 *Frank Leslie's Illustrated Newspaper* commented that the amount of business transacted was enormous. Even in 1860, when some effects of the panic still lingered, the totals remained imposing. Tryon notes that the five trade sales held in the country during that year grossed over $700,000.

The last few years before the Civil War saw the rise of a flashy Philadelphia publisher, G. G. Evans, who ignored the newly established sales channels and sold directly to the public with great success. He did so by the shrewd use of premiums. With every book a reader bought he would get a "free" piece of jewelry, a little watch, or a gewgaw. Evans mailed out 60,000 books through such lures in 1859. And during the period from 1854 to 1859 he gave away a million dollars' worth of shiny trinkets. But he was the exception; ordinarily publishers continued to sell their wares in wholesale lots to the bookseller.

The ways of book promotion were various. Using the same sources as Tryon, William Charvat has described the promotional activities of the remarkable junior partner in the firm of Ticknor & Fields, James T. Fields. In an article about him in the *Huntington Library Quarterly*, Charvat explains the different techniques of promotion that Fields employed. His problem was double. He had to get notices about Ticknor books to the public through the press and he had to see that those notices were as flattering as possible. To us the simplest way of doing the first might appear to be through paid advertisements in newspapers and magazines. However, when the 'forties opened there were ordinarily none of these to be found in the magazines and only a few in the newspapers. In the 'fifties this would change, but meanwhile Fields and other publishers had to depend on short critical notices, in many cases by hack critics trying to make a little money or add a new book to their personal library.

Charvat has noted that between 150 and 250 review copies were scattered among the more than 1,500 magazines and newspapers of the time. Since editors were not yet releasing space for comprehensive reviews, that indicated that any one book would probably receive only a few sentences here and there.

Fields set out to make friends with as many of the book-notice men as he could. He quickly displayed as much talent for winning their regard as he did for that of the writers he published. Rufus Griswold, J. S. Dwight, E. P. Whipple, G. W. Curtis, and T. B. Aldrich were some of the better reviewers he charmed. By and large they and most others seem to have treated Ticknor books tenderly. In 1855, however, according to Charvat, Fields overreached himself. The *Boston Traveller* condemned Longfellow's *Hiawatha*, one of the firm's most salable items, and Fields withdrew his advertising. The newspaper retorted with noble statements about how the press could be neither bribed nor coerced; the issue was also raised in New York and elsewhere; and the result was that Fields dropped much of his personal missionary work. Notwithstanding, the trend toward giving more space to books was on his side. After the middle of the 'fifties book advertising emerged as one of the major items in many an urban paper. With this paid advertising came the unspoken agreement on the part of editors to allow more space for book notices, and favorable ones, in their news columns. By the Civil War the system had become fairly well intrenched in both newspapers and magazines.

The proof of the pudding remains in the eating, and we may ask how many books these various techniques helped to sell. For Ticknor & Fields we are fortunate in having figures; their account books survive and have been printed by Charvat and Tryon. This is, though, the only firm for which we have all the records. Fortunately there are two other places where important sales figures have been collected. To these we shall go again and again. The first is S. A. Allibone's valuable *Critical Dictionary of English Literature and British and American Authors*. The first of its three heavy volumes appeared in 1858, the remaining two in 1870. Working with enormous industry

Allibone apparently queried publishers, searched publishers' advertisements, and checked booksellers' records for sales and publication figures of many of the best-selling works he listed. For the most part we are not able to check on his accuracy; in those few cases where it is possible—especially in connection with Longfellow's works—Allibone comes out well enough. If he is somewhat high in his estimates it is probably because he has relied on a publisher's optimism.

Our second source for sales figures is a series of nine articles, on writing in this country, which appeared in the *Boston Post* during the last months of 1859. They took as their theme "Who Reads an American Book" and they marshaled statistics in an impressive answer. The articles were signed "Nor'wester." Whoever the author may have been, he plainly knew his way about in publishing and bookselling. He wrote from New York but he had equally full information on the two other publishing centers, Boston and Philadelphia. His estimates agree with Allibone's; in fact he cites Allibone frequently enough to make him his principal source. However, there are many statistics in Nor'wester's columns not found in Allibone. Between them the *Post* and Allibone will provide our soundest data.

Most generalizations about book publishing hold for magazine publishing as well. (In fact, several of the outstanding publishers, including Harpers and Putnam, issued magazines as a supplement to their book production.) One of the few important differences was that the devices used to secure subscribers were generally more flamboyant. Premiums, prizes, and discounts were all employed. The most alluring bait was the club system, basically a discount device but sometimes with prizes added. Anyone could form a "club" by going to his friends and persuading them to subscribe in a group to a certain magazine. Often if he persuaded five or more, the subscription bill might be reduced by half. If he proved successful in forming larger clubs he might receive a free subscription himself or even a book dividend.

On the whole, the magazines prospered handsomely. The panic of 1857 alone had much effect, and that was transient.

Only during the months from, say, August 1857 to December 1858 did magazines, like books, prove to be something of a luxury. Newspapers, on the other hand, thrived like weeds throughout our entire period—in twenty years both dailies and weeklies more than doubled in number. And in the long run, it should be emphasized, all forms of print flourished. With each passing year the printed word meant more and more to Americans. The tide of printer's ink rose higher all the time.

SUMMARY OF TRENDS

	1840	1850	1860
Population	17,000,000	23,000,000	31,000,000
Number of literate	6,440,000	11,000,000	15,300,000
Number of illiterate (white, over 20)	nearly 500,000	nearly 1,000,000	over 1,000,000
Farm income	$545,000,000	$737,000,000	$1,264,000,000
Manufacturing income	$162,000,000	$291,000,000	$495,000,000
Value of books manufactured	$2,850,000	$5,900,000	$9,500,000
Number of nonpolitical magazines	nearly 500	over 600	575
Average circulation of magazines			3,370 quarterly 12,000 monthly
Number of newspapers	138 daily 1,266 weekly	254 daily 2,048 weekly	372 daily 2,971 weekly

Part Three

POPULAR PRINT: I

9
Manuals for All Things:

WITH MORAL TALES FOR SOME

　　When you open the pages of Orville Roorbach the panorama of ante-bellum publishing spreads itself before you. For booksellers before the Civil War, his *Bibliotheca Americana* was the best and only full list of books in print. The first fat volume covered 1820 to 1852. Three slimmer supplements brought the list up to the opening of the war. If you start at the beginning of the first volume and leaf through some of the pages, it will not be long before a significant fact strikes you. It is the high proportion of handbooks and manuals, of books that tell Americans how to do things. There are probably more how-to-do-it titles than any other kind. They vary from advice on saving an immortal soul to recipes for bird food.

　　Here is a handful of examples from the first few pages under the letter *A*: Abbott's *Rollo Code of Morals*; Mrs. L. G. Abell's *Woman in Her Various Relations, Containing Practical Rules for American Females*; *Accordeon Preceptor*; Ackerly on the

Management of Children in Sickness and in Health; Eliza Acton's Modern Cookery; F. A. Adams' *The Singer's Manual;* T. F. Adams' *Typographia, or Printers' Instructor;* T. S. Arthur's *Advice to Young Ladies;* Arthur's *Advice to Young Men;* H. R. Agnel's *Chess for Winter Evenings; Aids to Mental Development;* W. A. Alcott's *Slate and Blackboard Exercises;* Alcott's *House I Live in, or The Human Body;* James Alexander's *The American Mechanic and Workingman's Companion;* R. L. Allen's *Farmer's Muck-Book;* and so on and on.

Within the broad range of manuals two kinds dominate. The first deals, in several ways, with what Ralph Waldo Emerson called "The Conduct of Life," using that title for a book of his essays issued in 1860. The second deals with how to make things.

One way to approach the question of how to conduct your life is from a religious point of view. Some of the manuals in the group do that. These appeared before the public in the form of collections of sermons—sermons shorn of their sectarian nature for the sake of a wider audience, yet sermons notwithstanding. The great majority of the morality manuals have an ethical rather than a religious orientation, however. Without bothering to quote Scripture, they tell young men, for instance, as persuasively as possible that they ought to behave themselves and young women that they should be inwardly modest as well as outwardly demure.

Standing out above all other writers of the behavior books in the early pages of Roorbach—and these pages will be sample enough—are two persons. One is now remembered only because he wrote *Ten Nights in a Bar-Room,* the other because he was Bronson Alcott's cousin. But in their time they were considered major figures. No information is available on the total sales before the war of W. A. Alcott's many volumes but T. S. Arthur's are said to have sold almost a million copies.

They came to the writing of manuals through different doors. Wide-eyed Timothy Shay Arthur made his reputation by penning didactic fiction, of which *Ten Nights* remains the most famous example. He produced moral tales by the dozen. Many of them were merely sketches that first came out in magazines and then were collected. It is hard for a present-day reader to understand the original popularity of such dramatized little homilies as "The Pic-Nic, or The Young Lady Who Was Not Punctual," but it was indisputable. In this one, pretty Anna Milnor lost her very eligible beau because she always, always made him wait. First her tardiness made Henry's cheek burn and his lip quiver, then it drove him sorrowfully off, and finally it made him sigh in relief, "Thank heaven for my escape. . . . She would have killed me!"

The lessons in most of the others are betrayed by the titles. "Charity Begins at Home," "Living It Down," "Happy on a Little," "Speak Gently," are cases in point. In partial compensation for their banality, the sketches have a certain amount of zest. Though the incidents are trivial they are also abundant. Something always seems to be happening. The characters look as flat as the movie heroes and villains of the present, yet every now and then they come to life as a result of Arthur's grasp of psychology. And the sketches do not lack humor. Its dry light plays over enough of the action so that the nineteenth-century reader could curl a lip instead of shedding a tear when a character got what he deserved. If Anna Milnor's man broke away, the reader could simply congratulate him mentally, feeling at the same time no need of tears for Anna's sake since she was scheduled to marry a less discriminating suitor anyhow.

Notwithstanding the popularity of the sketches, Arthur made his reputation as a writer of didactic fiction through his longer works. Of these, *Ten Nights*, with its blood pudding of horrors, found so many readers that it finally passed into American folklore. Published in 1854, it sold over 50,000 copies in the next five years. It remains the leading representative of a once-popular genre, the temperance novel. (Walt Whitman published one in 1842, called *Franklin Evans, or The Inebriate*, which was even worse than most.) The ten nights are spread over ten years. They cover the time between the first visit of the traveling narrator to a new tavern in Cedarville, the "Sickle and Sheaf," and the last visit, when the wretched alehouse is forced out of business and, in a symbolic gesture, the ax is put to the tavern sign.

"The false emblem which had invited so many to enter the way of destruction fell crashing to the earth."

The opening of the tavern lets misery and crime into an innocent village. Their effects are pictured by Arthur in a series of Hogarthian scenes. Each portrays a further degradation in most of the characters. The main ones are the tavern keeper himself, Simon Slade, and his son Frank; a blackleg or gambler of truly satanic cast, Harvey Green; the Hammonds, father and son; and Judge Lyman, a venal congressman owned by the liquor interests. Joe Morgan, who had worked for Slade in his days as an honest miller, appears at the beginning and end of the novel; sobered by tragedy he emerges as the only person to reform.

With their passions fanned hotter and hotter by drink, the main characters inevitably bring violence on one another. Young Hammond is murdered by the devilish blackleg. His crazed mother dies of grief; his father becomes a broken man. Judge Lyman is brutally beaten, his features stamped flat by the boots of his enemies. Simon Slade has an eye gouged out during a brawl in his tavern and ultimately is slain by his own corrupted son.

The death of Slade is an echo of an earlier tragedy which served to wring the heart of many a reader. This was the accidental killing of a little girl, Morgan's daughter. She had come to convey her drunken father home from the tavern. Slade, who had just been arguing with Morgan, threw a glass at him. It barely grazed his temple but crashed full into the forehead of the child. Arthur devotes most of the next sixty pages to her lingering, pathetic demise. He squeezes every drop of emotion out of the deathbed scene, ending it with Joe Morgan's promise to his heaven-bound Mary that he will never touch liquor again. She starts up from her bed with joy, her father draws his arms tightly about her, and when he unclasps them, she is "with the angels of the resurrection."

Arthur ostentatiously repeats the symbolism of the glass in the manner of Slade's death. It occurs when Frank, "infuriated by drink and evil passions," hurls a liquor bottle at his father and shivers it against his skull. There is nothing more horrible than parricide for Arthur to write about; so he stops there and the book concludes shortly afterward with the shutting down of the nefarious tavern.

Arthur rings the changes on the disastrous results of drink, with one exception. In a left-handed tribute to the literary puritanism of his time, he carefully says nothing about drunken debauchery. The only pretty young woman in the book is Slade's daughter, and she easily avoids Harvey Green's dishonorable intentions. But the other alarming effects of liquor are fully explored, and decried. Arthur naturally has no hesitation about stopping the progress of his story to underline his moral. Often, in the person of his narrator, he will describe the arguments against prohibition and then proceed to demolish them point by point. Appropriately enough, the final chapter of his novel, "Night the Tenth," includes a mass meeting in which all the arguments against drink are summed up and a set of formal resolutions passed to make Cedarville bone-dry.

Though Arthur's purpose was as instructional as that of any writer of plain precepts, he customarily preferred to adorn a moral with a tale. It is obvious that his imagination tended to cast his lessons into dramatic, fictionalized form. Take the volume *Married Life*, published in 1851. In the preface Arthur announced his aims: to show husbands and wives how to get along together, and to warn young men and women against making bad marriages. With all the confidence of a writer who has a string of didactic best sellers behind him, Arthur added that he was sure he would succeed. To do so he employed his usual briskly anecdotal style. Clearly, he wanted to save those souls that did not ordinarily go to church, for he packed his morality as full of action-interest as possible. The plainest explanation of his method he liked well enough to make the title for his early volume: *Prose Fictions: Written for the Illustration of True Principles, in Their Bearing upon Every-Day Life.*

Besides the two score of manuals he dressed in fictional clothing, Arthur produced some works that were manuals per se. A pair of volumes of advice, for young men and young ladies respectively, have already been mentioned. He also turned out a series which included *The Young Maiden, The Young Wife,* and *The Young Husband*. In them the percentage of solid advice is much higher but the books are the duller for it.

By contrast with the delicate-seeming Timothy Arthur, William Alcott looked like a gargoyle. But his was an attractive, Lincolnian kind of homeliness. It gave an accurate index to the character of the man. Unselfish, industrious, thoughtful, he developed himself from a rather shallow country schoolmaster into the best-informed man on public education of his day. He got his start in the writing of manuals through his early teaching experiences. Because he became appalled by the ignorance that most of his pupils displayed about the mechanism of the human body, Alcott began, in simple terms, to teach its physiology. He fixed on the device of comparing the body to a house. Soon he was giving lectures to groups of teachers, using this method and choosing as his title "The House I Live in." The lectures developed into a book, first published in 1837, with the same name. Almost every year before the Civil War saw a new edition.

A truly pioneering work, it triumphantly avoided all the pitfalls involved in teaching physiology to a prim and touchy public. It did this by adopting a strictly matter of fact tone, by carefully using the metaphor of the house, and by shunning any mention of the reproductive system. Mindful perhaps of Bronson Alcott's disastrous attempt to reveal the facts of life to six-year-olds, William kept his physiology noncontroversial.

His preface indicated his purposes. Over and above the basic one—to introduce the reader to human physiology—he wanted the book to "have a good tendency on morals" and, he added, to increase the reader's reverence for the God who had created the human body.

With this disarming preliminary Alcott moved on to his first chapter. It was mainly a description, with pictures, of how an actual house was constructed. The succeeding chapters described, again with pictures, the framework of the figurative house (the skeleton), the covering of the house (the skin and muscles), the apartments, and the furniture. The language was simple, the incidental comparisons were as homely as the main metaphor, and the opportunities to preach about the proper use of the body were always employed to advantage.

When Alcott began to concentrate on the writing of his manuals of morality, he used his educational background with marked effectiveness. Throughout the entire 1840's and 1850's those manuals were printed and reprinted to an extent that must have made him one of the most read writers in this genre. By the time Fort Sumter was fired on he had directed manuals at more than a dozen groups. By then he had words of counsel in print for young men, young women, sisters, mothers, housekeepers, husbands, men (as opposed to young men), women (as opposed to young women), wives, young mothers (as opposed simply to mothers), and children!

Of all these groups there was no doubt which needed advice the most desperately. It was the young men. With a wild light in their eyes and a reckless smile on their lips, they stood ready to reel down the primrose path. To save them, when at all possible, became the ambition of many writers of morality manuals. If clergymen, they delivered their homilies to the young fellows on Sunday nights and published afterward. Henry Ward Beecher was only one among a number of ministers to do this in the 1840's, though he showed exceptional appeal, for his *Lectures to Young Men* soon gained a popularity that kept them in print until the mid-1920's. If the writers were laymen they dispensed with the preliminary stage and published their little volumes of warning at once. It is probable that the manual most in demand was the one which was copyrighted by Alcott in 1833 and reached its twenty-first edition by 1858.

By the 1840's his *Young Man's Guide* had eight chapters and a patriotic appendix: the Constitution of the United States. In those chapters Alcott covered almost everything he could think of, bringing a considerable amount of acumen to bear on his topics. Moreover, he had made enough mistakes of his own (they crowd his *Confessions of a School Master*) to give him humility. His errors had been minor ones but they served to take some of the wind out of his natural tendency to pontificate. And he spoke to his coltish audience directly, sensibly, and plainly, adding a liberal sprinkling of anecdotes to his observations. No Arthur, he nonetheless knew the value of a good story in driving home a point.

Chapter I was long. It exhorted the young man to form the noblest possible character and warned specifically against laziness, untidiness, and intemperance. Two sections of this chapter tie in closely with other writing in the field. The section on intemperance sharply criticizes drinking, as do almost all the corresponding manuals. And there is a section on good manners which well illustrates the growing tendency of the manuals to try to make Americans refined. Much aware of the gibes by such visitors as Dickens and Mrs. Trollope, the molders of American youth earnestly preached politeness. The typical manual of the 'forties also emphasized that good manners must be the fruit of good character, and never merely ceremony laid on for the sake of appearances. But as the next decade wore along, volumes on manners as such became popular. They were the first books of etiquette for the crowd. At the end of this decade, in 1859 to be exact, the ultra-aggressive New York firm of Beadle & Co. published their *Dime Book of Etiquette*, which the people purchased with alacrity.

Chapter II made a direct appeal to the young American's commercial side. "On the Management of Business" provided a fine early example of the literature of success. Avoid debt, work hard, be honest, do not be too trustful, do not speculate, put everything in writing. *Calculate*, advised Alcott, and he underlined the word.

As befitted a moralistic nation, Chapter III, "On Amusements and Indulgences," devoted nine-tenths of its space to warning against bad amusements and only one-tenth to proposing good ones. Alcott bore down hard on what he considered the chief recreations of the time: gambling ("every gambler a robber"), lotteries ("a species of swindling"), the theater ("a school of vice"), smoking ("a most powerful poison"), chewing ("tobacco *does not* preserve teeth"), and taking snuff (disgusting and dangerous). The only ones he could recommend were out-door sports and lyceum-going.

In his next chapter, on the improvement of the young man's mind, Alcott furnished an interesting insight into what kinds of reading were considered useful and what were not. He stressed "practical studies," praising geography, history, arithmetic, chemistry, grammar and composition, in particular. In the field he chose to call "mere reading" he pronounced voyages, travel, and biography worth attention—and these were, as we shall see elsewhere, all highly regarded forms of nonfiction. As to novels: "not recommended."

In Chapter V Alcott considered social and moral improvement together, further illustrating the belief that manners should be the fruit of character. He advised the young man how to act especially in female society, though he also threw in some more admonitions about the value of attending lyceums and Sunday schools. Chapter VI stemmed from part of the preceding chapter; it gave fifty pages of sane if pedestrian counsel about marriage. Chapter VII, bleakly headed "Criminal Behavior" and spiced with rather lurid anecdotes, inveighed against the various kinds of sexual misconduct open to young men. The final chapter was a catchall of miscellaneous cautions, followed by the Constitution in the appendix.

In Alcott's *Guide* we have a prime example of a work that echoes the sentiments of the time, becomes enormously popular, and because of that popularity helps to reinforce and keep alive those same sentiments.

But there is more, a good deal more, to the matter of the vogue for manuals. Exactly what were the sentiments that stimulated the sales of such books? And what conditions helped to make the sentiments what they were? Suppose we speculate about one Horace C. Wilcox to help us see. Wilcox ended up as the wealthy, mustachioed president of a railroad, a silverware company, and an organ company. But he began as a Connecticut country boy who stayed on the farm until 1844, when he reached twenty. Such formal education as he had came from the modest public schools of Middletown. In his twentieth year he went, in a manner of speaking, into business. Starting with a capital of $3 (borrowed), he peddled tinware from door to door. His more important capital, in the words of *Representative Men of Connecticut, 1861–1894,* consisted of "a strong will, a clear and vigorous brain, and a hopeful disposition."

There is no record of his father's giving him a copy of Alcott's handy *Guide* when he left the Wilcox farm, but we should like to assume that he did so. He might well have.

For this was a time of growing faith in the power of human nature to shape itself—with of course some assistance. The bitter puritan doctrine of election and reprobation was largely discredited. Only a modicum of Calvinists still held that a few of us were arbitrarily destined by God to go to heaven while the rest, in spite of anything they could do, were consigned to eternal fire. That hard doctrine lingered only here and there throughout the country. Elsewhere the doctrines of kindlier sects had won acceptance. The Methodists, the Liberalized Congregationalists (Horace Wilcox was one), the New-School Presbyterians, and the individualistic Unitarians now set the religious tone. They agreed with the old Calvinists that human nature was depraved. But they denied that anyone could not conquer that depravity, through faith and good works, and thus find his way to heaven. Eternal life could be his if a man would believe in God—and if he would behave.

Behavior was important. During the decades of the first half of the nineteenth century, the emphasis on it mounted. Everyone could perform good works if he wanted to, for he enjoyed the blessings of free will. Practically speaking, he was, through his soul, the master of his body. He could make it do what he wanted.

Yet this was not always easy. Anyone could look around at others, or within himself, and see that the body became at times a very balky servant. It drank, it stole, it committed adultery, it did nameless other things. Nevertheless, conduct in general was becoming better, after having dropped to a moral low following the Revolutionary War. The onset of the nineteenth century had seen a flood of "godless" immorality, for which it was fashionable to blame the excesses of the French Revolution. But thereafter religion had reasserted itself. The evangelical sects, such as the Methodists, had burgeoned and in addition the whole moral impulse had apparently grown stronger. Though puritanism as dogma was dead, puritanical standards of conduct revived and then flourished. Reinforced by Queen Victoria's influential example, ante-bellum puritanism erected public standards of propriety which have made succeeding generations snicker. Legs became limbs, nude statues were supposed to be draped (except for Hiram Powers' "Greek Slave"), taboos multiplied.

If this was merely another indication that the age was conscious of its inherited shortcomings, it is also true that it was confident of surmounting them. In 1851 Emerson Davis published *The Half Century, or A History of Changes That Have Taken Place*. He devoted an entire chapter to the moral reformation that had occurred in the preceding fifty years. He sketched the history of the vigorous crusades against drink, slavery, prostitution, and other ills of the time. He evidently felt that in these crusades the printing press assumed a vital part. The most obvious weapons were the published sermons, leaflets, and periodicals. But we can deduce that much public support of reform also came from the attitudes inculcated by the manuals of morality.

We should like to think that Elisha Wilcox felt all this when he proffered his departing son that hypothetical copy of Alcott.

The other thing in Alcott's *Guide* which would have recommended it strongly to a father such as Elisha was the section on business. In it Alcott preached the gospel of commercial progress. He announced that anyone could get ahead if he really applied himself. This positive doctrine found an echo in son Horace's own optimistic outlook. He and Alcott were in tune with the times, for America devoutly believed in progress. To Americans, greater size and greater superiority went hand in hand; we were getting bigger all the time and, accordingly, we were getting better. At the lowest level in the scale of values, that meant simply that a man could make more money this year than last. At the highest, it became a cosmological optimism that saw both this world and the next advancing serenely under the calm hand of God.

Many a manual tried to assist the reader in improving his mind, making it a better, sharper, stronger instrument for the service of God and Mammon as well. The tips about proper business practices we see in Alcott supplement the counsel on good conduct.

Thus far we have talked, first, about shaping character and, second, about the general education of the mind. But if we are to give a proper picture of the America that thumbed through hundreds of thousands of manuals of every sort, we must not forget the ones that explained how to make a specific thing or to learn a specific skill. The opening of this chapter only began to suggest their variety. How to keep books. How to render olive-oil soap. How to build a staircase with curving balustrades. How to make a rocking chair. How to survey a field. How to build a locomotive. How to take a picture. How to mine coal. How to construct a telegraph. How to mill flour. How to tell a precious stone from an imitation. How to dye. How to cut marble. How to make perfume. How to (or rather, officially, how not to) counterfeit bank notes. How to mold. How to make iron. How to carve gravestones. How to sail a ship. How to treat a fever. How to breed poultry. How to speak with eloquence. How to cultivate taste. How to grow grapes. How to keep bees. How to write letters. How to raise silkworms. How to fatten swine. How to invent—anything (and patent your invention). And even how to fly (this was Wise's *System of Aeronautics*, 1850).

The remarkably varied need for instruction which these manuals satisfied resulted from a series of circumstances. An expanding America called urgently for a myriad of material things but did not have large enough factories to satisfy its desires. Our country had not yet entered the age of mass production. In the twenty years between 1840 and 1860 the net income from manufacturing swelled from $162,000,000 to $495,000,000; but that increase becomes less impressive if we remember that even as late as the start of the Civil War, this was still an agricultural nation with a net income from agriculture, in 1860, of well over a billion dollars—$1,264,000,000 in fact.

Since mass production, with its simplified operations, had not yet appeared, workmen had to maintain a relatively high level of skill. Consequently, they either had to train themselves or be trained by others. This of course was before vocational schools existed. In addition, the system of long apprenticeship that trained European workers very well never got a foothold in our haste-ridden country. The ultimate result was that the main method of independent technical instruction became, by default, the how-to-do-it book. It taught embryo craftsmen how to make the material things America insisted on wanting. It trained other workers in the nonmanufacturing skills the country also required.

It is clear that American aggressiveness (typically, Horace Wilcox was "full of push") saw an opportunity in the manuals and seized it. American materialism, furthermore, set a high value on the products and skills to be gained by poring over their pages. And in added testimony to the pervasiveness of the manuals we should remember that some even made their appearance in the field of recreation. If these did not go into edition after edition as the vocational manuals did, they nonetheless sold steadily enough. Tired of bringing business home at night, it may be that a now middle-aged Wilcox decided to take up chess. He might have asked some friend to teach him the rudiments, but for the finer points he would have done well to pick up a copy of Hyacinth Agnel's thorough *Chess for Winter Evenings*.

Today Wilcox' descendants can easily buy things at stores, mass production having long since arrived. The people whose services they also buy have been formally schooled. Yet the vitality of the how-to-do-it book is not gone—quite the reverse. You can still order a book anywhere telling you how to repair your sink, sell goods, make people like you, or win peace for your troubled heart.

10

Steps to the Temple

༄༅ The religious strain was one of the most prominent in the ante-bellum character. Manifest in many phases of
our culture, it found its greatest expression and satisfaction—so
far as the printed word was concerned—in the reading of tracts
(those prayerful little leaflets that combined a story with a sermon) and the Bible. And in the half-dozen years immediately
preceding the war it discovered a new genre to enjoy, the
Biblical novel especially as exemplified in *The Prince of the
House of David.*

If we were asked to guess the name of the most prolific publisher in the United States of a century ago, we might think of
several commercial giants, among them Ticknor & Fields, Harpers, and T. B. Peterson. Or we might think of the federal government. Either way we should be wrong, for it was actually an
organization of devoted Protestant laymen and ministers, the
once-famous American Tract Society. The extent of its operation was astounding. It issued both little unbound tracts and

bound volumes of religious books (other than the Bible, which it left to the American Bible Society). By 1840 its yearly production of tracts amounted to more than 3,000,000; in 1850 it rose to almost 8,000,000; and in 1855 it passed 12,000,000. Even in 1860, when the effect of the panic of 1857 still lingered, the figure was over 10,000,000. The number of bound volumes printed was likewise great: 325,000 in 1840; almost 1,000,000 in 1850; over 1,000,000 in 1855; and 731,000 in 1860.

No publisher ever had a more ambitious aim than the American Tract Society. As early as May 1835, according to its *Brief History*, it resolved to try to "supply with its standard evangelical volumes the entire accessible population of the United States." Of course it failed, but so strenuous were its attempts that it achieved a far wider circulation of such volumes than any other publisher. It once announced that it had "produced a body of as rich spiritual instruction, adapted to the varied ages, capacities and conditions of individuals and families, as can be found in the same compass in any land or language." And that, as far as we can tell, was true enough.

The society started in 1814 when a thoughtful Massachusetts minister named Ebenezer Porter suggested that it might be good to print a few Christian tracts for general distribution at a low price. There was evidently a market for them—people were buying even poorly made and relatively costly ones from commercial printers. Porter's proposal at once attracted support, and an organization to carry it out was formed in New England. A policy of vigorous, economical publishing was established at the very beginning. In the next few months fifty tracts were printed and the total number of copies at the end of the first year came to 300,000. This remarkable pace was maintained in succeeding years. In 1823 the New England group officially became the "American Tract Society" and widened its field of operations. Two years later the important New York Religious Tract Society combined with it, and in this augmented form it continued its epic labors during the remaining decades before the Civil War.

Before we see what publications the society circulated, it

would be useful to understand how the circulating was done, for the success of the society was due partly to the methods it evolved.

Colportage, first employed in 1841, became the best-known and most characteristic one. The thirty-first annual report of the society, for instance, dated May 1856, describes the flourishing state of the system the year before the panic. The colporteur was a combination of part-time missionary and tract salesman. Originally he was supposed to work among unchurched settlers on the frontier, but the managers of the society soon realized that even in populous New England many a family existed without direct contact with Christianity. They became convinced, in fact, that the need was nationwide. As a result, colporteurs traveled throughout the whole country to sell their inexpensive publications (or give them away to such families as could not pay for them) and "to converse on personal religion or to unite in prayer."

Colporteurs to a total of 662 labored devoutly during the year summarized in the report. They covered thirty-one states and territories as well as part of Canada. Some were employed on a full-time basis. The rest, including 115 college students hired for the summer vacation, were employed as part-time workers. Indicative of the widespread distribution of the agents was that 210 among them traveled in the northern and middle states, 254 in the southern and southwestern states, and 166 in the west and northwest. In all they managed to visit over 600,000 families.

Manifestly, some of the colporteurs were embryo revivalists, lay preachers. About one of them, for example, a minister testified, "A new interest in religion has followed his labors. I feel truly thankful that he has been among us, and I have learned that similar results have followed him in other congregations." And the colporteurs did not confine their efforts to Protestants. During this year nearly 60,000 Roman Catholic families were visited in an attempt to persuade them to cast off what the report austerely termed "the bondage of Rome." Because of the colporteur, "Many a Papist . . . exchanged his symbols of superstition for the word of God, borne to his door."

Here is the record of a typical colporteur for the year of the report. L. L. Bonnell, whose territory embraced Licking County in Ohio, wrote that he had sold 1,393 volumes, had given away 683, had participated in thirty-five public or prayer meetings, had found twenty-three families destitute of religious books, had found sixteen destitute even of the Bible, had visited forty Catholic families, had found 141 families which habitually neglected evangelical preaching, had conversed or prayed with 292 families, and had visited a grand total of 768 families. To these and the other families throughout the nation, according to the report, the colporteurs sold over half a million books, at the rate, on the average, of four for a dollar. Over a hundred and fifty thousand more were distributed free.

Thus in attaining the unsurpassed popularity that distinguished the publications of the society, colportage played the leading part. There were, however, two additional methods of distribution. The first, by sale through normal commercial channels, was quite impressive when its results were compared with those of most commercial publishers. But the results of the second method, free distribution (by other than colporteurs), were naturally far more striking. By means of this free distribution hundreds of thousands of copies reached every corner of the world. The report for 1856 reveals the scope of this operation. Missionaries in Asia, Africa, Europe, and South America all received their share of copies. The society gave other copies to the shipping lines for their seamen. Still others went to ships' chaplains, and to the army and navy. Even the canal boatmen were not overlooked. For them the American Bethel Society was given over half a million pious pages. American Indian mission stations received some; so did literary institutions such as the YMCA's; so did "humane" institutions and Sabbath schools. Lastly a large number went to the many individuals besides missionaries or chaplains who, while not regular colporteurs either, nevertheless spread the Gospel and the volumes of the American Tract Society at the same time. Often these were ministers and Christian laymen in the small towns. The 1856 report estimated that 10,000 persons had taken part in such volunteer efforts, thereby bringing "incalculable good" not only to the people visited but also to themselves.

Among the volunteers was a spindly young girl, Susan Warner, who rose to fame in the 1850's as the author of a best-selling sentimental novel, *The Wide, Wide World*. In the early years of the previous decade she had jotted down some of her experiences. "Today began my tract visiting," she noted in her journal for September 12, 1843. Then she told the seriocomic story of her first venture. Although she dreaded the idea of going, she nerved herself to the effort and took her shy sister along for support. Susan knocked at one door after another. The mistress of the first house told her huffily that people making a profession of religion were sometimes not a bit better than their neighbors. Susan politely agreed—and left a tract. Next she visited some "ostensible Christians" and then called upon an old lady who defiantly pronounced herself a liberal thinker. Susan prayed with her, left a tract, and moved on to another old lady's house. In that more Christian atmosphere Susan was thanked for coming and asked when she would return. Then she sought out other people nearby, including a young woman who laughed at Susan when Susan began to talk to her. But everyone got a tract.

Firm in the belief that she was doing the Lord's work, Susan went forth regularly thereafter. "Have been abundantly satisfied that I am not out of the path of duty in the matter," she commented with Yankee understatement.

It was a varied assortment of tracts and bound volumes that the society provided for Susan, Mr. Bonnell, and the rest to carry. To understand the attractions the works had, the best place to go is to a little manual for colporteurs which the society printed in the late 'forties. It lists the titles of the publications and suggests the nature of the appeals they made, for most of the widely circulated volumes are here characterized from the reader's point of view.

The cardinal principle of all the publications, as stated in this same *Circulation and Character of the Volumes of the Amer-*

ican Tract Society, was that they should teach evangelical Christianity—"exhibiting 'Christ and Him Crucified' "—but without dealing in matters of denominational dispute. This principle the managers of the society clung to, though the slavery question, which was already dividing some of the greatest denominations within themselves, offered the severest test. The last report before the opening of the Civil War noted that the society still held to the printing of only those Christian publications that did not involve controversy. When a Boston group of the society split away because of the refusal to take a stand against slavery, the steadfast answer to the Bostonians was, "The teachings of this Society in previous publications are retained in the unchanged stereotype plates."

In *Circulation and Character* itself the books are divided into several kinds. First come the "Standard Spiritual Works" of the seventeenth century, then those of the eighteenth and first half of the nineteenth centuries, and then "Elegant Practical Works" —that is, those more "elegant" in style than the average. These sections are followed by ones headed "Romanism," "Biography," "Missionary Memoirs," "Volumes for the Young" (a large section), and "Pocket Manuals."

Perhaps the most successful of all the volumes in the seventeenth-century list was gentle-eyed Richard Baxter's *A Call to the Unconverted*. Its key word was "reasonableness." By a combination of logic and emotion it developed its theme of "Turn ye from your evil ways." In a brief series of sermons Baxter asked the reader if he was saved, stated that God wanted him to be saved, announced that if the reader went to hell it was his own doing, and concluded with directions for his salvation. The society had printed 250,000 copies of the *Call* by the late 'forties. One of many testimonials came from two illiterate daughters of a couple in Virginia who had had the beginning of the *Call* read to them by a man in the neighborhood. "He had not read three pages when one of them, in tears, stopped him and begged him to pray. The other wept. They read and prayed alternately. Truth reached their consciences—they trembled—repented, and were converted. By and by the parents returned. They had the same blessed book read to them, and they too were brought to rejoice in hope of the glory of God. Here were four souls saved in one house by means of Baxter's *Call*."

Among the seventeenth-century works of less but still considerable popularity, Bunyan's *Pilgrim's Progress* was an excellent example. *Circulation and Character* analyzes its twofold appeal. The book is "as an allegorical narrative, so entertaining that the heedless youth is attracted to it; while yet it so illustrates the windings of the human heart, and the ways of God in bringing sinners to himself, that the Christian pilgrim finds here his own history, in all the dangers, temptations, sins, falls and rising again, struggles and conquests of the spiritual life."

The list of volumes for the eighteenth and nineteenth centuries included Doddridge's *The Rise and Progress of Religion in the Soul* ("warnings against temptations and spiritual decays"), Pike's *Persuasives to Early Piety* ("written in a style of tender entreaty"), and Andrew Fuller's *Backslider*. Among the "Elegant Practical Works" were numbered Wilberforce's *Practical View of . . . Professed Christians* and Paley's *Natural Theology*. The "Miscellaneous" group included *Hymns for Social Worship and Anecdotes for the Family and Social Circle* (308 of them, "each conveying some valuable lesson"). The "Volumes for the Young" included Jacob Abbott's *Child at Home* and *The Tract Primer*. A favorite theme in this portion of the list was the history of the spectacularly pure young lady who died young. *Amelia, the Pastor's Daughter* is such a story. The summary mentions her premature death and then adds, "This is in all respects a pleasing and delightful memoir."

These bound books proved remarkably popular, yet their circulation was dwarfed by that of the tracts. Modest pamphlets, paper-covered and ranging from four to about forty pages in length, the tracts cost only a few cents. Because they were cheap they could be more widely circulated than any other kind of publication. True, their flimsy construction made them ephemeral—they failed to survive the rereading or receive the care of such volumes as Baxter's *Call*—but the extent of their over-all distribution is astounding.

Up to the opening of the 'fifties, 526 different tracts had appeared. The twenty-fifth annual report of the society gives the number of copies printed for each of those tracts from its time of original publication to mid-century. The smallest number was 6,000; and only one tract, "A Plea for Sacred Music," had so small a printing. At the top of the ladder, "Quench Not the Spirit" led all the rest with 908,000 copies as of 1850! The pace slackened only slightly as the Civil War approached.

"A Traveler's Farewell," Number 124, illustrates the characteristics that made for those sales of hundreds of thousands of copies. No "Quench Not the Spirit," it nevertheless had already risen over the 400,000 mark. The author treats his theme simply. If two friends must say farewell, there is always the question of when they will meet again. Will it be in this world or the next? Will it be in hell or heaven? No one can say, for it depends on the kind of life they go on to lead. At any rate, they will meet at the Last Judgment; and when they do, the author hopes that they—and we—will be among the saved.

The tract begins casually enough by remarking, "There is always something painful attending the separation of friends." It continues in a natural, conversational tone, quickly addressing the reader as "you." Then the sentences shorten and soon the exhortations come thick. By the time the fourth and last page is reached, every phrase is clutching at the reader. "If you have hitherto lived unconcerned, oh! reflect—the time is short—your days are fast spending and wasting." In the final few lines the tension is broken; the tract ends with what amounts to a benediction: "Now the God of hope fill you with all joy and peace in believing that you may abound in hope through the power of the Holy Ghost."

The famous "Quench Not," taking as its topic the idea that religion must be sought now, opens with a vivid directness that accounts in part at least for its mass appeal. " 'My children,' said the old man, 'the words of your dying father will be few. I wish them to sink deep into your hearts.' " For the nineteenth century such a start would be almost impossible to improve. The father then explains how he promised repeatedly—as a boy, as a young man, and finally as an old one—that he would become a true Christian. Each time he broke his promise to the Lord; and now, when about to die, he knows he is "in the hands of a justly offended God, from whom [he can expect] no mercy." "Profit by my example—quench not the Spirit—seek religion now," he gasps to his children with his last breath. The remainder of the tract spells out the lesson for every reader. Hurry! it says in essence. "O! be about it." Seek salvation at once!

Among the other highly popular tracts were "The Lost Soul," "Why Are You Not a Christian?," "The Way to Heaven," "Procrastination," and "Do You Want a Friend?" Their character is evident from their titles. They preached an earnest, loving Christianity, avoiding Calvinistic hell-fire on the one hand and Unitarian intellectualism on the other. They proved themselves indeed " 'agents' of the Lord."

Perhaps the clearest way to sum up the appeal of these publications is to read the eulogy of the Reverend Richard Knill. When this English clergyman, a skilled tractarian, died, the thirty-fifth annual report noted his passing with deep regret. Observing first that the American Tract Society had printed eight of his tracts with a total of 3,256,000 copies, the report then asked, "What secret had Mr. Knill, as a tract writer, that writers of cultivated intellect have failed to discover or employ?"

The answer could be found, was the reply, in the analysis of his tracts made by the London Tract Society's *Reporter*. Cited first was their brevity; then their strong narrative character; their plain, natural, forceful style ("His short, quick sentences are like rapid blows of a hammer"); and their straightforward, earnest teaching. His art, in other words, was the art of "The Traveler's Farewell" and "Quench Not." It was effective in the years before 1850; it maintained its effectiveness throughout the decade that followed.

Permeating the spirit of the American people more than any other book, the Holy Bible went into hundreds of thousands of homes throughout the nineteenth century. The Bible, as F. L. Mott has remarked in *Golden Multitudes*, was *the* best seller.

Compared to it, all other books—no matter how great their popularity—have been merely better, not best, sellers. The colporteurs of the American Tract Society visited more widely among American families than any other religious group; yet even they, according to the society's report of May 1856, could find only one family out of every twenty-one without a Bible.

Year after year in the 1840's and 1850's new editions appeared. They ran from the Large Pictorial Bible down to the small Pocket size. They varied from one volume to at least three. Some were elegantly bound, others wore only the plainest cloth; some were designed especially for family use; some were for children's Sunday school; and others were intended for advanced students. But regardless of external variety, the basic text was generally the authorized one of the King James version. There were only two exceptions. The Catholic Bible was the Douai version; and the rigid fundamentalists among the Protestants—the Baptists in particular—kept to their own version of Scripture based on their strict translation of the Greek and Hebrew originals.

The words most Americans were taught to love were still, however, those penned more than three centuries earlier by the learned ecclesiastics whom James I commissioned. How well they labored they would never know, but their language continued to inspire the rising generations. By the mid-nineteenth century it was true that a host of other books and periodicals existed in America, so that a family did not need to depend principally on the Bible for reading matter. Nor would antebellum American prose style be formed in the Biblical image as much as style had been in Britain or colonial New England. Yet the appeal of the majestic simplicity of Biblical language refused to disappear. This was still a time of the ornate instead of the plain style, yet it is probable that America's energies might have overflowed into a style almost baroque but for the restraining influence of the King James version.

The vast popularity of the Bible had another effect on American culture: it contributed a common stock of reading experiences and literary references. The Bible served as the prime source for parable and citation, for quotation and allusion. The poet Whittier could call Daniel Webster "Ichabod" for deserting the cause of the abolitionists, and everyone would recognize that here was a statesman from whom, in the poet's eyes, the glory had departed. Not only in the sermon and prayer but also in the poem, the lyceum lecture, the novel, and the essay would this common body of knowledge be evidenced.

Harder to measure than any other factor was the Bible's supernatural significance to the millions of believers who pored over it. For every atheist like the voluble Abner Post who denied its supernatural truth or every scientist who preferred to believe in geology instead of Genesis, there must have been hundreds of thousands who felt that they were reading the literal word of God.

The prime agent in distributing the Bible throughout the nation was the American Bible Society. Founded in 1816 through an amalgamation of local Bible societies, it elected as its first president the benevolent old Revolutionary statesman Elias Boudinot. From the start it was a nondenominational, nonprofit institution dedicated to printing and passing out as many Bibles as it could. To those able to buy Bibles it sold them at cost; to the poor it gave them cheerfully, "without money and without price." Like the American Tract Society it spread its activities over the entire world; but the focus of its attention was always the United States.

The mid-'fifties saw the American Bible Society at its greatest vigor. Progress during the previous years was uneven, though the trend was clearly upward. In its first year it issued 6,410 Bibles; in its tenth year it issued 31,154 Bibles and 35,980 New Testaments also; in its twentieth year the Bibles numbered 65,974 and the New Testaments 155,720; in its thirtieth year the totals rose to 161,974 and 321,899 respectively; and in the fortieth the society issued 240,776 Bibles and 427,489 New Testaments. During that period the annual income of the society rose correspondingly, from less than $38,000 to nearly $400,000.

The most imposing symbol of this progress was the Bible House. The cornerstone of the American Bible Society's headquarters was laid in New York in June 1852. The handsome brick building, six stories high and covering an entire city block, was completed the next year. The activity for which the Bible House became both the center and the symbol was no less striking. Between 1851 and 1856 the production of Bibles and New Testaments averaged almost three-quarters of a million a year. At the annual meeting of May 1856 the society boldly resolved, for the second time in its history, to place a free Bible in the hands of every poor family in the United States willing to take one.

The channels through which the myriads of Bibles and New Testaments passed differed somewhat from those used by the American Tract Society, for the Bible society worked mainly through its "Auxiliary Societies." During the first half of the 'fifties, for instance, hundreds of such groups sent remittances to national headquarters, while additional hundreds received Bibles from the American Bible Society without cost. Scattered throughout the country, the auxiliary societies inevitably showed a great variation in effectiveness. Most of them, however, did a good job. To stimulate their work the national society sent around its professional agents. In 1856 there were thirty-three. Suffering hardship and at times even danger, they traveled from one place to another, helping to build up the auxiliary groups. In a few cases they acted as colporteurs, distributing the volumes themselves; but their main mission was to organize and energize the work of the local Bible groups.

The progress of the society received a sharp check in 1857. This was the year that H. O. Dwight entitled "Storm Clouds" in his *Centennial History* of the society. Three things threatened then. The first was the business panic. Donations fell off until the total for the fiscal year was less than a hundred thousand dollars. Execution of the great plan to supply a Bible to every poor family stopped "as if struck by lightning." The auxiliary societies could not raise money to pay even the freight for the books they wanted, let alone for the books themselves. Although several legacies were received, they were not enough.

The second threat might be termed textual rather than financial. What had happened was this. The various editions of the Bible printed by the society were found to contain typographical errors as well as differences in editorial style. Its standing Committee on Versions began removing these in the late 'forties. Completing its work in 1851, it presented the society with a new "Standard Bible," which was distributed during the next six years almost without criticism. In 1857, however, a gale of protest was whipped up. Fundamentalist journals and some newspapers charged the society with what they belatedly termed tampering with the sacred text. The Committee on Versions had discovered 24,000 discrepancies among the editions it compared. The assailants of the Standard Bible adroitly distorted this fact into the accusation that the committee had made 24,000 changes in the Holy Writ.

The next year the shaken society yielded to its critics by ordering a recollation of the Standard Bible to remove any verbal differences between the old version and the new one. The concession proved great enough to let the society ride out this part of the storm.

The third threat that the year 1857 brought to the society was political. Like the textual problem, it had been long in the making. It was the increasingly bitter debate over slavery, now made still more bitter by the Dred Scott decision. For the society the main issue, first raised some twenty years earlier, related to the Negro slave and the Bible. The abolitionist members demanded two things: that Bibles be given to all literate—and illiterate— slaves and that some means be sought to teach the illiterate ones to read. In 1857, despite the heightened tension, the society as a whole kept to its established position. Through its managers it affirmed that free Bibles should go to the literate everywhere. But giving Bibles to the illiterate and helping them to read seemed to the society's managers to be beyond the scope of the organization. There the matter rested, to be settled by the coming of the war itself and the splitting away of more than six hundred auxiliary societies in the Southern states.

Despite the troubles of 1857 the society survived and, once the Civil War was past, would flourish anew. Meanwhile, throughout the 1850's Bibles ranging from the little Diamond at 30 cents to the elegant Imperial Quarto at $12 poured from its presses. Besides the large number of Bibles printed in English, Bibles in foreign languages, both major and minor, continued to come from the society. It advertised Bibles, for instance, in Syriac and Bohemian as well as in German and French. But the emphasis was, as has been said, on America; and here through the work of the society the Bible consolidated its position as the most popular of all books.

The amazing thing about the Biblical novel in American culture was that it had not appeared earlier. *The Prince of the House of David* itself did not come out until the mid-'fifties. When it did emerge, however, its literary roots were obvious. Along with the Bible itself, these were the domestic novels with their loud and recurring note of Christian piety; the fictionized manuals, of which T. S. Arthur's *Ten Nights in a Bar-Room* proved to be the most widely circulated example; and the tracts we have already described.

Nothing less than a conversion called the author of *The Prince* to his task. Before beginning the book, Joseph Holt Ingraham had been known only as the writer of a flood of sensational pseudohistorical novels. His first success of this kind was *Lafitte* (1836), in which he exploited to the full that Gulf pirate's gory career. For ten years afterward he continued in the same course. On April 6, 1846, he went to see Longfellow; and the poet mentioned the visit in his journal. "In the afternoon, Ingraham the novelist called. A young, dark man, with a soft voice. He says he has written eighty novels, and of these twenty during the last year; till it has grown to be merely mechanical with him. These novels are published in the newspapers." Longfellow added, with the professional writer's normal interest in literary earnings, "They pay him something more than three thousand dollars a year."

But by 1849 Ingraham had put all this behind him. He undertook theological studies and was soon ordained as an Episcopal minister. When that happened, he found his lurid novels so embarrassing that he is said to have destroyed any of them he could lay his hands on. Yet writing came so easily to him that he could not abandon it.

He found the solution to his problem in penning a work that turned out to be one of the outstanding religious best sellers of the century. It was an epistolary novel whose synopsis can be gleaned from its well-filled title page alone: *The Prince of the House of David; or Three Years in the Holy City. Being a Series of the Letters of Adina, a Jewess of Alexandria, Supposed to be Sojourning in Jerusalem in the Days of Herod, Addressed to Her Father, a Wealthy Jew in Egypt, and Relating, as if by an Eye-Witness, All the Scenes and Wonderful Incidents in the Life of Jesus of Nazareth, from His Baptism in Jordan to His Crucifixion on Calvary.*

The first edition came in 1855 with others following, first slowly and then with heightened speed. In three years 180,000 copies went out to the eager public. The reasons for the book's appeal still can be seen. The style is as a rule simple as well as commonplace but there are times when it becomes both vivid and ornate. The tone is emotional, exclamatory. The management of incident and action is quite effective—the author's many profane novels had taught him something of his craft.

The mass appeal of *The Prince* was based on a lucky combination of literary strength and weakness; the general reader cared little for critical subtleties and so the book's crude power, though it repelled the critics, held him hard. Its impact must have been great even in as bathetic a passage as the one where Adina describes the Jewish mob surrounding Jesus shortly after he has been taken by the Roman soldiers:

> With renewed uproar, they [the Jews] tumultuously pressed forward, their way lighted by the red glare of a hundred torches, insulting the Roman soldiers with seditious cries. John followed, but being recognized as one of his disciples, by a soldier in Aemilius' legion, he was seized and only escaped by leaving his apparel in the grasp of the rude Roman; for

such was the prevalent hatred to Jesus that they threateningly called for his followers, and would have taken them also had it been in their power. Five of the disciples, who have escaped arrest, are now in this house, whither John fled also, on eluding the grasp of the soldier, leaving his linen garment in his hand. We are all so sad and anxious! To move in favor of Jesus is only to share his fate, and do him no service; besides, I am pained to say, two or three of his disciples begin to doubt whether he *is* Messias, since, instead of establishing his promised kingdom, he is now held a prisoner, and even menaced with death.

To compensate for the bathos, the whole book contains a measure of tragic suspense. Everyone knew that the account of the crucifixion was to come, and yet Ingraham was able to keep attention on the immediate moment being described. The result for the reader was a kind of brooding Olympianism because he knew how the story was going to end, but Adina, being in the middle of it, did not. At times indeed, the author attained a genuine poignancy through this device. When he came at last to the scene on Calvary, he described it through Adina's eyes with an imaginativeness that was graphic enough to arrest anyone of the time. In the final few pages after the crucifixion there is a feeling of release and optimism. As Adina says at the end of the book, just before Jesus ascends, "We are filled with expectation of some great event, which will conclude the brilliant and wonderful succession of marvels that attend his footsteps and presence on earth."

There is little doubt that *The Prince of the House of David* not only accomplished its primary purpose but also had incidental effects. Perhaps the chief of these was the sanction it gave the novel as a respectable genre. The book helped to show that the novel was not necessarily a noxious literary form; in the right hands it could be a positive good. Other religious novels followed *The Prince*. Two more before Sumter came from Ingraham's own pen, *The Pillar of Fire* (1859), a story about

Moses, and *The Throne of David* (1860), about David himself. Ingraham had inaugurated a best-seller tradition that would thrive for a century and more, with Lloyd Douglas as its most important exponent in our day.

11

Strong Meat:

When the 1850's arrived, the moist but sparkling eye and the heaving bosom would become epidemic. The sentimental domestic novel would reign unchallenged, and unharmed by Hawthorne's now famous denunciation of its authors —"A d——d mob of scribbling women." But the 'forties were more masculine years, with a liking for richer fare.

Interestingly enough, two of the three most popular novelists in America during this decade were British. The third was a sensation-loving Philadelphian. In the eyes of the reading public they had little in common. The first and oldest, Sir Walter Scott, they universally accounted a gentleman. The second, Charles Dickens, so enthralled his American audience that even the South—which felt badly injured by his caustic criticisms of slavery—for the most part ignored the question of his gentility, or the lack of it, as it paged eagerly through his newest novel. The third, George Lippard, was considered no gentleman at all.

149

One significant—and obvious—thing they did have in common was their extraordinary ability to tell a story. They could each start a narrative briskly, complicate it with a swift succession of incidents, bring it sweepingly to a climax, and then end with a hasty knotting of the final strands of the plot. British novels were long, but both Scott and Dickens wrote with so much verve that the public wished for more chapters instead of fewer. And Lippard wrote so luridly that he secured the same result.

The 'forties grew up on Scott. By the time the decade opened, he had ranked for a generation as the most widely enjoyed of all novelists writing in English. Before turning novelist he had been poet, editor, antiquarian, and historian. His poetry had aroused such enthusiasm that even today *The Lady of the Lake*, issued in 1810, has not been dislodged from conservative high-school English courses in America. In 1814 he experimented with the novel form and published *Waverley*, though he did not sign his name to it. This story of a young English army officer, Edward Waverley, and his defection to the cause of "Bonnie Prince Charlie" mixed excitement, romance, and antiquarianism together. Highland chiefs, outlaws, and two romantic heroines (a brunette and a blonde—"jetty ringlets" vs. "paley gold") pursued their adventures in an atmosphere of heather and Scottish history.

So gratifying was the success of *Waverley* that Scott continued to write novel after novel, producing on the average one anonymous three-decker a year. As time went on, the identity of their author became the worst kept of literary secrets, and thus Scott added to his already magnificent reputation.

Waverley and its successors clearly show all the reasons for his popularity in ante-bellum America. To understand them best, we must start with Scott's opinions about fiction when he wrote *Waverley*. For he composed it in whimsical rebellion. Somewhat like Cooper, he revolted against the kinds of novels then in vogue. Chief among those he repudiated were the Gothic romance and the novel of sensibility. He announced his objective in the first chapter of *Waverley* and held to it for the rest of his life. It was to replace the elaborate lushness of Gothicism and sensibility with a simple return to the truth of human nature. And he specified where his emphasis would go: "upon the characters and passions of the actors;—those passions common to men in all stages of society."

It is usual to think of Scott in terms of joustings, dungeons, disguised identities, and beautiful women in peril; in terms of nobles, clansmen, knights, and outlaws. It is true that these fill his fiction. In his most famous book, *Ivanhoe*, for instance, we can find every one. Notwithstanding, *Ivanhoe* and the rest also represent truth to human nature in the sense that the characters are portrayed in a spirit of realism, of fidelity to life, with their actions developing organically. Prince John behaves as meanly and stupidly as one would expect him to; Wilfred of Ivanhoe acts with characteristic bravery, Brian de Bois-Guilbert with appropriate arrogance; and so on. Their creator proved himself a careful observer of humanity, often in fact stopping briefly in a chapter to explain why somebody acted the way he did. But Scott's psychologizing was made palatable to the mass audience by his habit of establishing dramatic settings and situations for his realistic characters. He served, if you will, realistic cake with romantic icing.

The major limitation of Scott as an expositor of human nature was that he failed to demonstrate much understanding of its range. He appeared at his best when depicting brave, highborn men but he made his lower-class characters rather too simple. Some of his women were vivid—Rebecca of York is a fine example—but in drawing heroines he suffered his only striking failure. Along with nine-tenths of the other authors of his day, he found it nearly impossible to keep a good, beautiful woman from seeming insipid. The stately blonde Rowena is no exception. Yet this caused him no trouble then, and for a good reason: he was in tune with the times.

The first half of the nineteenth century demanded that its heroines be pretty and pure. And it revealed the same simplicity of ethical standards for the remaining characters. Purity above all, with rewards for goodness and punishments for evil. Scott proved more than satisfactory on this score. His and the readers' sympathies always lie with the good characters and against the bad. The ethical values are painted in black and white, with no grays to complicate the problem. And good invariably wins out. It would be unthinkable for the wicked Brian to succeed in seducing Rebecca or slaying Ivanhoe.

Beyond these characteristics, Scott's novels had various other claims on public approval, as the contemporary American reviews show. The novels were historical, and many people asserted it was profitable to read about the past. In this way they answered critics of William Alcott's kind, who dismissed the novel as a waste of time. Another claim would not have been avowed as readily. But there is little doubt that it had a widespread existence, attested most clearly by the vogue of travel books—particularly those with touches of sensationalism in them. It was escape: escape for men from the deepening rut of business, even profitable business, and from the deadening routine of family life; escape for women from the never-ending labor of housework and the perfunctory attentions of a bewhiskered husband.

The appeals that Scott made were nationwide but one section of the country, the South, responded—for better or worse—with unusual ardor to his work. In *Life on the Mississippi* Mark Twain indicted Scott, as bitterly as he ever did any writer, for having greatly harmed the South. Mark Twain charged him with having blighted liberty, humanity, and advancement there. "Then comes Sir Walter Scott with his enchantments, and by his single might checks this wave of progress, and even turns it back; sets the world in love with dreams and phantoms; with decayed and swinish forms of religion; with decayed and degraded systems of government; with the sillinesses and emptinesses, sham grandeurs, sham gauds, and sham chivalries of a brainless and worthless long-vanished society." To Mark Twain the rest of the world got over its disease; the South stayed sick. "It was Sir Walter that made every gentleman in the South a major or a colonel, or a general or a judge, before the war; and it was he, also, that made these gentlemen value these bogus decorations. For it was he that created rank and caste down there, and also reverence for rank and caste, and pride and pleasure in them." And Scott molded Southern character: its prewar complexion "can be traced rather more easily to Sir Walter's influence than to that of any other thing or person."

On this angry arraignment of Scott, today's sociologists look coldly. They ask for proof and demand some examples of Southerners who performed specific actions under the influence of *Waverley* or *Ivanhoe* or *Quentin Durward*. They ask for statistics, furthermore, and receive none. Nevertheless, after all the necessary allowances have been made for the fact that Mark Twain was writing impressionistically, there is probably some truth to what he said.

If the Southerner found nothing else in the Waverley novels than a confirmation of his preconceptions, that was still a good deal. For he found a world of action rather than thought. He found a class society with the gentry and nobility as heroes, with the middle class almost unnoticed, and with the poor acting as the faithful, simple retainers of the rich. He found an agrarian, uncommercial culture, which he felt resembled his own. And he found an elaborate sort of writing that suited his notions of what literary style ought to be. "Wordy, windy, flowery 'eloquence'" Twain called it, forgetting that for his time Scott wrote in a relatively direct manner. To sum it up, Scott was the celebrator of chivalry, and the South was sure that it was more chivalrous than any other part of the country.

To this array of reasons for his enormous vogue not only in the South but everywhere else in America, one more must be added. It is neither literary nor psychological, however, but economic. His novels were boundlessly accessible. Because no international copyright existed, American publishers pirated him with unflagging zeal, and by 1840, as our period opened, a Waverley novel could be bought for twenty-five cents!

In his workmanlike *Golden Multitudes*, Mott tells the copyright story as it affected Scott's writings. They and the American practice of pirating appeared simultaneously. Competition among the buccaneering publishers developed with such fierceness that an American publisher would try anything to gain an edge over his opponents. He might even pay the British author a small sum for the privilege of using the advance sheets of the original edition so that he could get his American edition on the streets ahead of his competitors. These competitors could, and would, quickly set their type from his but he would have enjoyed a brief advantage. Even a day or two might mean that a first edition of 3,000 could be sold out in the United States.

The Philadelphia publisher, hard-faced Mathew Carey, seized the lead in publishing Scott for the American market. Through his English agent he paid up to £75 for advance sheets and presumably Scott received some of that. When the sheets arrived, the fortunate publisher strained every resource to bring out the book swiftly. Carey's firm set a record in 1822 when it produced *Quentin Durward* in twenty-eight hours. A notion of the riches to be quarried out of the sale of Scott can be gained from the fact that by 1830 nearly a dozen publishers in Philadelphia alone profited from printing him. When the day of the complete sets of Scott arrived, American publishers produced them at all price levels. The last and most spectacular set before the war came from Ticknor & Fields. From 1857 to 1859 they issued their Household edition, in fifty volumes, for $37.50. By the time Sumter fell 300,000 volumes of it had been sold.

Scott's reputation moved into the 1840's with all the courtly assurance of two decades of applause. But the fame of Charles Dickens, the sanguine-looking, cocky ex-reporter of Parliamentary debates, reached the 'forties in full bloom after only four short years. Sniffing eagerly for British best sellers, actual or potential, Mathew Carey's firm picked up the *Sketches* by Boz and published them in the first American edition in 1836. *The Pickwick Papers* followed in 1836–37. In the latter year *Oliver Twist* began going through Carey's presses also, Carey having paid £60 for part of the advance sheets. The *Sketches* merely prepared the way; the *Pickwick Papers* and *Oliver Twist* opened it wide. Critics in American magazines praised Dickens with a warmth matched by men on the street, for he proved to have some appeal for every level of his audience. "Dickens reigns supreme," Longfellow wrote in 1839 to a friend in Rome.

Carey and his successors in the firm continued to be Dickens' prime publishers until 1842 when an exceptionally aggressive competitor entered the publishing melee. It was Harpers. Harper & Brothers reprinted *American Notes* almost as soon as it came out in England. At that, a sly weekly newspaper, the *Brother Jonathan*, beat them by bribing a London pressman for the advance sheets and printing the entire book as an "extra" in a single day. But the Harpers had their own resources and soon fought back by publishing *Martin Chuzzlewit* in parts at six cents each. They could afford to. Henry Thoreau, when trying to establish himself as a writer, made the rounds of the New York publishers. He wrote to his mother on August 29, 1843, "Among others, I conversed with the Harpers—to see if they might not find me useful to them; but they say that they are making $50,000 annually, and their motto is to let well alone."

The battle continued during the rest of the decade, reaching its climax with the unprecedented sales of *David Copperfield*, whose first American edition was dated 1849. Harpers had withdrawn from the field for the time, leaving it again to Carey's successors plus some other enterprising printers. No one can calculate, or come close to calculating, the number of copies of *Copperfield* sold from 1849 on. But the book turned out to be the best-liked of all Dickens' novels, and the passing of more than a hundred years has not dimmed its popularity.

The opening of the 'fifties saw the development of what the publishers called the "courtesy of the trade." By this they meant that if one publisher paid a royalty to a foreign author, the remaining publishers were duty-bound to give him a year or two to recoup his investment before they began publishing their own editions. The firm of Harpers itself advocated courtesy of the trade and, now re-entering the field to become Dickens' chief American publisher, invested some rather handsome amounts in his writing. By paying him, or his English publishers to be precise, they were usually able to get the advance sheets of a new Dickens novel and thus give themselves a slight advantage over their competitors in the United States. As Mott points out, Harpers paid £400 apiece for *Bleak House* and *Little Dorrit* and £1,000 for *A Tale of Two Cities*.

But it would be inaccurate to conclude that Harpers had succeeded in monopolizing the field. They simply became first among a large number of avidly interested printers, many of whom were issuing more than one edition. In an advertisement in the *American Publishers' Circular and Literary Gazette* of January 1862, T. B. Peterson & Brothers of Philadelphia, who had bought the Carey plates eleven years before, announced that they themselves were at the moment publishing twenty-nine different editions of Dickens' works. They ran in price from $8 for a twenty-two–volume set bound in cheap paper to $90 for a thirty-volume set bound in full calf and with gilt edges.

Of all the novelists native or foreign whose works were printed in the United States, Dickens best managed to attract and hold the public's interest—except in the South, for reasons easy to understand, and even there he ran second only to Scott. Throughout the country as a whole his reputation dipped at times and occasionally the public seemed fickle, but those times turned out to be few. Certainly the 1840's were not among them.

Dickens' magnificent popularity was based during the 'forties on *Pickwick, Oliver Twist, The Old Curiosity Shop, Dombey and Son,* and *David Copperfield*. These novels testified, first of all, to the steady increase in his narrative skill, a skill that had made itself apparent, however, even from the beginning of *Pickwick*. They testified, furthermore, to the peerless fertility of Dickens' invention. He was able to invent incident after heightened incident with a minimum of effort. He showed that he could create a gallery of characters far more diverse than any of his competitors; yet these characters were all gifted with a personality that made readers feel they would know them at once on the street. No one writing in the 'forties could draw character as Dickens could; later decades would see him equaled at times but never surpassed.

Plot and character combined to wring the maximum of emotion out of his scenes. He reveled in sentiment, in feeling. Anthony Trollope, over in England, christened him "Mr. Sentiment" and the nickname had a point. This was not, it should be added, the womanish sensibility that Scott had reacted against. This was the ancient and honorable arousal and discharge of human emotions. It had sympathy as its main ingredient but a wide variety of other emotions were, from time to time, mingled with it. *Oliver Twist*, for example, has nearly all. The reader feels indignation, for instance, when Mr. Fang, the police magistrate, roughly sentences Oliver to jail. He feels contempt for Oliver's villainously conniving halfbrother, Monks. He feels helpless anger at the way Bill Sikes beats his drudging Nancy and horror at his clubbing her to death.

Dickens was also skilled in arousing gentler emotions in his public. A tender sorrow was one of them, and he surpassed himself when he treated the favorite topic for pathos of the time: a dying child. The two most heart-rending examples in his work both appeared during the 1840's. They were the death of little Nell in *The Old Curiosity Shop* and poor Paul in *Dombey and Son*. Believing in his characters, living with them, Dickens found himself in tears when he had to end the existence of these children. There is no doubt that his emotion was sincere as he took the reader into the bedchamber to look down with wet eyes at Nelly:

> For she was dead. There, upon her little bed, she lay at rest. The solemn stillness was no marvel now.
>
> She was dead. No sleep so beautiful and calm, so free from trace of pain, so fair to look upon. She seemed a creature fresh from the hand of God, and waiting for the breath of life; not one who had lived and suffered death.
>
> Her couch was dressed with here and there some winter berries and green leaves, gathered in a spot she had been used to favor. "When I die, put near me something that has loved the light, and had the sky above it always." Those were her words.

She was dead. Dear, gentle, patient, noble Nell was dead. Her little bird—a poor slight thing the pressure of a finger would have crushed—was stirring nimbly in its cage; and the strong heart of its child-mistress was mute and motionless for ever.

Where were the traces of her early cares, her suf-ferings, and fatigues? All gone. Sorrow was dead in-deed in her, but peace and perfect happiness were born; imaged in her tranquil beauty and profound re-pose.

And still her former self lay there, unaltered in this change. Yes. The old fireside had smiled upon that same sweet face; it had passed, like a dream, through haunts of misery and care; at the door of the poor schoolmaster on the summer evening, before the fur-nace fire upon the cold wet night, at the still bedside of the dying boy, there had been the same mild lovely look. So shall we know the angels in their majesty, after death.

But such copious emotion would have overpowered the reader or, if long continued, would have dulled his sensations had it not been for Dickens' other great gift, humor. It could be discovered at its peak in his group of grotesques and eccentrics but it extended to every class of characters except his heroines. It played over the wicked even more effectively than over the good. Dickens was, in fact, never so potent a humorist as when he grimly caricatured a rogue. Mr. Bumble, Uriah Heep, Samp-son Brass: these are only a few examples out of many. Yet he did almost as well with his more kindly characters; Mr. Micawber, Sairy Gamp, and Sam Weller are distinguished mainly by being the best known among a large and memorable company.

When analyzing Dickens' popularity Mott suggests that his greatest appeal to Americans lay in this humor. It was certainly powerful. But if we set Dickens' novels in their context of other ante-bellum best sellers, the conclusion might well be that his sentiment was even more attractive than the humor. As it worked out in practice, one reinforced the other. Dickens quickly learned how to set off his sentimental passages against his humorous ones, as well as how to mingle the two. He was doing it brilliantly by the time he finished *Oliver Twist*, in 1838, and he kept it up the rest of his life.

Mott is certainly right, on the other hand, in ascribing Dickens' popularity partly to a cluster of subsidiary elements: his "preoccupation with the fortunes of the lower and middle classes, with a disparagement of aristocracy; a reformer's burning sense of the injustices against childhood and against the poor and the weak generally; a flair for the rhetorical, and a love of fantasy and grotesquerie."

Though this was no longer the Age of Jackson it remained a democratic age, a time of leveling. Any writing that accorded with our republican preconceptions as well as most of Dickens' did was bound to be popular in America. And all the more so if the disparaged aristocracy was English. This was an age of reform, furthermore, and the reformer's zeal in Dickens was matched in many Americans. Theodore Parker and the poor in the slums of Boston, Dorothea Dix and the maltreated insane of Massachusetts, John Gough and the temperance legions, and —above all—Wendell Phillips and William Lloyd Garrison and Negro slavery: these were the most noted captains of the most notable causes; but there were many others of less importance. When Emerson Davis surveyed the period from 1800 to 1850 in *The Half Century*, published in 1851, he proudly described the various movements for better care of lunatics, for improved prisons, for temperance, for universal peace, and for moral uplift in general. All these had been maturing while Dickens wrote his first group of great novels.

Dickens' flair for rhetoric appealed to a public that still admired some decorative language, and not merely on the Fourth of July. Congress itself led the fashion. Despite the inroads of the plain style of public speaking under John Calhoun, congressional speeches continued to favor the florid. Full-blown diction, rhetorical questions, periodic sentences, repetitions for emphasis, and the numerous other devices that Dickens adapted to literature and the politicians still used in their addresses, provided another bond between him and the American reader.

The relish for the fantastic and grotesque which never left Dickens has already been cited as an element in his humor. To those Americans who loved the tall tale, the frontier brag, the horror story, he likewise had something to give. Throughout all his novels his strain of exaggeration, his delight in strange extravagance, showed itself abundantly.

Built on such foundations, Dickens' popularity in every region of the United States except one became enormous. The South, it should be kept in mind, however, judged every writer first by how he wrote about slavery. Dickens was no exception. Yet so great was his appeal that even the South could not help buying his books.

Southern literary circles showed that they had as long a memory for an injury as did Southern politicians. They never forgave that climactic, scorching chapter on slavery in *American Notes*. There he had pictured the slaveholders as venomous, cruel, and vile. Among other things he had assembled, as illustration, over two score newspaper advertisements for runaway slaves. For example: "Ran away, a Negro woman and two children; a few days before she went off, I burnt her with a hot iron, on the left side of her face. I tried to make the letter *M*." "Ran away, a Negro man, named Henry; his left eye out, some scars from a dirk on and under his left arm, and much scarred with the whip." "Ran away, a Negro girl called Mary. Has a small scar over her eye, a good many teeth missing, the letter *A* is branded on her cheek and forehead." Dickens' acid commentary left no doubt about who knocked out the teeth and left the burns and scars.

As a consequence, Southern critics turned their fire on Dickens. The South never had more than a handful of established literary magazines during the 'forties; they all attacked Dickens but in various ways and in varying degrees. The most eminent was the *Southern Literary Messenger*, which set a reasonably high standard through, at least in part, the caustic genius of Edgar Allan Poe. Later it maintained its influential position under the long-time editorship of J. R. Thompson, who was no friend of Dickens.

The magnitude of Dickens' popularity constituted a substantial problem, however. As a matter of strategy, the critics adopted two indirect methods of attack. Either they jibed at him in passing or else they simply announced his works in a line or so without comment. "*The Cricket on the Hearth* . . . is a late creation of the once magic pen of Dickens, which has not yet lost its power." Such was the detraction offered in one *Messenger* notice of March 1846, and this kind of thing continued for a decade. After the mid-'fifties a grudging alteration occurred, and even the *Messenger* faced the realities of popular taste. Commenting in May 1857 on the publishing of *Bleak House* in book form, the *Messenger* conceded, "We need say nothing at this late day of the merits of this remarkable work of the most popular of English novelists, but can only express our gratification that so excellent an edition of it has been laid before the American public."

As the 'fifties drew to an end, the *Messenger* felt it had to acquiesce in the widespread praise of the great Englishman. Of all the novels *David Copperfield* became the most highly regarded, and the *Messenger* added its praise. But always reluctantly. As late as July 1860, eighteen years after the issuing of *American Notes*, the *Messenger* would still allow one of its reviewers to comment on a recent volume of Dickens' short stories by insinuating that he really had not written them all himself. "But they are none the worse for that, probably all the better," since some of his job-hands could by now write as good a story as the master.

The reaction of the *Messenger* typified on the whole that of the Southern literary journals. There were a good many of them which, like the so-called little magazines of the twentieth century, began and ended almost with the same issue. Of enduring and celebrated periodicals there were only two during the 'fifties besides the *Messenger*. And one of these, *De Bow's Review*, was basically a commercial journal though it continued to give space to literary news after the decade opened. The other, the

Southern Quarterly Review, came out from 1842 to 1857; *De Bow's,* started in the same year, continued into the war period. The *Southern Quarterly Review* assumed a slightly more judicial attitude than the *Messenger.* It granted humor, liveliness, and sentiment to Dickens but found him too often ludicrous, grotesque, and mawkish. Moreover, his writings showed a lack of refinement, for he himself was (one recalled) not quite a gentleman. In spite of the fact that *De Bow's* paid increasing attention to literature, its files for the 'fifties contain only one brief review of a novel by Dickens, *Bleak House.* It remarks on his tens of thousands of readers.

Among the short-lived little magazines, with names such as the *Magnolia* and the *Orion,* scant mention of Dickens was normally to be found—a fact to be expected—but when a reference did occur it was perhaps a little more likely to be judicious, with space for both praise and blame, than were those in the *Messenger.*

From all this, the conclusion can be drawn that Dickens represented a rare occurrence in the South. He was a writer who retained, or at any rate, quickly regained, his popular standing despite his criticism of slavery. Though the critics censured him, the average Southerner found Dickens' fiction so interesting that his lone if outrageous deficiency could be overlooked. Despite a slightly bitter taste to the concoction, the general reader drank deep.

Even today novels of Dickens are reprinted time after time. Correspondingly, every schoolboy knows something about Sir Walter Scott. But George Lippard has disappeared from public notice to such an extent that the Library of Congress itself, the fullest storehouse of American writing in the world, does not contain a single copy of some of his works. It seems almost inconceivable that *Godey's Lady's Book* could, in 1849, call him "unquestionably the most popular writer of the day." Yet it did, adding that his books were currently being sold "edition after edition, thousand after thousand."

This lost figure in the history of American culture was born in Pennsylvania in 1822. As a child he was left an orphan and homeless. When he reached adolescence he tried studying for the ministry, rejected it, tried studying law, and left that too. He then decided he wanted to write and was starving for the privilege when he got a job as assistant editor of a Philadelphia daily, *The Spirit of the Times*. He stayed there long enough to make a local reputation as a satirist. In 1842 *The Saturday Evening Post* ran his first published romance, *Philippe de Agramont*. Then he began to compose historical fiction, publishing *Herbert Tracy, or The Legend of the Black Rangers*, which centered on the Revolutionary War battle of Germantown. In 1844 he offered the public stronger fare in *The Ladye Annabel, or The Doom of the Poisoner*. And this same year he issued the Gothic novel that became the most avidly read and bitterly criticized work he ever wrote.

This was *The Quaker City, or The Monks of Monk-Hall*, which had as an additional, tantalizing subtitle *A Romance of Philadelphia Life, Mystery, and Crime*. According to Randall's laudatory *Life and Choice Writings of George Lippard*, it proved a "really splendid success." In five years it reached its twenty-seventh edition, with each edition comprising from one to four thousand copies.

The furor it created in Philadelphia was especially intense. Its aim was to expose aristocratic lechery there. Randall says that it divided the city into two parties, with the workingmen on Lippard's side and the rest against him. An enterprising local dramatist turned the book into a play and when the play was to open, a riot brewed. Lippard flamboyantly presented himself outside the theater, "wrapped in an ample cloak, and carrying a sword cane to repel assaults." At the peak of excitement the mayor of Philadelphia appeared and persuaded him to call off the performance and thus quiet the mob. But the agitation about *The Quaker City* did not die down; the novel was soon sold in many parts of the country. Conservatives of all kinds were scandalized and did their angry best to besmirch the author. The controversy he aroused was so extraordinary, in fact, that it made him a public figure and the novel common gossip.

But it was not surprising that he attracted attention; he would have done so even without the aid of his sensational book. At this time Lippard was still in his early twenties and he dressed like a character out of Poe. He rather resembled Poe, moreover, but was better favored. In a contemporary daguerreotype he looks at the viewer from under finely arched black eyebrows. His head is large and symmetrical; his hair is long, reaching almost to his shoulders, and slightly wavy. He wears a black coat, a white vest (he always did in summer), and an open white shirt, with a flowing silk tie. In his hand he holds a scroll of manuscript, thereby making it plain to everyone that he is an author. Enveloped in his cloak and armed with his sword cane he must have made a truly romantic figure.

Dedicating *The Quaker City* to Charles Brockden Brown, dead for a generation but then still the best-known writer of Gothic novels in America, Lippard showed that he was consciously writing in the Gothic tradition. With its gloomy castles, hidden staircases, bedeviled heroines, and mystic melodrama, the Gothic novel had been a prime favorite in Europe but not in the United States. Except for those produced by Brown, none of any note had appeared till *The Quaker City*.

Lippard's sensational book, however, used the Gothic form only as a foundation. On it he built a tale whose lurid equal was not to be seen until the twentieth century. It was no wonder that it hit the American public like a blow in the face, for one of the earliest incidents finds the narrator bedded with a prostitute. A bare outline of the main plot is sufficient: the virginal and lovely Mary Arlington, daughter of a Philadelphia merchant, is tricked into a false marriage by the handsome, rakish aristocrat Gus Lorrimer. As a member of a diabolical fraternity that makes its headquarters in an old mansion called Monk Hall, Lorrimer brings her to a bridal chamber there and ruins her. Her brother Byrnewood Arlington tries to find her and avenge the wrong. Four hundred pages later, on Christmas Eve, he succeeds and shoots Lorrimer to death in a boat. As he holds the dead man's head on his knees, Byrnewood trembles with horrible joy. Then he opens his mouth.

" 'Ha, ha!' the shout burst from his lips. 'Here is blood warm,

warm, aye warm and gushing! Is that the murmur of a brook, is
that the whisper of a breeze, is that the song of a bird? No, no,
but still it is music—that gushing of the Wronger's blood!
Deeply wronged, Mary, deeply, darkly wronged! But fully
avenged, Mary, aye to the last drop of his blood! Have you no
music there, I would dance, yes, yes, I would dance over the
corse! Ha, ha, ha! Not the sound of the organ, that is too dark
and gloomy! But the drum, the trumpet, the chorus of a full
band; fill heaven and earth with joy! . . .'

" 'This, this is the vengeance of a brother!' "

Before he described that final revenge Lippard filled his
chapters with turbulent events. In no other ante-bellum novel, it
is a safe guess, were as many jammed together. Besides seduction and murder, they included attempts at rape (graphically
portrayed), tortures, poisonings, diabolical revels, mesmerism,
the machinations of a "Wandering Jew" type of cult leader and
his elegant harem, disguised identities (swiftly assumed and
dramatically discarded), abductions, escapes (which reach their
height when a regenerated prostitute spirits away not one but
two beautiful girls—one on each arm—from the horrors of
Monk Hall), and the resurrection (on the anatomist's table) of a
beautiful and of course unclothed woman.

The characters could not possibly be as remarkable as the
plot. After a time one villain—and one wronged maiden—begins
to resemble another. Nevertheless, a few characters stand out.
Devil-Bug reigns as the leading grotesque. He was "a strange
thickset specimen of flesh and blood, with a short body, marked
by immensely broad shoulders, long arms and thin distorted legs.
The head of the creature was ludicrously large in proportion to
the body. Long masses of stiff black hair fell tangled and matted
over a forehead, protuberant to deformity. A flat nose with wide
nostrils shooting out into each cheek like the smaller wings of an
insect, an immense mouth whose heavy lips disclosed two long
rows of bristling teeth." And he had only one eye.

To such type characters as the rake, the wronged maiden, and
the old crone, Dora Livingstone offers something of a contrast.
She individualizes her role of a bold, beautiful, wicked woman.

Pastor Pyne too, though cast as the lecherous minister of anti-clerical tradition, manages to exhibit marks of individuality. The others are the customary creatures of melodrama.

His greatest impact Lippard made not through character but through portraying melodramatic happenings in a manner highly sensational for its time. When rape was about to be attempted or seduction take place, every other writer of the 'forties and 'fifties dropped the curtain hastily and left the rest to the reader's imagination. It was Lippard's doubtful distinction that he waited until the last possible moment before letting that curtain fall. He relished describing beautiful girls in turmoil. His account of the unsuspecting Mary Arlington having her feelings aroused by Lorrimer is vivid considerably beyond the proprieties of that time. The scene midway in the book where Pastor Pyne gives a lovely girl named Mabel a potion is another set piece of this sensational kind. Mabel first becomes pliant and yielding, then begins to realize what is happening to her, fights him off, prays for help to her mother in heaven, is seized in triumph by the fat villain, and is saved at the last moment by—of all people—Devil-Bug.

But this does not happen until Lippard has had a chance to savor the scene. For instance:

> A gleam of malignant triumph shot from the Preacher's eyes.
>
> "I have you at last!" he muttered as he knelt by her side. His watery eyes grew expressive with a look of gloating admiration. For a moment he gazed upon the girl in silence. She lay prostrate upon the floor, her form quivering with a slight convulsive motion, while she gazed upon his face with her large black eyes dilating in an expression of utter horror.
>
> "Oh tremble, trem-b-l-e!" whispered the good Dr. Pyne. "It does me good to see you laying there, helpless as a baby! You may cry for help—no one will hear you! You may attempt to escape—but the doors are locked! Tremble, oh trem-b-l-e!"

In his picturing of the lightly clothed feminine form, finally, Lippard displayed preoccupations that, in the novel at least, were a full century ahead of his time. He seemed unable to look at a young woman in *The Quaker City* without staring at her bosom and the way it heaved. There are more "milk-white globes" and also more "voluptuous limbs" in this single book by Lippard than in all the novels of Scott, Dickens, and the female novelists of the next chapter.

Yet Lippard thought he could justify his sensationalism. He had, he announced firmly in the preface, a moral purpose. It was to demonstrate that the seduction of an innocent girl was a deed as heinous as deliberate murder and ought to be punished as such.

This kind of disclaimer has a long history, and readers could be excused if they raised an eyebrow at it. The chances are, however, that Lippard was at least partly sincere. He himself was the only protector of his orphan sister and was especially apprehensive about the evil a rich man could do to a poor girl.

His moral purpose was buttressed by his social aim, which Lippard shared, it happened, with Dickens. They both possessed a sympathy for the poor which had developed from their early struggles with poverty. But Lippard went beyond that. He became a genuinely proletarian writer whose interest in the class struggle could be detected in many of his pieces.

Further evidence of his radical sympathies can be found in his historical fiction. To an abnormal degree he interpreted the Revolutionary War as the glorious victory of the people over the aristocratic tyrants. His veneration for the conservative Washington was great but he also esteemed and defended the deist radical, Tom Paine. Lippard did not content himself with words as his only weapons. For a number of years he had been hoping to found an association of workers, and in 1850 he finally did so. It was called the Brotherhood of the Union. He became its first president and an energetic one. Although he constantly maintained that the brotherhood was not intended to set workers against capitalists, he termed it in its platform "the Union of the Workers against the Idlers who do not work, but who do steal the fruits of Labor's toil—the Union of Labor until Labor ripens into Capital." This was nothing if not pre-Marxism.

In and out of his brotherhood, Lippard fought the battle of the proletarian reformer. He campaigned against the money monopoly, against monopoly of land, against imprisonment for debt, against wage slavery (and chattel slavery too), and against the low status of women. He campaigned for the oppressed and for the poor wherever he found them.

As Lippard moved into the 1850's, nearing the end of his short life, the public's attitude toward him was strikingly ambivalent. As a preserver of the historical legends of the Revolution, he had earned their esteem. On the other hand, as the author of a series of scandalous stories, he was condemned even while many thousands continued to peep at his pages. But the public judged him somewhat too harshly in that respect. He was not a literary pander; he was a radical reformer who obviously enjoyed using the novel as a tool and incidentally enjoyed sensationalism for its own sake.

12
The Scribbling Women:

THE DOMESTIC NOVEL RULES THE 'FIFTIES

One of the best ways to understand the place of the domestic novel of a century ago is to remember that it was the great-grandmother of the sentimental radio or television serial that we call the "soap opera." The needs satisfied, both at the conscious and unconscious levels, are largely the same; where they are not, they illuminate some of the changes in cultural patterns which the passing of a century has seen.

Still with us are the complicated plots, with dismal doings strung throughout their length. So are the loud lamentations of the characters. Sorrow, not joy, continues to be the keynote. The main character is still female; around her revolve a variety of male and female types. The settings remain domestic for the most part. Home is where the heart is and, correspondingly, the heart is at home. Yet there is also a major difference. The central character in the novels was usually a girl, growing through a sad adolescence into adulthood. Now in the serials she is a mature woman. Though the little heroine of a century ago was taught to respect her elders and bend her will obediently to men —to good men, of course—today's heroine dominates her drama. She displays far more insight and stability than the attractive but feckless males who attach themselves to her. She may still be too young to play the matriarch but she is the matriarch in the making.

At least two factors, of different kinds, help to account for these changes. One is the altered audience. Today housewives alone are exposed to the serials, and the serials are aimed squarely at them. But the audience for the domestic novel was male and female both. Sentiment and even sobs were not purely for women. A man could spot the pages of a novel with tears almost as often as his wife did. The other factor is the improved status of women in America. They need no longer be submissive wives. Other careers, as well as the privilege of easy divorce, have opened to them. And the cult of what is sometimes called "momism" flourishes unabated. Mother is lavished with praise, father now sits smoking in the corner.

Today the man in the serials is expected to look up to the woman; a hundred years ago it was the reverse. But either way, the equal mating of equals was shunned. No sexuality appeared in the best-selling domestic novels of the nineteenth century, nor does it in the twentieth-century serial. Queen Victoria is dead but a new Victorianism keeps the heroine of the serials from melting in a man's embrace.

The passing of time has seen another change, the diminished role of religion. Most of the best-loved novels of the 1850's had a strong religious tone and made their lessons plain and clear. Today religion is taboo in the serial. Only its ghost lingers in the homely philosophy the matriarch may murmur while the organ plays softly in the background. Here we have an obvious reflection of life, for it would be hard to deny that religion (including the church as a social institution) means much less now than it did before the Civil War.

But the most important psychological elements have not changed. If we explore them we are bound to come to the conclusion that the domestic novel satisfied certain basic needs of the unconscious as well for its time as the astutely contrived serials do today.

Those needs were satisfied especially through the repeated appearance in this fiction of several of the archetypes later described by the great Swiss psychologist C. G. Jung. He considered archetypes to be primordial images in the collective unconscious, that is, the unconscious we all possess in common. Five of the main archetypes that can help us understand the appeal of the domestic novel are the anima, the animus, the earth mother, the old wise man, and the self as child.

Among them the anima was perhaps the most important. Jung described it as the female image in man. Born within him and first shaped by his view of his mother, it symbolized his womanly side. Jung believed that every man had female elements within him just as a woman had male ones. What made someone a man, so far as character was concerned, was merely a preponderance of male elements. In man, then, the female elements were represented by the anima. But it should be added that though the anima was molded by the child's experience with his mother, the anima of the grown man was the image of a nubile woman.

The domestic novel, invariably written from the female point of view, made a powerful appeal to the anima. A girl or woman customarily acted, moreover, as the central character, and it was her trials that aroused the softer side of the male's emotions. Tears, tenderness, sensitivity: these were all characteristics of the anima; and the domestic novel had in its pages occasion for every one. Thus a man could read such a novel with unusual satisfaction.

The animus, the male principle, found an almost equally significant expression. Ordinarily the central female character —with whom the feminine reader identified herself—would lack decisiveness, aggressiveness, and wisdom because these were all supposedly male qualities. But the animus would furnish them in the shape of other characters in the book who would bring the benefits of those qualities to the heroine. Jung has described the form the animus takes with perfect appropriateness for the domestic novel. It is, he says, something like an assemblage of fathers and other authorities who pronounce incontestable judgments. In novel after novel, the heroine listens to these opinionated sages and obeys meekly.

Two other archetypes were met with less often than the anima and animus. Unlike them, they were not sexual inversions. The archetype of the old wise man was found in the male sex; the archetype of the earth mother was found in women. Usually, of course, the earth mother was the mother of the heroine. But she could well be a kindly grandmother, an elderly aunt, or an especially understanding friend of the family. The old wise man was often cast as the wealthy benevolist who counseled the little girl. He taught her patience and aided her in the battle against "pride" or willfulness, which was her most frequent failing. But he did not need to be old so long as he was wise. He might be a young minister, for example, and still fulfill the image. For the male reader he was primarily an extension of himself but for the female reader he was likely to merge at times into her animus. Then he would simply be chief in the assembly of elders.

By the self, lastly, Jung meant the unified personality, which integrated its conscious and unconscious. Customarily, real selfhood developed only after years of thoughtful effort, hence the normal form of this archetype was the maturely integrated man, at its best the Buddha. But in many cases the child was another form that the archetype took, for the child represented the unity of the human being at birth, when the conscious and the unconscious were not yet divided. This primitive innocence and wholeness lingered in the typical child-heroine of the domestic novel, making her psychological appeal doubly strong for both men and women readers.

The most talked-about domestic novel as the 1850's opened was probably Susan Warner's *The Wide, Wide World*. Through it the Jungian archetypes run like a red and yellow thread. But there is more to the book than archetypes; other reasons for its wide-ranging popular appeal also manifest themselves.

The Wide, Wide World has many distinctions, few of them aesthetic. Not the least is that the little heroine cries more readily and more steadily than any other tormented child in a novel of the time. That she had her reasons, and that certain of them were rooted in her creator's own disheartening experiences, we must admit.

The book opens with a lawsuit—just lost—and the poverty and heartbreak that it brings with it. The life of Susan Warner's family abounded in such litigation; Anna Warner has told the story in a biography of her sister. Their father turned out to be the kind of man who was perennially plagued by commercial disasters. He improved his land by diking it, and his enemies breached the dikes. He sued them for it and won, but won years later when it did him no good. He mortgaged his land, and his enemies gained control and foreclosed. For long years he and his motherless daughters lacked the money to buy adequate food and clothing. Early in November 1850, for example, while *The Wide, Wide World* was going through the press, Susan wrote in her journal: "Mem.: that we burn tallow candles these many weeks, our oil-can being at the grocer's and no money existing to fetch it thence full. . . . That father wants clothes immediately, and we proximately. . . . That father has also borrowed from Mr. ———." The sugar they used was brown sugar, the cheapest kind, yet at the end of November they had less than two pounds of that left. And they still had no oil for their lamp.

Religion was Susan's comfort. It weakened neither with literary success nor with the mild kind of prosperity that later accompanied it. Even when *The Wide, Wide World* came out and was praised by the critics with unexpected warmth, she wrote characteristically, "A Newark paper sent me by Mr. Putnam with such a notice of the W.W.W.!—above everything I have seen yet. Very grateful indeed—and I—what shall I say? My Lord and my God, sanctify me entirely to Thy glory. My face is in the dust, and I say, if I have done iniquity I will do no more." Then after this self-abasement—to avoid "pride"—a brisk little note about her second novel, *Queechy*, "Copied out near seven pages."

When *The Wide, Wide World* appeared Susan was thirty-one. A tall, skinny young woman—she called herself a Maypole —she owned to a long nose and a long upper lip. She had always been a reader, from childhood days. She loved stories and when she was in her late twenties her aunt suggested that she write one. It took her over a year, but when she was through there was *The Wide, Wide World* ready for publishers to refuse. Finally George Putnam agreed to print it, and it made its hesitant appearance with "Elizabeth Wetherell" signed to it, the name of one of Susan's great-grandmothers.

Ellen Montgomery is the child heroine soon to be cast out into the wide, wide world of the title. Her mother is still alive when the book begins, but for her to remain so, she must shortly go to England in company with Ellen's father. To Ellen the prospect of separation is as bad as death itself, and the initial chapters are devoted to this harrowing matter. It is anticipated by and then accompanied with a multitude of tears, but they are not out of keeping.

Who will take care of Ellen while her parents are overseas? The shrewish aunt of course, whom she has never seen. This aunt, sharp-nosed Miss Fortune Emerson, lives on a farm near the Yankee village of Thirlwall. She treats Ellen as harshly as one might expect. However, a protector emerges in the blunt, taciturn hired man, Brahm Van Brunt. He is abler and better off than average, having his own farm too. Rough, good-humored, almost handsome, he sees to it that Ellen's lot is ameliorated as much as possible.

Ellen needs feminine help also. Alice Humphreys, delicate daughter of a nearby minister, provides that. She gives the little girl love and needed advice, for by now we know, without surprise, that Ellen is guilty of pride. Chiefly through long talks with Alice and ardent reading of the Bible, Ellen begins to control her emotions (aside from the melancholy ones) and attempts to meet Aunt Emerson's unfairness with humility and downcast eyes.

Then Alice's undefined yet mortal illness sets in. Ellen's mother has already died abroad and her father is missing at sea, so Alice's sickness means a breaking of the child's closest ties. But Alice does not die until Ellen has been brought under the kindly guidance of her brother John Humphreys.

To Ellen, Alice announces her approaching death and after part of the initial shock has worn off, she "looked sadly for a minute into the woe-begone little face, then clasped her close and kissed her again and again."

" 'Oh, Alice,' sobbed Ellen on her neck,—'aren't you mistaken? maybe you are mistaken?'

" 'I am not mistaken, my dear Ellie, my own Ellie,' said Alice's clear sweet voice;—'not sorry, except for others. I will talk with you more about this. You will be sorry for me at first, and then, I hope, you will be glad. It is only that I am going home a little before you.' "

In the solemn months following Alice's burial John, now a minister, is Ellen's comforter and teacher. He guides her through a classical education as well as a moral one. Ellen responds readily to his admonitions. Here she is, after having done a thoughtless thing and upon being asked by John if she feels right:

" 'Why?' said Ellen, the crimson of her cheeks mounting to her forehead. But her eye sunk immediately at the answering glance of his. He then in very few words set the matter before her, with such a happy mixture of pointedness and kindness, that while the reproof, coming from him, went to the quick, Ellen yet joined with it no thought of harshness or severity. She was completely subdued."

As the novel went into its last chapters Miss Warner gave it a twist. Ellen's grandparents prove to be a wealthy Scottish couple, so she must go to them, leaving John, Mr. Van Brunt, and the rest behind. She tries to settle into her new life but succeeds only tolerably well. However, she gradually perfects her submissiveness under a new tutor, her stately uncle Mr. Lindsay. On one occasion, for instance, after a slip on her part (the flesh is still a little weak):

> "Now lift up your head and listen to me," said he, taking both her hands,—"I lay my commands upon you . . . that you answer simply according to what I have told you, without any explanation or addition. . . . Do you understand me?"
>
> Ellen bowed.
>
> "Will you obey me?"
>
> She answered again in the same mute way.
>
> He ceased to hold her at arm's length, and sitting down in her chair drew her close to him, saying more kindly,
>
> "You must not displease me, Ellen."
>
> "I had no thought of displeasing you, sir," said Ellen bursting into tears,—"and I was very sorry for it last night. I did not mean to disobey you—I only hesitated—"
>
> "Hesitate no more. My commands may serve to remove the cause of it."

Every now and then Miss Warner flirted with the ethical complications of complete submission. What should Ellen do when Mr. Lindsay orders her to drink wine? She drinks it, after a brief moral struggle. But finally even Mr. Lindsay's lordliness meets its match when John comes masterfully to see her in Scotland. It is a dull reader who fails to realize that the attractive, budding Ellen loves him. Miss Warner shyly leaves us to guess whether John loves Ellen too, but the guess is not hard to make. And we are promised that at the end of three or four more years of "Scottish discipline" Ellen will be allowed to return to America, through John, and rejoin the "friends and guardians" she loves best.

The Wide, Wide World provided its ready public with every one of the five Jungian archetypes. Ellen is both the anima and, even if imperfectly, the self as child—a fertile combination.

Alice Humphreys, young but because of illness prematurely wise and kind, is the earth mother who ministers to the orphaned Ellen. Van Brunt, John Humphreys, and Mr. Lindsay constitute the assemblage of fathers; they become the animus. John also acts as the old wise man. Like his sister he is young for the role but is already able to play it acceptably at the beginning and unusually well later on when he becomes a minister.

From *The Wide, Wide World* Miss Warner went on to write *Queechy*, which proved almost as popular. Both books reached the mass of people so effectively that they became bywords. Anna Warner dryly mentioned some evidence that she saw—for example, the advertisement: "In the 'Wide, Wide World' cannot be found better undergarments and hosiery than at James E. Ray's, 108 Bowery"! And *Queechy* made famous the upriver region where its scene was laid. The local pond became Queechy Lake; a local rifle maker stamped his product "Queechy Rifles"; and so on. Other "Queechy" articles appeared in distant parts of the country.

The heroine of *Queechy*, incidentally, was another little girl, nicknamed Fleda. She refused to cry as often as Ellen but her opportunities were fewer. On the other hand, Miss Warner allowed a considerable love interest to enter this novel; and when Fleda and her young man at last embraced, her tears gushed forth readily. This time, though, they were joyous, "illumined with heart-sunshine."

In the train of Susan Warner the rest of the scribbling women followed, their pens scratching busily. Some of them had started writing years before; others began their writing in the early 'forties. All contributed to impressing on that decade the seal of the domestic novel.

After Miss Warner, the leaders among these ladies were Caroline Lee Hentz, Maria Cummins, and Mary Jane Holmes. Each had her individual peculiarities of course, but the work of each shows many more similarities to the stereotype of the domestic novel than differences from it. And the archetypes are everywhere.

Mrs. Hentz was a rather sweet-faced woman with a cork-screw curl dangling in front of each ear. Born in New England in 1800, she belonged to the generation ahead of Miss Warner's but started writing late. She developed into a person of unusual culture. This was partly because, her husband being French, she came into contact with another national background besides her own. In addition, he was a teacher by profession, who had something to teach his wife. A lady from Mobile, quoted with approval in John S. Hart's *Female Prose Writers*, declared that she was "admirably accomplished, and a perfect classic and belles lettres scholar."

She started by writing tragedies, winning a prize with *De Lara, or The Moorish Bride*. She composed two others afterward, and it is probable that from this kind of composition her novels and novelettes benefited. They show a management of scene and an understanding of dramatic construction that distinguishes them from the large number of amorphously plotted novels of the time. *Rena, or The Snowbird* (1851), *Eoline, or Magnolia Vale* (1852), and *Helen and Arthur, or Miss Thusa's Spinning Wheel* (1853) are representative products of her prolific pen; and each has a better-than-average plot structure.

Two further characteristics of Mrs. Hentz's work were well described by the lady from Mobile. One is a piety equal to Miss Warner's. "A calm and holy religion is mirrored in every page. The sorrow-stricken mourner finds therein the sweet and healing balm of consolation, and the bitter tears cease to flow when she points to that 'better land' where the loved and the lost are waiting for us." The other is the detailed realism of her domestic scenes: "Home, especially, she describes with a truthfulness which is enchanting."

All Mrs. Hentz's novels were popular but one created a sensation—though not for literary reasons. It was *The Planter's Northern Bride*, a novel with a thesis. The thesis was that—contrary to *Uncle Tom's Cabin* and lesser-known abolitionist fiction—slavery was really beneficial. Because Mrs. Hentz was a transplanted Yankee, she could write with a measure of appreciation for both the Northern and the Southern points of view. She inclined toward the South, though, and many of the readers who delighted in *The Planter's Northern Bride* were doubtless either proslavery or else averse to grappling with the problem of the peculiar institution.

A single book, *The Lamplighter* (1854), lifted shy young Maria Cummins into national popularity. It sold 40,000 copies within eight weeks after publication and 70,000 in its first year. Its orphaned heroine, little Gerty, is being brought up in grimmest poverty as the novel opens. Daily she waits for the kind old lamplighter to pass, for he brings the only spot of warmth in her dismal life. Aptly named Trueman Flint, he rescues her when the brutal woman she lives with drives the spunky little girl out. Succeeding scenes take her through an eventful, tear-stained and sometimes rebellious childhood, into a self-sacrificing adolescence, and ultimately to a young womanhood of happy marriage, wealth, and emotional security.

The Lamplighter, like *The Wide, Wide World*, made its appeal through various means, including elements so diverse as ostentatious piety and, once again, the unconscious use of archetypes.

Ultimately the novels of Mary Jane Holmes, the wife of a Massachusetts lawyer, sold—according to several estimates—over a million copies. She was born in 1825 and saw her first article set in type when she was fifteen; her first novel, when she was under thirty. She was a kindly woman, a former schoolteacher, and she carried the qualities of kindliness and didacticism into her fabulously successful fiction. She managed to write almost a volume a year. Representative of her achievement in the late 'fifties is *Meadow Brook*.

Meadow Brook is the Massachusetts village that furnishes the main setting for Mrs. Holmes's engaging novel. Typically, it starts out as the story of a plain little girl much given to tears and temperament. However, this book lacks the heart-wringing quality of most domestic novels, for the heroine, Rosa Lee, is by no means rejected or orphaned. Death visits the story more than once but somehow its bitterness is not so great as usual. Grief even if intense is short-lived.

Since Rosa Lee is bright she is allowed to teach school at thirteen. Her adventures and misadventures at school parallel some of Mrs. Holmes's own experiences. One of the overseers is darkly handsome Dr. Clayton, with whom the novice teacher falls in love. Surprisingly he is attracted too. But after considering carefully, he decides to marry a haughty eighteen-year-old who is reputed to have money. He does and soon gets the unhappiness he deserves. Rosa goes south to teach in the wealthy Lansing family. On their Georgia estate she tutors the angelic Jessie, whose proud uncle Richard Delafield soon falls in love with the new tutor. The course of love, naturally, fails to run smoothly. Rosa is plagued by Richard's ward Ada, is lied about and tricked, and is made generally unhappy by a series of domestic tribulations. Yet there are happy times for her too.

The climax of the story comes with the arrival at the Lansings' of the now widowed Dr. Clayton. Rosa realizes that she is no longer infatuated with him but has instead a deep, mature affection for Richard. Richard, however, through a perverse sense of honor, gives her up nobly and only her sudden illness keeps her from being maneuvered into an unwilling marriage with Dr. Clayton. Ultimately events untangle themselves: Richard and Rosa marry; the doctor finds himself a pleasant, prosperous widow; and all is well.

The lessons of humility and Christian piety abound in the pages of *Meadow Brook*. So do sorrows and trials. But the whole novel is in a quieter key than the usual domestic fiction. Mrs. Holmes announced in her preface that she was going to try to be natural, and she succeeded. Nothing is overstrained; even the deathbed scenes do not become emotional orgies. The dialogue is realistic. The descriptive passages go along without the purple rhetoric that accompanies them in the books of others.

Mrs. Holmes's effort to write "naturally" had another and equally favorable result. Through describing her characters, their actions, and talk with calm realism, she created genuine local color. She brought to her pages a number of New England village types that later novelists would develop to their advantage. Her naturalness, finally, overflowed into an unassuming humor that plays objectively over nearly all the characters including even Rosa Lee. Aunt Sally Wright, for instance, is a professional gossip whose mixture of motives is delightfully described by the author. And Ada's uncomfortable wrigglings when she wants to avoid being found out as a liar are painted with an engaging touch that few other writers could employ.

Although her humor and unassuming realism distinguish Mrs. Holmes, her work remains in the tradition of the domestic novél. Our picture of the work by the women writers of the 'fifties, however, would be incomplete without a mention of two notable exceptions to most statements about the fiction of the time.

One exception is the work by Mrs. E. D. E. N. Southworth; the other, that by the little woman who helped start a big war, Harriet Beecher Stowe. Suppose we look at Mrs. Southworth first. Poor, sickly, but diligent, she poured out a stream of turbulent stories that circulated all over the country. The opposite of Mrs. Holmes, she attempted the stagiest possible literary effects. Melodrama in plot, character, and even setting marked her manifold novels. Something was always happening in them and (except in the final chapter) it was almost always bad.

Yet she had her reasons. They lay partly in her own career, which was bitter from the beginning. "I was a child of sorrow," she once wrote sadly, "from the very first year of my life." A thin, dark infant, she had no touch of beauty except for her large, wild eyes; and blindness, though temporary, effectively tarnished that. Her young sister turned out to be a beautiful child, and Emma suffered through the contrast. Then family misfortunes began and soon piled up. Her father died, leaving the family poor. Evidently they did not have to taste the penury that the Warners endured so long, but Susan Warner was loved while Emma felt that everyone rejected her. In consequence: "Year after year, from my eighth to my sixteenth year, I grew more lonely, retired more into myself, until, notwithstanding a strong, ardent, demonstrative temperament, I became cold, reserved, and abstracted."

Her girlhood was sad, her young womanhood was worse.

She married Frederick Southworth in 1840; he stayed with her long enough to father two children, and then ran away. After going through what must have been heavy trials, she moved to Washington, D.C., from the Midwest where Southworth had left her. Here she started to teach school and also to write for publication. She went on to pen half a hundred novels, beginning with *Retribution,* which was issued in book form in 1849. Several of the succeeding ones were composed in the face of exceptional misery. "Sorrow, sickness, death, litigation, the parting from friends identified with our lives": she listed all these in describing her troubles between 1852 and 1854.

But *Retribution* proved a success. Two prominent periodicals, the *National Era* of Washington and the *Saturday Evening Post* of Philadelphia, now published what she wrote and urged her to hurry up with more. Book publishers readily collected and reprinted her serials. She found a market, and since she had to support herself she learned to pour out the type of stagy fiction she could sell most quickly. Even after she made money and her health improved, her novels kept their dank theatricals.

The Curse of Clifton is a fair sample. Melodrama permeates each page. It shows itself not only in the spectacular incidents of the plot and in the dramatic scenes but also in the descriptive passages and the routine dialogue.

Here, for example, early in the book, is the haughty Captain Clifton of Clifton describing to his friend Fairfax a trout stream, which is the source of a river:

" 'From the Western cliff there springs a torrent that with many a leap and fall, and rebound, tumbles tumultuously down the side of the mountain, and falling into a channel at the foot of the lawn flows calmly on, until it meets a second fall, from whence it goes hurrying on, through forests, fields and rocks, taking tribute from many a mountain-torrent, and many a meadow-stream, and widening as it goes, until it becomes a mighty river, rushing on, to pour its floods into the majestic James.' "

This was the sort of bombast that numerous readers of the 'fifties confused with good writing. Mrs. Southworth's general dialogue fooled them further. As for instance when Captain Clifton, riding along after describing the stream, denies Fairfax' charge that he is in love with a girl named Georgia:

" 'Impossible, sir! The perfect beauty of the young girl struck me forcibly, as it strikes *all others*—nay, more—impressed my imagination deeply perhaps. I confess to a *penchant* for female beauty—and—observe—it is the artist's taste, sir, not the sultan's. But in love with Georgia! Impossible, sir! She was a girl of humble parentage!'

" 'Ah! then you think it quite "impossible" that a gentleman born should be in love with a girl of "humble parentage?" '

" 'Preposterous, sir!—utterly preposterous! Pray, let us hear no more about it!' "

And so on for a few more lines until Mrs. Southworth startles the reader by having Fairfax' horse nearly plunge him into an abyss. As soon as that scene has its dramatic possibilities drained, she moves to another type of titillation, this time a meeting with an innocent mountain girl. From that point the action in *The Curse of Clifton* proceeds spasmodically but inexorably to the end of the book. Mrs. Southworth's energy is always up to the task of varying her incidents and driving her plot on to its conclusion. Even in the middle 1850's while seriously ill, she could huddle on her bed and dictate her current novel to an amanuensis.

Doubtless in the ordinary course of events Harriet Beecher Stowe would have made a modest contribution to mid-nineteenth-century American culture. She would have published several domestic novels, each with an average sale. They would have been marked with unusual earnestness and perhaps with the ability to dramatize a thesis. On the other hand, they would have been flawed by an exceptional awkwardness in technique. The plot would probably have wandered away from the subplot early in the story, never to rejoin it till the last few pages. The transitions would have been made as clumsily as this: "A while we must leave Tom in the hands of his persecutors, while we turn to pursue the fortunes of George and his wife, whom we left in friendly hands, in a farm-house on the road-side." Melo-drama worthy of Mrs. Southworth would have thrown its garish light over far too many of the incidents. The characters would have displayed a comparable weakness in literary technique, for almost without exception they would have been simple and two-dimensional. Their motivations would have been described with almost childlike directness. Their thoughts and actions would have proved them almost at once to be either thoroughly good people or thoroughly bad ones. Only here and there would the author have created a character tinged with gray.

Little Mrs. Stowe, in other words, would not have been stig-matized as a poor novelist for her times but neither would she have compared with Mary Jane Holmes or Susan Warner. But if this is a fair appraisal of her literary worth, it still leaves us with the massive fact of her popularity. The best way to ap-proach it is by following the appearance, installment by install-ment, of a serial tentatively titled *Uncle Tom's Cabin, or The Man That Was a Thing*.

Forrest Wilson has told the story well in his *Crusader in Crinoline*. Harriet got her idea while sitting in church in Febru-ary 1851. The conception of the central scene, the saintly old slave flogged to death by two of his brutalized fellows at his master's order, burst upon her. She began the writing promptly; it affected even her husband Calvin, who told her to compose the entire work around this harrowing scene. In March she queried Dr. Gamaliel Bailey, the editor of the same *National Era* in Washington which had just published Mrs. Southworth's *Retribution*. He agreed to publish the work in three or four parts.

From the start he realized that he had something remarkable. Subscribers began writing in, praising the story more with every issue. In September, Dr. Bailey announced, "We receive letters by every mail inquiring whether 'Uncle Tom's Cabin' will be published in book form after its completion in the *Era*." The installments grew fuller, the scenes even more moving. As it gripped the readers of the North increasingly, it similarly shook Harriet with the effort of creation. When she had to kill little Eva St. Clare, she took to her bed, no more able to continue writing than Dickens was after killing little Nell. By the time of the last chapter, the story had stretched out into forty installments, but the nation was waiting with patent eagerness to reread it in book form.

Harriet had accepted the offer of a flashy book-publisher in Boston named John Jewett. Speculator though he was, he had his qualms at first. But gradually he too felt the public fever. Accordingly, he ran off a first edition of 5,000 copies—a larger-than-average number. The price ranged from one dollar to two, depending upon the binding. Publication day was March 20, 1852. It saw 3,000 copies snatched up; the remaining 2,000 disappeared the next day. Jewett hastily put another printing through his presses, and then another, and another. Twenty thousand copies went in three weeks. And in that first tremendous year he sold 305,000 copies! When the panic of 1857 arrived, *Uncle Tom* had sold half a million—and that without counting the many pirated editions in Great Britain, France, Italy, and elsewhere. By 1861 it had become the most popular novel ever written by an American.

The question is, What made it so; and the query has added point if we remember that purely as a novelist Mrs. Stowe never reached any literary heights.

The answer lies in several factors, one of which clearly is the presence of two powerful archetypal figures, little Eva as the self as child and Uncle Tom as the old wise man. Their importance is evident. But the most significant factor is of course the timeliness of *Uncle Tom*. By the opening of the 'fifties, the struggle over slavery was shoving all other political issues into the background. And it was becoming much more than a political issue; it was reaching into all departments of American life. In the South, especially, the touchstone which was applied to everything was its relation to slavery. The same touchstone was also applied to everybody; by the time Harriet's book had been out six months, no one in the South could praise it in public and hope to remain unscathed. In the North opinion on slavery was split but excitement was growing monthly. There the population was divided into the relatively few bitter abolitionists, the large number of defenders of slavery, and the much larger number of independents not yet committed to either side of the great controversy but more and more aware of its importance.

Mrs. Stowe took all these Northerners by the hand and showed them what slavery meant. The most shocking chapters are the gruesome "Select Incidents of Lawful Trade," the superficially wry "The Slave Warehouse," and the terrifying "The Martyr"; but the horrors of slavery are the very stuff out of which the entire book is made. The mark of slavery lies on every page. The reader can never overlook it.

Uncle Tom probably made few friends among the pro-Southern element in the North. But it enlisted every abolitionist on its behalf. And it caused a soul-searching among the many independents which obviously ended with large numbers of them convinced that Mrs. Stowe was right and slavery wrong.

The story was true, Mrs. Stowe insisted, and that added to its impact. But when she put it into the form of fiction, it became not merely an accurate account but an experience that was happening to the reader. Some of the scenes proved so effective that they have been caught up into American folklore. Eliza Harris crossing the crumbling ice to freedom is now a classic example of the chase. Uncle Tom reading his Bible makes a picture every schoolchild is likely to recognize. The touching death of little Eva is the best-known instance in American writing of that popular kind of scene. Tom's beating at Simon Legree's orders and then Tom's death have become almost as famous.

Reinforcing the timely thesis and the highly effective dramatic scenes was the religious element. In a period that greatly valued the Bible and formal Christianity, Harriet's book had a significant advantage. Not that the other novelists were not pious; they were; but none of them outdid Harriet. None of them, so far as we know, contended that God dictated their novels. Harriet, though, believed throughout her life that *Uncle Tom* had been the result of God's direction. "It all came before me in visions," she once assured a woman friend. The book is rich with piety. The most powerful, and unexpected, religious feature was her development of Uncle Tom into the figure of Christ. Tom starts out as a devout and Scripture-quoting man, but it is not until he has been sorely tried through suffering that his religion deepens. Then he experiences a conversion and is so utterly at peace with the world that when Legree later orders him beaten to death—and Harriet emphasizes that he is being killed for being good, for being Christian—Tom suffers gladly for the sake of the heavenly life to come. Just before he loses consciousness he says to Legree, "I forgive ye, with all my soul!" He dies in the love of Christ.

In the epilogue Mrs. Stowe called on the slaveholders and their friends to repent while there was time. "A day of grace is yet held out to us." With that thought she prayerfully concluded.

13
The Sentimental Muse

☙ Everyone liked Erato. Or so it seemed. The extent of the audience for poetry a hundred years ago is almost inconceivable to the present-day American. Accustomed as he is in this Age of Prose to eying any poet suspiciously and dismissing his poems as either too difficult or too easy, the average man finds it hard to believe that housewives, merchants, ministers, and clerks often had a little volume of verse handy at their table or bedside. They read poetry for pleasure and profit both, and much of the poetry popular in the two decades before the Civil War gave them exactly what they wished.

What they wished particularly was poetry that would titillate their emotions, especially the gentler, melancholy ones, and then give them a moral turn. The popular poetry of both the 'forties and 'fifties, like the sentimental novels of the 'fifties, made a strong appeal to the softer side of the American character. While a page of poetry was being read, our usual aggressiveness and materialism were forgotten. Tears started with ease, it may be remembered. The melancholy that brought them on could stem from many a different cause, large or small. Often, however, it would be small and so allow the emotion to become sentimentalized by being out of proportion to it. The death of a household pet was as likely to be rhymed as the death of a child. And even when the sorrow turned out to be major—about the death of a human being—it was often treated in a minor way. The accent would seldom be on the tragic, frequently on the pathetic. The dying little girl, as opposed, say, to the dying warrior, would be the perfect subject for pathos. She could expire in tinkling rhyme almost as effectively as Dickens' Little Nell managed it in prose.

People felt that women poets were the natural masters of the pathetic, and of all the softer emotions, to a degree that few men could equal. Not surprisingly, the two best-known poets of the 'forties were women. Mrs. Felicia Hemans, the British Nightingale, had died five years before the decade opened but her poetry continued for a time to be read with unsurpassed enthusiasm. Then, toward the end of the decade, the American public began to prefer the verses of an extremely active competitor, the American Nightingale or so-called American Mrs. Hemans, Lydia Huntley Sigourney. By the mid-'fifties Mrs. Sigourney in turn lost her crown—and this time to a man, but to one who could write poems that occasionally at any rate combined intellectual depth with technical deftness, and thereby impressed the critic as well as the general reader. The man was Henry Wadsworth Longfellow.

With the notable exception of the poetry of Longfellow, who achieved fame considerably after the two ladies and reflected an increase in American literary sophistication, American poetry in our two decades might be represented only too well by the image of a woman appealing to womanly emotions.

At the level of the unconscious, several but not all of the same Jungian archetypes that drew readers to the best-selling sentimental novels drew them to the best-selling poetry of Mrs. Hemans, Mrs. Sigourney, and their school. And those several were female. The self as child was undoubtedly the most prominent, followed by the anima and then by the earth mother. The animus and the old wise man were ordinarily absent.

At the level of the conscious, the nature of the attraction was different but equally interesting to the social psychologist, and to anyone wishing to understand the history of the American character. We are fortunate in having a pair of contemporary essays that set forth the conscious appeals with considerable discernment. One is by a woman, the other by a man, and both take Mrs. Hemans as their subject. The first, by Mrs. Sigourney herself, appeared in 1840 as an introduction to a set of Mrs. Hemans' works issued by the Philadelphia firm of Lea & Blanchard. It was an "Essay on the Genius of Mrs. Hemans." The second (with, it happened, the identical title) came from the pen of the art critic and essayist Henry Tuckerman. It prefaced an anthology of her poems chosen by that literary man of all work, Rufus Griswold, and printed in 1845.

Mrs. Sigourney begins by sketching the influences on Mrs. Hemans. What proved the most significant one? The answer was inevitable: her mother, or as Mrs. Sigourney puts it in elevated prose, the agency of maternal culture. After that came nature: the rushing streams, the mountains of her childhood Wales, the shadowy dells. Then came several other influences, noted in passing. Finally—and this was important—there was sorrow. Indeed, the "high harmonies [of her genius] could have been perfected by no other teacher." "How else," Mrs. Sigourney demands rhetorically, could Mrs. Hemans have "become a soothing songbird to the sad of heart?"

The poetry resulting from this genius Mrs. Sigourney goes on to pronounce essentially feminine. "The whole sweet circle of the domestic affections," she explains, "—the hallowed ministries of woman, at the cradle, the hearth-stone, and the deathbed, were its chosen themes." Accurately—and revealingly—she omits the marriage bed from the list. She makes the Victorian point, moreover, that the tendencies of Mrs. Hemans' genius were "pure and holy. With dark and stormy passions it had no affinity."

And with holiness we come to the final element in her poetry. People read her lines not only with the conviction that she herself was spotlessly good but also with the belief that this reading made their own characters better. Here was poetry, in other words, with a moral purpose. Poem after poem ended with an ethical or pious reflection. "O happiness! how far we flee Thine own sweet paths in search of thee!" Mrs. Hemans will conclude. Or she may ask, "—Why should *we* dwell on that which lies beneath When living light hath touch'd the brow of death?" Or "A world sinks thus—and yon majestic heaven Shines not the less for that one vanish'd star."

By concentrating her praise on certain characteristics of this poetry, Mrs. Sigourney indicated the nature of Mrs. Hemans' appeal to the public. Henry Tuckerman dealt with the question of her popularity explicitly. He stated both the nature of her appeal in general, as he saw it, which was obvious enough, and the specific basis for her appeal to men.

What men value is her womanly insight into the human heart. Men do not expect "extensive knowledge and active logical powers" from a female poet. They do expect to feel from her verses "the influence and power of the affections." From Mrs. Hemans' lyrics they desire, and receive, the reflection of tender, melancholy love.

With insight comes ennoblement, and thus all readers—men and women both—can become better persons through perusing her poems. Although Tuckerman does not harp on their purity, he plainly recognizes its importance. Her lyrics, he says on this point, "lift the thoughts, like an organ's peal, to a 'better land,' and quicken the purest sympathies of the soul into a truer life and more poetic beauty."

Griswold knew what he was doing when he gathered the poems that follow Tuckerman's pithy little essay. They are poems of feeling, and the note of sentimental sadness is struck over and over. The titles alone are enough to prove the point. "If Thou Hast Crush'd a Flower," "The Bride's Farewell," "The Homes of England," "The Hour of Death," "The Childe's Destiny," "The Landing of the Pilgrim Fathers," "Dirge of a Child," "The Funeral Genius," "He Never Smiled Again"—

in this group of nine consecutive lyrics only "The Homes of England" and the famous poem on the Pilgrims lack some sort of sorrow.

Of all subjects the one that Mrs. Hemans found almost an obsession was the deserted bride. Here her own experience shaped her verse. After a few short years of marriage her soldier husband left her and went to live in Italy, where he remained the rest of her life. It is true that this was desertion as modified by Victorian proprieties—Captain and Mrs. Hemans politely continued to correspond—but it was desertion nonetheless. In her verses this misfortune appears repeatedly. "Come back, my ocean rover! come!" she cries in one of her many variations on the desertion theme.

The dying child also appealed to Mrs. Hemans as a theme though in this case the poignancy of personal experience was lacking, for all her five children outlived her. Yet she found the subject rewarding, as this typical development shows:

> Yes! thou art fled, ere guilt had power
> To stain thy cherub-soul and form,
> Closed is the soft ephemeral flower,
>   That never felt a storm!
> The sunbeam's smile, the zephyr's breath,
> All that it knew from birth to death.

The sorrows of the heart which Mrs. Hemans intoned were nearly universal ones. Though most wives were certainly not deserted, doubtless they knew the feeling by projection at one time or another. And if most children did not sicken and die, infant mortality remained so great, notwithstanding, that it was a rare family that did not lose a tiny son or daughter. The statistics tell a somber story not only in England but also in America: in New York City in 1850, for example, one-fourth of all deaths were those of infants under one year, and one-half of all deaths were those of children under six. At any rate, regardless of whether the sorrow in a lyric echoed the reader's own or not, the effect of Mrs. Hemans' lines was to arouse his or her melancholy emotions and then to assuage them.

Yet it happened that two of the most famous poems for her American audience departed from the stereotype. Read and re-read, recited haltingly or declaimed with eloquence, they gained a place in the nation's memory. You had only to begin, "The breaking waves dash'd high On a stern and rock-bound coast," and any schoolchild could finish the stanza. The other standard piece was "Casabianca"—"The boy stood on the burning deck." With its lesson of absolute obedience, this poem must have made many a teacher and parent grateful to Mrs. Hemans.

Besides her talent as a poet, Mrs. Hemans had one other accomplishment that was distinguished by its perfect appropriateness. She could play the harp.

Adorned with a smile of buttery sweetness Mrs. Sigourney primly followed Mrs. Hemans onto the American Olympus. She had, however, less right to be there. For all her sentimentality, Mrs. Hemans proved herself a poet of some skill and taste. She was a minor poet but not a bad one. Mrs. Sigourney, on the other hand, was a classical example of an extremely popular bad poet. Her popularity, it should be added, was no accident.

Almost from the modest beginning of her career she made a business out of literature. Increasingly shrewd in negotiations with publishers, she accumulated more money than her banker husband was ever able to earn. And she was always adept at the arts of pleasing. For one thing, she made a practice of sending autographed copies of her latest volume wherever they would do most good. Snubs she accepted humbly; and she managed to soften even the pointed critical jabs of the irascible Edgar Allan Poe.

Like some present-day politicians, Mrs. Sigourney consistently kept herself in the public view. She was tireless in pushing the constant publication and republication of her poems and other writings. During the 1840's fourteen volumes came out under her signature, and the presswork slackened only moderately in the next decade. Often the latest volume was a combination of old poems with the new, as was the practice of the time. Although the new were always mentioned first, the old were always there as well. The publisher's notice prefacing *The Western Home* (1854), for instance, says that this volume contains poems previously unpublished, poems drawn from the collected *Poems*, and poems reprinted from periodicals.

Regardless of provenience, in the poems themselves it was the mixture as before. In tone, technique, and content, they showed almost no change during the half century she was engaged in producing them. Her twin formulas evidenced themselves almost immediately. In *Mrs. Sigourney: the Sweet Singer of Hartford* Gordon Haight has dubbed them the Historical Formula and the Religious Formula. The first consisted of picking out a historical personage and then basing a moral on something in his life, the second of taking a religious event and then celebrating its moral significance too. Included under both was her favorite single subject, death.

The climax of her career came in 1849 with the publication of her *Illustrated Poems* by the Philadelphia concern of Carey & Hart. This edition, republished in the 'fifties, was flatteringly uniform with those already issued for Bryant, Longfellow, and Nathaniel Willis. With her usual thrift she chose the poems from previously published as well as unpublished works. The handsome book showed off the Historical and Religious Formulas to great advantage. The Historical Formula is exemplified in such poems as "The Return of Napoleon from St. Helena," "Pocahontas," and "Anna Boleyn," each complete with a moral message. Mrs. Sigourney could no more have avoided moralizing than breathing; and so when Anne Boleyn, for instance, is about to be executed by order of the lustful Henry VIII, Mrs. Sigourney says:

> For him she prays in seraph tone,
>   "Oh! be his sins forgiven!
> Who raised me to an earthly throne,
> And sends me now, from prison lone,
>   To be a saint in heaven."

Among the examples of the Religious Formula is "Aaron on Mount Hor," a piece of semi-Wordsworthian blank verse with death, again, as its climactic device. The poem reminds us that the characters in Mrs. Sigourney's verse were even more given to tears than those in Mrs. Hemans'. Here, as Aaron died, his son "Remembering but the father that he loved, Long with his filial tears bedew'd the clay." Not infrequently the very presence of an old man could make someone sob. Still more moving was the picture of a dying child, a scene that Mrs. Sigourney painted far oftener than Mrs. Hemans. This was a grief that Mrs. Sigourney herself would know. She communicated it to her readers again and again. "Death of an Infant," once faultily ascribed to Mrs. Hemans (as Mrs. Sigourney noted with a touch of pride), is the essence of all her poetry on the subject. She explains in brief blank-verse paragraphs how Death has taken everything from this fair infant—the rose of the cheek and lip, the tender blue of the eyes, the murmuring sound of the little voice, but:

> there beam'd a smile,
> So fix'd, so holy, from that cherub brow,
> Death gazed and left it there. He dared not steal
> The signet-ring of heaven.

If we want to find the median, so to speak, of Mrs. Sigourney's verse, regardless of subject, it might well be discovered in one other piece collected for the *Illustrated Poems*. Called the "Parting of the Widow's Son," it deserves to be quoted in full:

> Yon slender boy his bark hath launch'd
>   On life's deceitful tide;
> His balmy years of childhood o'er,
>   He goes without a guide,
> Amid the stir and strife of men
>   His devious course to run,
> The tempter and the snare to bide—
>   God bless the widow's son.
>
> He turneth from the pleasant door,
>   And from the garden fair,
> Where with his little spade he wrought
>   Beneath a mother's care;
> He bears his head like manhood high,

> Yet tears their course will run,
> When on his stranger-bed he rests—
> God bless the widow's son.
>
> Say ye he goeth forth alone
> To dare the eventful field?
> No, no! a spell is round him thrown,
> Like adamantine shield,—
> A mournful mother's fervent prayer!
> So, till his life is done,
> Till time and toil and change are o'er,
> God bless the widow's son.

Small wonder that the public took Mrs. Sigourney's volumes to its bosom. They could be found in many a home, found—as she wished—"in the alcove of the library" and "on the centertable of the matron." The gradual spread of muttered criticism about the banality of Mrs. Sigourney's lines meant little. That a Griswold might condemn or a *North American Review* ignore the American Hemans had for years no weight for the mass of readers.

She always observed the public's proprieties; indeed she was, if anything, even more conservative than the mores of her time. Woman was meek, man superior; God was good and the world not bad. Just as she observed the cultural proprieties, she observed the political ones. Everywhere except in the South, humanitarian movements were attracting greater and greater attention; and the leading movement was abolitionism. Whatever her personal sympathies, Mrs. Sigourney kept appeals for political reform out of her poems. Almost without exception the New England poets best remembered today wrote bitterly against the slave system. Their condemnation of it grew until it included even the Great Compromiser, Daniel Webster of Massachusetts. "Ichabod"—the glory is departed—became Whittier's name, we recall, for the once-respected statesman. Emerson, Thoreau, Hawthorne united in their strictures against him. But Mrs. Sigourney stayed calm while he compromised, and then elegized him ("I Still Live") when he died. The result was no doubt increased sales for her books and the evident approval of the thousands of readers who still hoped that the Civil War could be avoided.

It was when the 1850's ripened that Longfellow incontestably became the most popular of American poets. The collected *Poems*, which Ticknor & Fields issued in two neat little volumes dated 1857, has an admirable engraving of him at his peak. This is Longfellow before the patriarchal beard. Here he peers out, a large-eyed man, with heavy brows gathered thoughtfully over a Roman nose. His graying hair is cut long, covering his ears. He seems to be more the poet than the professor, yet both can be detected.

The 1857 edition brought together all of his poetry that he wished to preserve up to that time. Among the individual volumes incorporated in the collected *Poems*, first came *Voices of the Night*. Originally published in 1839, it included those permanent favorites "Hymn to the Night," which opens "I heard the trailing garments of the Night," and "A Psalm of Life," with its famous exhortation, "Tell me not in mournful numbers, 'Life is but an empty dream!' " *Ballads and Other Poems*, issued three years later, added to the collected *Poems* even more of the extremely popular Longfellow. Four poems in the *Ballads* must have been as often recited during the rest of the nineteenth century as any. They were "The Skeleton in Armour," "The Wreck of the Hesperus," "The Village Blacksmith," and "Excelsior." People liked "Excelsior" the best perhaps:

> There in the twilight cold and gray,
> Lifeless, but beautiful, he lay,
> And from the sky, serene and far,
> A voice fell, like a falling star,
> Excelsior!

Next in the 1857 collection came *Poems on Slavery;* a dull verse drama, *The Spanish Student; The Belfry of Bruges and Other Poems;* and *The Seaside and the Fireside.* That concluded the first volume.

Volume II had only three works reprinted in it, but one, *Hiawatha*, was the most popular of all Longfellow's extended pieces. The others were the sentimental pastoral, *Evangeline*, and *The Golden Legend*, another verse play, in this instance about a sick German prince who, in effect, sells his soul to Lucifer for health but is redeemed by the love of a pure maiden.

All available evidence indicates that Longfellow was the most popular poet of his time and yet it might fairly be asked, How popular was that? In most cases, in too many cases indeed, we should have to content ourselves with an estimate or an approximation. But for Longfellow we are in luck. Thanks to the orderly way he managed his business affairs, we have the exact figures. The poet's account book has been found by William Charvat. In addition he and W. S. Tryon have printed the financial record of the poet's long-time publishers, Ticknor & Fields. One corroborates the other.

Longfellow proved even shrewder, we find, than Mrs. Sigourney. Like her, he started by selling verse to the magazines; but he soon learned that this paid inadequately and so he developed a better method. He concentrated on putting his poems in small volumes and thereafter publishing several of the small volumes in a collected edition. Repeating the cycle, he would write some more poems, print them in more small volumes, and then issue a new collected edition augmented with the most recent of such volumes. The 1857 edition, one of the most successful, is an excellent example of how the collected editions were made up. Furthermore, Longfellow early in his career began to buy and then keep the stereotype plates of his books. Thus he could sell copies to his publishers wholesale and they in turn sold them to the booksellers. This may sound like a burdensome procedure for a poet but it paid well. By using it Longfellow for decades earned almost double the average royalty rate.

Now the figures themselves. The typical edition of a single volume of new verse came to 500 copies. Exceptions were rare but they did exist. Most notable among them was *Hiawatha*. Its first run was 5,250 and even by the opening of the war Ticknor & Fields could still order an edition (by now the nineteenth) of 1,000 copies. Collected editions of the poet's works normally ran slightly higher than editions of single volumes. The collected edition of 1857, a handsome success, started at 5,000 with later issues, understandably, of a smaller size. Nevertheless, it demonstrated the solidity of Longfellow's reputation. It was reprinted twenty-one times up to 1864, the total number of sets amounting to nearly 20,000.

The grand totals up to the war appear still more impressive. We know from Tryon's study of the popularity of Tennyson and Longfellow that over 56,000 sets of the various editions of Longfellow's collected works were sold; we know that nearly 22,000 copies of individual volumes (the small ones such as *Ballads and Other Poems*) were sold; and we know that the total sales of Longfellow's books from 1839 to 1861 reached the breath-taking number of 179,000.

One piece of general reassurance should be mentioned at this point. In estimating book sales for most other writers, we have often been forced to rely on Allibone's contemporary figures. Obviously since he used sales catalogues and publishers' advertisements as his principal bases, he could not be exact. Yet his figures for Longfellow are not extremely inflated. They run about 15 per cent higher than Longfellow's own, and that is probably due to the normal tendency of a publisher to exaggerate sales. In other words, Allibone usually runs high but not much higher than he should have. It must be kept in mind, however, that in arriving at his total for an individual volume, say *Ballads and Other Poems* again, he adds in the number of volumes printed as part of sets. Thus *Ballads and Other Poems* actually sold only about 4,000 copies by itself, but when it became part of the various collected editions it sold enough extra to make Allibone's estimate of a total sale of 40,000 not much out of line.

From the outset the laurels for the most phenomenal popularity were of course won by *Hiawatha*. On New Year's Day of 1856, seven weeks after publication, Longfellow noted in his journal, "Went to town on business. Saw Fields, and heard that *Hiawatha* is going at the rate of three hundred a day." So great was its success that it immediately became the target for satire.

"*Hiawatha* parodies come in from all quarters,—even from California," the poet complained mildly in the journal for February 18th. But *Hiawatha* was only the brightest star in his constellation. How deeply and widely the public approved of Longfellow is best testified by one more figure, one that this time must be only approximate. It is Mott's: in *Golden Multitudes* he estimates that more than a million copies of the collected poems have been purchased since Longfellow began publishing poetry in 1839.

14

Person to Person

His essay may be a lay-sermon or a satire, a criticism or a reverie.

Henry Tuckerman, "Characteristics of Lamb," *American Quarterly Review* (1836)

It is not unreasonable for our purpose to assume that Calvin W. Marsh, salesman for Goodrich, Willard & Co., wholesale grocers of St. Louis, was spending the evening at home. It was January 1859, and the sleet drove against the walls and windows of his fairly large if cheap house at 232 Chestnut Street. Marsh and his family were gathered in the sitting room, around the center table on which stood the camphene lamp. His wife was mending clothes, his children were giving halfhearted attention to their lessons, and he sat reading. Though his station in life was average, his literary tastes were a bit above that. In testimony to his interest in books, he was now a director of the Mercantile Library Association. Instruction rather than pleasure had from the outset been the aim of this association, but Marsh himself often enjoyed a few pages or so of recreational reading.

The book he leafed through comfortably tonight was the most popular of all volumes of its kind, Ik Marvel's sentimental, tobacco-scented *Reveries of a Bachelor*. Within a year of its publication in 1850, it had sold 14,000 copies. Ultimately it is said to have sold over a million, though that is a suspiciously round number. Besides this highly successful book of sentimental essays Marsh owned several other volumes of essays. He kept them all in a tall, ornate, oak bookcase. The earliest, bought ten years before, was a copy of R. W. Emerson's first series of essays, originally issued in 1841. Young Marsh had alternately knitted his brows and cleared them while going slowly through Emerson. A little later Marsh had gotten Washington Irving's *Sketch Book*, in an old secondhand copy. On the same shelf of the bookcase stood two more collections. One, Henry Tuckerman's *The Optimist*, enjoyed a satisfactory enough success after its publication in the same year as the *Reveries*. But it could not begin to match the fame of the other, G. W. Curtis' *Prue and I*. A group of surprisingly affecting meditations about a poor bookkeeper who was rich with a wealth that money could never buy, it sold half a million copies between its publication in 1856 and 1900.

But regardless of whether their popularity throughout the nation was to be measured in thousands or hundreds of thousands, the books on Marsh's shelf looked well used. The spines were worn with handling. And their owner's interest was far from unique. Actually, his gathering of these volumes represented a nationwide trend toward the essay.

It was with all the glitter and sparkle of a Fourth-of-July rocket that the personal essay soared into public notice in the late 'forties. The fuse had been lit in the 'thirties; public interest was being created by then. But before that time relatively little existed. With the important exception of Washington Irving, no essayist of renown was writing during the first quarter of the century.

In sad fact Irving's best essays, in *The Sketch Book* and *Bracebridge Hall*, were among his earliest. By the beginning of the 'forties he had run almost completely dry. Yet his reputation as America's foremost literary man continued until the Civil War. With his unchallenged reputation went an unprecedented popularity at all levels of the reading public. When in 1859 the *Boston Post* published its figures on book sales, it estimated that 575,000 copies of Irving's works had been disposed of within the decade.

The sources for the steadfast favor that he found were several. One, and not the least important, was negative and nonliterary: he was tactful. Though he enjoyed foreign travel, and lived a good part of his life abroad, he never made the blunder of comparing the Old World with the New. Nor did he criticize American mores. How useful this tact proved can be seen when we look, in contrast, at James Fenimore Cooper. At one time Irving's leading rival, he blighted his popularity for a generation through his sour and often justified criticisms of his countrymen. It was not till after his death in 1851 that his novels again sold very well.

Among Irving's more positive virtues the major one in the eyes of the people was his remarkably winning blend of sentiment and humor. American sentimentalism continued undiminished during the middle decades. In *The Sketch Book*, for instance, the meditative little essay on "The Broken Heart" (he believes we can expire of one), the pathetic sketch of "The Widow and Her Son" (the long-lost son returns, to die a shattered man, and his mother soon totters after him), and "Rural Funerals" (they are "beautiful and simple-hearted") all exemplify the emotionalism in Irving's work. Yet the emotionalism is never mawkish. His "elegance"—the term is applied repeatedly to him—prevents that. It was compounded out of two ingredients, an Addisonian urbanity and a kind of balanced objectivity that allowed Irving to paint a pathetic picture and still be philosophical about its pathos. His elegance distinguished both his sentimentality and his humor. It shines through clearly in the two classic comic tales of *The Sketch Book*, "Rip Van Winkle" and "The Legend of Sleepy Hollow." It gleams more quietly in many a passage of such essays as "The Country Church" and "The Stage Coach."

Not the least tribute to Irving's genius was that he attracted many imitators. The pages of periodicals of the time such as the New York *Atlas*, the *Charleston Courier*, and the *Portland Transcript* contain more than a share of third-rate Geoffrey Crayons. Besides essayists of the school of Irving there were a fair number of writers of articles, especially on history, government, and theology. But of essayists in the graceful, whimsical, informal style popularized in England by Charles Lamb, there were almost none. Lamb and his fellow English Romantics gained surprisingly few American disciples at first.

In 1836, however, the American Henry Tuckerman announced in a review of Lamb's final book, "We confess a partiality for the essay." He went on to regret the current decline, as he saw it, in essay writing and then strongly urged the superiority of the essay over the novel as a vehicle of truth. He felt that in the essay ideas were presented clearly, concisely, and ornamentally, with none of the sensational distractions that the novel afforded. Lamb's essays aroused Tuckerman's warmest enthusiasm. He found in them many things to praise. They included the skillful variation of styles, the note of personal confession, the familiar address to the reader, the pathos, the humor, the evident and loving sympathy for struggling mankind. Important above these was the sincerity of the essays, and still more important was their devotion to the ideal.

Sincerity and devotion to the ideal: the critics of few periods, before or since, have seen fit to stress those qualities in Lamb. That he has them, no one is likely on reflection to deny; but they are ordinarily ignored in favor of the obvious elements in the essays. There are at least two possible reasons why Tuckerman singled them out. The first lies in his own writing. They exist there, and it may be that that is why he responded to them in Lamb. Even in his early travel sketches Tuckerman's thoughtful frankness and lack of posturing are evident. The sketches show his ideality less clearly, but it can be inferred from the moral and ethical judgments he sets down. The second reason must likewise be suggested rather than declared. It is that the climate of the time favored the qualities of sincerity and devotion to the ideal. Our culture was, in one of its aspects, announcing its democratic esteem for sincerity and in another, based on its personal puritanism, was showing respect for ideality.

The existence of these attitudes becomes more evident when we examine the rise of New England Transcendentalism in the late 'thirties and early 'forties. There if ever was a movement that advocated the qualities Tuckerman saw in Lamb. And in the works of the chief Transcendentalist, Emerson, this advocacy reached its apex.

No literary historian would assert that Transcendentalism had a marked influence on mass attitudes, however. Aside from Emerson, disciples of the new movement aroused more hostility than friendship in the crowd. But they did succeed in getting a good many people to talk about Transcendentalism. Emerson himself, through his lecturing as well as through his written essays, preached the gospel of sincerity and ideality to more and more people.

Yet Emerson was never a flashy success. Although he became America's most respected lecturer, his books of essays, often based directly on his lectures, failed to make a substantial profit until he was an old man. Not for him was the spectacular vogue of Ik Marvel or George Curtis. Emerson's genius caused him, though, to appeal to a significant proportion of the intellectual leaders of many a community. That gave his writing an added influence, which his lectures helped to maintain. (The lectures, in fact, probably did more than that: they probably created much of the market for the books of essays.) Public awareness of him grew slowly but steadily.

It started in 1837 when he delivered "The American Scholar" before Harvard's Phi Beta Kappa society. Today this essay is often considered America's intellectual Declaration of Independence. No one probably had foresight enough to realize this at the time, but the piece aroused enough interest to require a second edition the following year. The "Divinity School Address," given before the class of 1838 in the Harvard Divinity School and then printed, made a greater stir even though it failed to go promptly into further editions. To it Transcendentalists said amen, while conservatives of all sorts, including the luckless conservative wing of the Unitarians, shouted that its ideas were blasphemous.

But Emerson kept on lecturing and writing, without a pause to answer any of the charges launched against him. Half a dozen more essays had appeared either by themselves or in the pages of the new Transcendentalist magazine the *Dial* by March 1841, when Emerson's first volume of essays came out. Its success was modest but perceptible. Without doubt, what Emerson preached was finding at least a limited response in American culture. In the next few years two more editions of the same text were issued and in 1847 the first revised edition saw print. It was reprinted in turn, and in 1855 and 1857 Emerson's publishers brought out two other new editions. This was not a million copies nor even half a million but not a publisher's failure either.

In this little volume Emerson preached a series of lay sermons that contained the doctrines he would devote the rest of his life to reaffirming. He had some things to say that no one but a mystic—or a professional philosopher—could grasp. But he had others that anyone could understand because of the striking way Emerson put them.

These ideas were not those of a systematic thinker. Emerson felt rather than thought, announced rather than argued. But his main conceptions could be stated. They justified his being called a Transcendentalist. He believed enthusiastically that the world of the spirit transcended the world of the body. He believed that the knowledge we gained intuitively, from within, transcended the knowledge we gained through our senses, from without. He believed that the Over-Soul (his God) transcended the soul of any individual man, and that a human soul reached the ultimate of felicity when it merged with the Over-Soul.

In some ways these were, literally, un-American ideas and emphatically not those of a large majority of Americans. Most of Emerson's countrymen believed in a trinity of Father, Son, and Holy Ghost, instead of an Over-Soul. Scoffing at intuition, they believed instead in gaining all the knowledge from without that they could. The how-to-do-it books, the growth of the public school system, the popularity of the lyceum all demonstrate that. And though Americans officially admitted that the world of the spirit stood superior to the world of the senses, they nevertheless paid a great deal of attention to the sensory world.

On the whole, consequently, the essays constituted a minority report. There were some elements in them, however, which plainly made a wide appeal. These can best be seen in the most famous of the essays, "Self-Reliance."

What "Self-Reliance" asserted—luminously, movingly—was the innate worth of the individual. That was an impressive idea. In a dozen ways Emerson preached his inspiring gospel of personal independence. Looking straight at the reader, he said, "Trust thyself: every heart vibrates to that iron string." He preached to him alone in the first part of the essay, in language as quickening and evocative as that of any writer of the nineteenth century. A score of his sentences were so aptly put that they have become common coin. "In every work of genius we recognize our own rejected thoughts: they come back to us with a certain alienated majesty. . . . Whoso would be a man must be a nonconformist. . . . A foolish consistency is the hobgoblin of little minds."

After prescribing for the individual reader Emerson turned to the ways American society would improve if all individuals became more self-reliant. Religion would be purged of selfishness, meanness, dogma. Education would rise above servile imitation. So would art. Our country would shake off its naïve belief in mechanical progress. Property would no longer be the mainstay of government. Fate and Chance would cease to rule us. In urging these ideas in the last part of the essay Emerson again wrote sentence after sentence in a way to fix them in the American mind. "As men's prayers are a disease of the will, so are their creeds a disease of the intellect. . . . Traveling is a fool's paradise. . . . Insist on yourself; never imitate. . . . The civilized man has built a coach, but has lost the use of his feet. . . . Society is a wave. . . . Nothing can bring you peace but yourself."

Complementing his ideas and aphorisms, one more thing had a share in Emerson's widening appeal: his mastery of the quietly arresting phrase. The aphorisms remain the best of his expression, of course, but even his relatively ordinary writing is full of phrases and sentences that cling to our attention and cause us to return to them. The opening sentence of "Self-Reliance" is a fine example. "I read the other day some verses written by an eminent painter which were original and not conventional." We gather its surface meaning and quickly pass on. But while one part of our mind absorbs the next sentences, another lingers, piqued and stimulated by the fact that those verses were penned not by a poet but by a painter. And they were original—always an interesting thing. What were they? The sentence echoes below our consciousness as we read further; and we realize after a time, and in discontent, that Emerson will not quote the verses for us.

But the discontent merges, as we go on, into the general feeling that we have been reached by the words of a remarkable man, who will plumb our reservoirs of emotion. He will persuade us of our own nobility. He will demonstrate to us that we are good, mankind itself is good, and a good God rules our universe.

Henry Tuckerman—to return now to him—shared Emerson's optimism and preached some of the same ideas, though in more ordinary tones. Today he is one of the forgotten figures of American letters, but a century ago he stood foremost. When he published a collection of his essays in 1850, called *The Optimist*, significantly, the *Southern Quarterly Review* said, "Among the essayists in America, Tuckerman perhaps deserves the highest distinction." If we are inclined to dismiss praise of this lavish kind as coming from a minor magazinist, it is worth noting that Washington Irving too commended Tuckerman. He greeted the volume, *Biographical Essays* (1857), for instance, with unrestrained enthusiasm. "I do not know when I have read any work more uniformly rich, full, and well sustained. . . . The work is a model of its kind."

The qualities in Tuckerman which his contemporaries delighted to praise reveal themselves pleasantly enough in *The Optimist*. Three essays among the twenty-two collected there can clearly illustrate the fact.

"New England Philosophy," the opening essay in the book, reveals the man of thought rather than of feeling. It justifies the admiration then expressed for Tuckerman's accurate analysis and penetrating insight. Under the guise of describing New England's ruling ideas, he criticizes American attitudes. Looking closely at his countrymen he finds them slaves to society and so speaks out for a higher regard for the individual, as Emerson had. (He cites Emerson a little later on.) He finds them greedy, restless, devoted to logic at the expense of sentiment, and grossly unpoetic. At the end of the essay, when custom and patriotism would both call for a strenuous attempt to picture the more attractive American attitudes, Tuckerman declines. Travel on two continents has made him a realist. He says explicitly that nothing can be done about the attitudes of Americans as a group. But the individual remains, and to him Tuckerman addresses his final plea. Look for beauty in nature and literature; look for richness of feeling at home!

When we remember how his fellow citizens scourged Cooper for criticism not quite so harsh and how they used the whip on some of his successors, it is a wonder that Tuckerman escaped. But he did, and the reason lies in the way he wrote his strictures.

His tone in "New England Philosophy" though firm is modest and appealing; he tries to lead, not push or drive. His style is formal, roundabout, and heavy. Accordingly, it loses much of its potential sting. Here, for example, he is moving from one strong criticism to another: "Next to the danger of subserviency to society, the unhealthy prominence of the idea of thrift is the most baneful feature in our philosophy of life." He is aiming point-blank at the American character, but how many readers would realize that they were a part of the target? If the sentences move weightily, so do the paragraphs. They are pages long at times, and their thread is easy to lose.

Yet that kind of essay, in Tuckerman and others, had a measure of popularity because it was a lay sermon. It could not compare with Emerson's in strength or beauty; but this was a period when Americans liked to be preached to—and the lay sermon obliged.

It was by no means Tuckerman at his best, however. That could be found in the essay "Art and Artists." Here was a field in which he moved with unequaled assurance and authority. The fact shows on every page.

He begins conversationally, describing a sketch he has seen of a youthful painter dreaming of fame. The ill-starred young man who painted the sketch ended by losing his mind, Tuckerman tells us; he stands as the type for the over-strained artist who is talented but not great. Then Tuckerman makes a plea for the artist of that sort. He has his role in life too if he is "a sincere worshipper of the beautiful and the picturesque."

What even the mediocre artist can communicate to us is his feeling. In asserting this, Tuckerman fixes firmly on the main point in his personal aesthetics: feeling or sensibility instead of form or rationality. He himself loves essayists as diverse as Lamb and Emerson because they are advocates of sincere emotion. He loves artists for the same reason. Dedicated to the pursuit of beauty, they help mankind to enrich a life otherwise coarse and commercial. A man in love with beauty will be a better man because of it. The artists themselves show that, for they have "a remarkable simplicity and truthfulness of character." They have learned the lessons nature can teach and will pass them on to us if we will permit it.

As Tuckerman describes the dedication of the true—even if not great—artist, examples crowd into his mind. He draws on his remarkable knowledge of art history and suffuses it with his sympathy for the artist and his love for art. His sentences grow shorter, more familiar as well as more fluent. The sober, unleavened assertions of "New England Philosophy" are replaced by mild aphorisms. The whole essay glows with a quiet warmth. The piece becomes itself the creation of a faithful artist who wishes to share his gentle faith with us.

The third of the essays to be mentioned is "The Weather."

In its overblown triviality, it represents half a dozen others in the book. If Tuckerman was dismayed by the triteness of his topic, his essay fails to show it. His commonplaces are jaunty, his phrases are whimsically turned. Quotations from literature ("poetical authority" he calls it in his preface to *The Optimist*) adorn his text. In all this he was doing indifferently what Lamb had done wonderfully well. Yet the American public liked it, and a dozen other essayists during the 'fifties worked this superficial vein instead of the other, deeper ones in Tuckerman's writing. A passage from the final paragraph of "The Weather" plainly illustrates the characteristics of this side of Tuckerman: "The weather is eloquently symbolical. It is a perennial fountain of metaphors. The clouds that fly over the star-gemmed sky typify the exhalations of earth, which, ever and anon, shade the spirit in its pilgrimage. The wreaths of vapor circling on the gentle breeze, and made rosy and radiant by the sunlight, present an apt similitude of the rise, expansion, and glow of the enthusiast's visions."

It would be unfair, however, to leave Tuckerman with his trivialities uppermost in our mind. After all, he developed an aesthetic theory unusual for his time and place; he warmly defended the implications of the theory for everyday life; and he usually put his ideas into decent and orderly language.

Tuckerman wrote many essays, some of which he reprinted several times. His literary life was a long one, and accordingly the total number of volumes from his study proved considerable. But he never could attract the wealth of readers which Donald Mitchell attracted with the publication, in his twenty-eighth year, of *Reveries of a Bachelor*. It left the press at the same time *The Optimist* did, it may be recalled, but other similarities are few.

Mitchell, a well-traveled, rather sickly Yale graduate, realized early that he liked to write. Several years after leaving college he made an extended visit to Washington, D.C., for his health. While there he wrote a series of light satires, calling them "Capitol Sketches," which he published in a New York newspaper.

He signed them "Ik Marvel," a pseudonym he probably created by coupling Izaac Walton's first name with Andrew Marvell's last. The sketches caused a pleasant little commotion but were nothing in comparison with Mitchell's next important group of satires, on New York society, published in pamphlet form and called *The Lorgnette*. Its two dozen numbers drew New York's attention at once. Using a new pseudonym this time, "John Timon," Mitchell satirized various metropolitan foibles. It seemed as if the whole town, as well as a considerable part of the adjoining eastern seaboard, enjoyed *The Lorgnette*'s sly ridicule and itched to identify the unknown author. It was a good game, ending a year later when Mitchell in effect admitted authorship by signing a collected edition of the sketches with his already well-known "Ik Marvel."

Meanwhile, writing as Marvel, Mitchell had begun publication of an entirely different venture. The *Southern Literary Messenger* for September 1849 had printed his essay called "A Bachelor's Reverie." Here was something new and evidently attractive; the *Messenger* printed a continuation of it in March. With such a promising start Mitchell thought he had the subject for a book. He submitted what he had written so far to the Boston publishing house of Ticknor & Fields. They rejected it, thereby making one of the most colossal wrong guesses in nineteenth-century publishing history. Charles Scribner knew better and accepted it at once.

The finished book was composed of four reveries: "Over a Wood Fire," "By a City Grate," "Over His Cigar," and "Morning, Noon and Evening." They have at least the ghost of a plot, for some of the dream figures seen early in the book reappear later on. And the final reverie makes a casual effort to wind up the action by bringing some of the figures together.

But it was not of course for plot that a multitude of readers bought the book. It was for emotion. Mitchell had given the *Reveries* the subtitle *A Book of the Heart*, and rightly so. He luxuriated in sentiment, expressing it, shaping it, indulging in it, and stepping back every now and then simply to enjoy looking at it. In his central figure of the Bachelor he revived one of eighteenth-century England's noted literary types, the Man of Feeling. Like him, the Bachelor made cultivating his sensitivity a profession. He was particularly fond of sadness. The joy of young love, the placid kisses of mature marriage, the unselfish devotion of parenthood—all such happiness detained him only briefly. He sketched the way it made him feel and then proceeded to relish sorrow.

In one section of an early reverie, for instance, he sits watching the flames of his fire while his fancy creates the ideal wife for him. "*Her* face would make a halo, rich as a rainbow, atop of all such noisome things, as we lonely souls call trouble. Her smile would illumine the blackest of crowding cares." He describes exactly how she will assuage his sorrows. "Your friend—poor fellow!—dies:—never mind, that gentle clasp of *her* fingers, as she steals behind you, telling you not to weep—it is worth ten friends!" When his sister dies, *she* will be a sister to him. When his mother dies ("Is there any bitterness . . . like this?") his beloved wife's grief will solace his own. When his children die she, their mother, will love him with such a wealth of devotion that his "heart grows pained with tenderest jealousy, and cures itself with loving."

Now there are only two other possible deaths left, the death of the dream wife and the death of the Bachelor. In this reverie Mitchell generously decides to sacrifice the Bachelor. He speedily sickens and his end nears. Mitchell envisions his final moments. "Kind hands—none but *hers*—will smooth the hair upon your brow as the chill grows damp, and heavy on it; and her fingers—none but hers—will lie in yours as the wasted flesh stiffens, and hardens for the ground." Then Mitchell breaks off while the Bachelor, his reverie over, sits by the fire with only his dog—his faithful dog, naturally—beside him. The fit of necrophilia is past.

Out of the success of *Reveries* came *Dream Life*, published at the end of 1851. Mitchell divided it into four parts, as he had *Reveries*, "Dreams of Boyhood," "Dreams of Youth," "Dreams of Manhood," and "Dreams of Age." Again there was a thread of plot, for the dreams described the life of the Bachelor, now called Clarence. Again the emotionalism was lush though the connoisseurship in it was not quite so obvious. The scenes melted into each other as they followed Clarence from boyhood to his deathbed in contented old age. Its first year the book sold even better than its predecessor. After that its sales settled down to about a third less than *Reveries*—still substantial enough to make any publisher happy.

Three years after *Reveries* came another best seller, by someone new. It was *Fern Leaves from Fanny's Port-Folio*, a collection of newspaper sketches and essays. Succeeding generations have taken one look at that ludicrous title and smiling broadly have declined to open the book. They have been less than fair.

Fanny Fern was the pen name of tall, high-nosed Sara Payson Willis, a sister of the glossy New York littérateur Nathaniel Willis. Left a widow with two children to support, she tried to earn a living by writing. Her brother snubbed her, so she was forced to place her pieces without any help. She succeeded in spite of some rebuffs, and the reasons for her success are manifest. For one thing, she worked the same wide vein of sentimentality that Mitchell had. With her little exclamatory sketches of orphans, meager old men, and downtrodden women she asked, and doubtless often received, the tribute of a tear from her readers. But she evoked it partly through the convincing realism of the sketches. And it was a humanitarian tear. She wrote about poor people, whereas the Bachelor of the *Reveries* confessed he had a tenant to work the farm he owned, a maid to do his room in town, and could travel abroad when the fancy seized him.

Furthermore, Fanny Fern never teased out an emotion, as Mitchell did, to prolong it for its own sake. Even when she was sentimental, she was brisk. "Two in Heaven," for instance, which reworks the well-known theme of Wordsworth's "We are Seven," occupies less than a page. Fanny sets the mood at once, goes through a series of pious apostrophes to the mother who has lost two of her children by death, and then concludes with a brief, high-pitched final paragraph. "Mother of angels! Walk softly!—holy eyes watch thy footsteps!—cherub forms bend to listen! Keep thy spirit free from earth taint; so shalt thou 'go to them,' though 'they may not return to thee!' "

In a long-winded age she knew the value of coming promptly to the point. That fact took some of the amateurishness out of her sentimental writing and also added greatly to the effect of her comic writing. As her career developed, it should be noted, she turned more and more from sentiment to humor. Fittingly, her later collections have such lighthearted titles as *Folly As It Flies* and *Ginger Snaps*.

Her wit became much admired by the reviewers. They found a rare flavor in it. Frontier farce was a staple of the times, as was social satire of the kind that Mitchell did unusually well in *The Lorgnette*. But Fanny attempted something in between, something that resembled the work of the seventeenth-century "character writers." She would sketch a type with all the resources of her sharp eyes and bustling, quick-paced style. It might be an Irish housemaid or a crotchety grandfather, a good wife or a model minister. The phrases and sentences would hurry across the page, separated only by dashes and exclamations. The highlights of the portrait would be painted in a moment and there, before the reader, would stand the type of person he saw every day but had never stopped to analyze.

And she was good at giving advice. Readily, breezily, but amiably. Somewhere she had also acquired the ability to scold —particularly to scold men—without being irritating. This characteristic intensified her popularity. The women lauded Fanny for taking their side, the men scratched their heads and agreed that she had spunk.

Fanny Fern proved above all both observant and imaginative, but the additional characteristics that aided in her success were never summed up better than by an unidentified critic quoted in Hart's *Female Prose Writers*. He wrote of her that "she had a warm, sympathetic, loving heart, a brilliant wit, a deeply religious nature, an irrepressible love of fun, and a most thoroughly independent, democratic, and '76-y spirit." The loving heart and the religious nature appealed to one side of the American character; the wit appealed to another; and the independent spirit appealed to a third. That the combination was effective, figures cited by Hart can testify. In a single year after its publication *Fern Leaves* sold 70,000 copies. Halfway through that year the eager publishers put out another volume entitled (save the mark!) *Little Ferns for Fanny's Little Friends*. It sold 32,000 copies during the six months remaining. Even that extraordinary record may have fallen when the second series of *Fern Leaves* came out a week before the end of the first series' initial year and supposedly sold 30,000 copies the first seven days.

Fanny's blend of humor and pathos was unique. No one successfully imitated *Fern Leaves* or her later volumes. George William Curtis, however, the last of the outstandingly popular essayists of the time, produced writings of a more usual kind. This is not to say that they were imitations: everything that Curtis published bore the impression of his high-minded character.

A New England boy, he went to college, so to speak, at that most progressive of all institutions, Brook Farm. There he mingled for two fruitful years with the Transcendentalists and their followers. Emerson became his God. Since the Concord man did not take an active part in the affairs of the Farm, Curtis had to be content with occasional meetings with him, plus the reading and rereading of Emerson's published works. After leaving Brook Farm, Curtis made it a point to visit Concord as often as he could. In 1844 he moved there and stayed for most of the next two years. However, he had other lives to live, and in August 1846 he made his break. He borrowed money from his father and sailed for Europe and the Near East.

While on his grand tour he sent back letters for publication in the New York newspapers, as young Bayard Taylor had done a year earlier and as Tuckerman and Nathaniel Willis had done a decade before that. Then Curtis selected the most exotic portion of his travels and on these based his first book, *Nile Notes of a Howadji* (or traveler). It exploited eastern materials that other travelers had previously used, but *Nile Notes* was exceptional in its vigor and tone. The highly colored oriental scenes were described in short, ejaculatory sentences, loaded with adjectives. The paragraphs were short too and made the overripeness of the text easier for a reader to accept. The book sold well enough to bring Curtis a mild kind of celebrity in the literary circles of New York and Boston.

His next and considerably greater success came with the publication of *The Potiphar Papers* in 1853. It resembled Mitchell's earlier satirical series, *The Lorgnette*, though the subject was suggested independently to Curtis. He satirized New York society, with its greedy, ambitious new rich, its rather stale old families, and its brainless, party-going young men and women. He concentrated on the showiest, wealthiest New Yorkers but found time to ridicule some others in passing. He painted his principal portraits—of extravagant Mrs. Potiphar, the unctuous Reverend Cream Cheese, and gossipy Minerva Tattle —with superficial blandness. Underneath lay a good deal of indignation. Curtis had not forgotten the Transcendentalist scale of values and he retained a lively social conscience. (His greatest contribution during the late 'fifties and thereafter would be, as a matter of fact, civic rather than literary.) The result was that his criticism proved at times considerably more severe than it seemed at first.

But all this—the severity, the sauce of humor, the exaggeration, the ridicule—was laid aside when Curtis wrote his next book. *Prue and I* played on the tritest of themes, that happiness comes not from wealth but from love. But the calm meditations of the old bookkeeper, devoted to his faithful wife, about his own happiness and others' discontents still have the power to move readers. There is no touch of smugness in him though he knows best what is important in life and what is not. He draws the picture of his own happiness modestly, and his sympathy for the unhappiness of others is surely if gently expressed.

"My Chateaux," the second essay in *Prue and I*, has the bookkeeper soliloquizing about castles in Spain. He owns some but not alone, for he shares them with his ever-young Prue. He pays a call on Mr. Bourne, a millionaire merchant whom he knows, to see if he likewise has castles in Spain. Many, says

Bourne sadly, and no employee has ever directed him properly to them. One Sunday, later on, the bookkeeper goes walking in the country with white-haired old Titbottom, his subordinate at the office. The two men talk placidly about their castles, since Titbottom owns several as well. But it is not long before the reader realizes that Titbottom leads a life of dreariest routine. Only the thought of his castles keeps him from killing himself. Then the bookkeeper comes home quietly. Prue smiles at him and says, "I see it has done you good to breathe the country air. . . . Jane, get some of the blackberry jam, and call Adoniram and the children." And they go in to tea.

Sentiment gleams in the long, easy-winding sentences, yet the emotion seldom cloys. Curtis will not luxuriate in feeling as Mitchell does, and the result is better literature. The scale of values is one of Emersonian integrity but its manifestations are never forced for effect. They never become extreme.

The whole book, as a matter of fact, is in a minor key. It may frequently go to the edge of a profound emotion but it soon retreats softly. It has a respect for moderation that is classical even if the atmosphere of the book is romantic. Curtis himself was in love and about to be married when the book was being written. Perhaps it reflects the richness of that phase of his life.

In Curtis mid-nineteenth-century America saw the last of its phenomenally fashionable essayists. Never before had the essay attracted so many readers as it did in the decade preceding the war; it would never attract so high a proportion afterward. Creatures of their time these leading essayists were (aside from Irving and Emerson); their work has since found oblivion. Yet the writing of at least two of them can still be read with pleasure. Especially in *Prue and I*, Curtis has felicities of tone and style which deserve to endure. And Fanny Fern has an unfailing feminine verve that no writer of her sex can equal today.

Part Four

POPULAR PRINT: II

15
Foreign Ports and Exotic Places

ℤℤ Take a weak-eyed Harvard boy and have him ship as a common seaman on a voyage round the Horn, thereby toughening his body, sharpening his sight, and bringing out all the basic strength of his character. This was the recipe for the most popular of marine travel books during the two decades before the Civil War. Richard Henry Dana, Jr., had barely reached twenty-five when he published *Two Years before the Mast*. Harper & Brothers issued it after giving him only $250 for the copyright. Since they seemed far more interested in pirating English authors than in paying American ones, they allowed Dana's book to try to sell itself—and it did. With several reprintings and editions in its first two years, it quickly became a success. Later on, sales dropped for a time but then a completely unexpected occurrence, the gold rush, drove them up again. Dana had devoted the whole middle section of the book to his adventures in California, the farthest point of his voyage. When the gold fields opened there in 1848, his proved to be the only easily available book on the region. Copies promptly disappeared from the bookstores and Harpers' book-bins. On returning to California a generation later, Dana said with pleasure that he found that almost every American in California had read him.

Even if we discount an author's optimism, little doubt exists about the popularity of *Two Years*. At the beginning the acclaim it earned in England exceeded that which it received over here, but by the 1850's its high quality was acknowledged universally. Yet it was only one of many such books. Works on travel dot the pages of Orville Roorbach's ante-bellum bibliographies; lectures on travel became one of the staples of the lyceum system; and novels and short stories with a faraway setting grew in number.

The origins of this interest in travel books lay in a noteworthy complex of American characteristics. Restlessness was perhaps the main element, betraying itself in manifold ways. "Men are in constant motion," Tocqueville observed. Our population demonstrated what the demographer would call a high degree of mobility. That meant that a family had relatively few qualms about picking up and moving away to improve its situation. The American seldom felt a compulsion to endure misery when he could alleviate it by settling somewhere else, preferably in the West. If times grew bad in New England and rocks seemed to multiply in the field, the Yankee farmer heeded Ohio's call or Iowa's.

But travel did not have to be purely a means of reaching richer land. It was also, as other foreign observers remarked, a recreation. Going somewhere for the sake of going. This had not yet become the land of the summer-vacation trip but notwithstanding, the riverboats and packets were crowded, the trains were full, and even the jolting stages and carriages kept their share of business.

Visitors to this country noted still another, more personal, aspect of American restlessness. That was the habit we had of walking fast, of being unable to sit still, of erupting into all sorts of brisk motions from drumming our fingers to tapping our feet. And deeper than all this lay the psychological restlessness of a people without the security and fixity of class status, the restlessness created by a break from the European tradition without a new tradition to replace it.

Restlessness, in its different manifestations, was the main but not the only thing that favored the circulation of travel books. Allied to it was a thirst for new experience and knowledge. The desire to explore deserves to be called an American trait too. If this desire could not be satisfied in real life—and of course circumstances often barred even a mobile American's way—it might be satisfied secondhand through travel literature. And that is what happened. It found such varied fare to feed on as the trappers' tales of the great West, the South Sea idyls, and the sagas of the frozen North.

These travel books furnished at least two, considerably different, kinds of vicarious experience. The first is a glorying in physical hardship, in the surmounting of rugged obstacles. In literature even more than in life, one can climb the Rockies and cross the ocean, treating Nature as an opponent to be tricked and then beaten down. As athletic Bayard Taylor wrote at twenty, "Sometimes I almost desire that difficulties should be thrown in my way, for the sake of the additional strength gained in surmounting them." Anglo-Saxon poetry often displays a similar relish for the trials and ordeals of seafaring life, based on the conviction that they can be endured.

The other kind of experience is a sybaritic, sensual escape, an escape from the cramping confines of a prim Victorian existence to a land of sinuous dancing girls. Rich in its appeal to the somewhat starved senses of the mid-century American, it brought him —and her, through identification—the release that motion pictures today provide. Satisfactions that would be unthinkable in the United States could be savored vicariously if the scene were a Turkish harem or a South Sea isle.

The classic example of hardship endured and conquered is Dana's book. It appeared in 1840, at the opening of our period, but similar volumes came out all during the years before the war. Elisha Kent Kane's account of his Arctic explorations dominated the new books of the 'fifties by selling a remarkable 130,000 copies before the decade ended. The pioneer in the field of South Sea idyls was Herman Melville's *Typee* (1846), but the full flowering of the sybaritic species did not come until the publication of Bayard Taylor's lush *Lands of the Saracen* in 1854.

In form if not content, *Two Years before the Mast* is actually a far better book than young Dana knew how to write. The strenuous experience was all his—no one has ever maintained (as is now done for *Typee*) that the author mingled fiction with his fact—but even its minor incidents fall into an artful order. The basic plot is almost certain to satisfy the reader: the green young fellow overcomes the hazards set up by circumstance and grows into a man. Furthermore, the plot is defined and limited in a perfectly natural way: the brig *Pilgrim* sails from Boston Harbor, makes its long voyage, and returns.

For this voyage, in other words, reality itself supplied an Aristotelian beginning, middle, and end. The beginning is the time the brig is outward bound, a time of increasing misery for all the crew, a misery temporarily accentuated by the cold of the Antarctic and crescendoed, when the California coast is reached, by the captain's flogging of two crew members. The middle is the extended period, full of descriptions of California life, when the *Pilgrim* sails back and forth along the coast exchanging her cargo of Boston wares for bullocks' hides. Dana helps to collect and stow the hides on board ship. In addition, he picks up a knowledge of Spanish which facilitates his frequent meetings with the Spanish inhabitants when he travels on shore. The end is the journey home. Once the Horn is rounded, even the physical rigors disappear. The brutal captain has already been transferred to another ship. Morale rises. The winds are good, so is the weather, and the whole ship seems quickened by the wish to reach port. The *Pilgrim* sails into Boston Harbor with the now robust Dana keyed up in excitement at coming home.

The tone of the book is an outgrowth of the man. It is never exclamatory or shrill. Even its few formal passages of description are modulated. One of the finest examples is his picture, given at the end of a lazy, sparkling Sunday on the return trip, of the *Pilgrim* at full sail. Dana had clambered and crawled to the end of the flying-jib boom and, on turning back, was struck with the beauty of the sight below him. "There rose up from the water, supported only by the small black hull, a pyramid of canvas, spreading out far beyond the hull, and towering up almost, as it seemed in the indistinct night air, to the clouds." Then in ascending order he enumerates the sails from the lowest ones to the sky-sail at the very apex of the pyramid. The cumulative effect is almost grand. He continues: "So quiet, too, was the sea, and so steady the breeze, that if these sails had been sculptured marble they could not have been more motionless." But now he needs something to round off his description. He finds it in the remark of an old sailor who had climbed up with him but whose presence has not been mentioned till now. This seaman gazes down quietly too before he speaks. At this point the risk of emotionalizing the scene is considerable, but Dana avoids it perfectly by letting him say of the full, still sails only, "How quietly they do their work!"

The style is in keeping. Harvard's Professor E. T. Channing described it in the *North American Review* shortly after the book came out. He thought the writing "plain, straightforward, and manly, never swollen for effect, or kept down from apprehension. There is no appearance of seeking for words; but those that will best answer the purpose come and fall into their proper places of their own will; so that, whatever the transitions may be, the composition flows on. . . . This we suppose is the perfection of style."

One more thing, which has already been noted but needs to be stressed, is important in appraising the story. It is the fact that *Two Years before the Mast* was a democratic book. It took the side of the crew, not the captain. Probably no nation disliked absolute power as much as nineteenth-century America. In the Jacksonian era just closing when the book appeared, even the rich often concealed their strength behind a democratic manner, and tyranny was hateful. When Captain Thompson ordered two seamen spread-eagled and then flogged them in a frenzy with his rope, Dana, "disgusted, sick, . . . turned away, and leaned over the rail, and looked down into the water." Other instances of cruelty in the book, less dramatic, were nevertheless many. In every case the reader's sympathies lay with the miserable sailors.

Herman Melville, like Dana, was a young seaman when he went through the experiences embodied in his first travel book. There, though, the resemblance ends. *Typee* is the arch example of the South Sea island adventure, spiced with as much sex as a Victorian publisher could permit. The nature of *Typee*'s appeal is shown at once. The first chapter begins with an exclamatory address to the reader, goes on to describe the ship with a richness of sensory detail that Dana never achieved, and then sets the slight plot in motion by the announcement that the next stop of the untidy ship *Dolly* will be the Marquesas Islands. "The Marquesas!" Melville marvels. "Naked houris—cannibal banquets—groves of cocoa-nut —coral reefs—tattooed chiefs—and bamboo temples; sunny valleys planted with bread-fruit trees—carved canoes dancing on the flashing blue waters—savage woodlands guarded by horrible idols —*heathenish rites and human sacrifices.*"

Having established his genre, Melville ends the chapter with a coy account of how a native queen was prompted to display all her tattooing to a crew of astounded French sailors. The second chapter concludes similarly, with a variation of this theme, for as the *Dolly* prepared to drop anchor in Nukuheva Bay, she was boarded by a lovely group of native nymphs. "Their extreme youth, the light clear brown of their complexions, their delicate features, and inexpressibly graceful figures, their softly molded limbs, and free unstudied action, seemed as strange as beautiful." In the evening they danced on the deck for the sailors, but, says Melville piously, it was with an "abandoned voluptuousness" that he would not dare describe. The night ended with an orgy and prompted Melville's reflections about the way European civilization corrupted native trust.

Thereafter Melville's own, and more proper, adventures began. He jumped ship, made his way across the island with difficulty, took sick, and fell into the hands of the cannibal Typee tribe. In spite of his initial fears, he found that the Typees treated him well though they refused to let him leave. To minister to his needs they gave him a faithful retainer named Kory-Kory. And he soon found a female companion. In the household where Melville was assigned there lived the lovely Fayaway. With her "free pliant figure," she became the prototype of a school of friendly South

Pacific charmers whose number is not exhausted yet. Gentle, playful, she devoted every hour to Melville.

Melville tasted most of the experiences of native life. He loafed in the hut, he enjoyed the men's club (tabooed for women), attended the important Feast of the Calabashes and twirled a finger in the savory poi-poi. And he swam, or bathed rather. As he blandly remarked, "Bathing in company with troops of girls formed one of my chief amusements." Most of the adventures Melville recounts would have held the attention then even more than today. None of them would have a more searching psychological claim, probably, than the Eden-like bathing parties with Fayaway and her lithe friends.

To the hard-working American male, if not to his spouse, such parties doubtless represented the pagan peak of idleness. The form of idleness had its significance too. To a generation used to being muffled in heavy clothes, the idea of bathing naked was a shocking, tantalizing thing. Swimming itself constituted more of an exciting innovation than one might expect. It would not be until twenty years after Melville published *Typee* that American men and women would begin to enjoy their oceans, lakes, and rivers; and when they did it would be with three-quarters of their bodies covered by woolen bathing suits. Lastly, the genial waters of the South Pacific were a perfect fertility symbol, regardless of whether the nineteenth-century readers of *Typee* consciously recognized the fact or not. With Melville, eyes alight, they watched the girls in the water, "springing buoyantly into the air, and revealing their naked forms to the waist, with their long tresses dancing about their shoulders, . . . and their gay laughter pealing forth at every frolicsome incident."

Most Americans associated Dana with only one book; they associated Melville with only two. Having attracted widespread attention with *Typee*, he followed it with an almost equally popular sequel, *Omoo*. But his succeeding works, works of fiction now considered among the best in our literature, were given less and less applause. To the public even as late as the Civil War he remained "Marquesas Melville." From Bayard Taylor, on the other hand, readers gratefully received travel book after travel book. A man of fewer literary gifts by far than Melville or even Dana, he established himself as the prince of professional travelers. He went everywhere, and then talked and wrote about it. His books spanned the last two-thirds of our period. *Views A-Foot, or Europe Seen with Knapsack and Staff* (1846) was his first one; *Travels in Greece and Russia, with an Excursion to Crete* (1859) was the last before the war began. And there were five in between.

Before Sumter more than two dozen editions (totaling 30,000 copies) of *Views A-Foot* had been exhausted. A brisk, breezy account of a grand tour of Britain and the Continent, it captivated its audience the more because it was the tour of a personable but poor young man. Taylor had only $140 with him when he started out, yet he managed to stay in Europe for nearly two years. They proved to be memorable ones, crammed with every kind of interesting incident. He went to Abbotsford and gazed reverently at Sir Walter Scott's study. He wandered through Westminster Abbey. He remained in Germany for months, learning to love the ancient university town of Heidelberg in particular. He went to Vienna and sat in a beer garden listening to Strauss play his own waltzes. He crossed the Alps to Italy, meeting Hiram Powers in Florence and praising the statue *Eve*, which the sculptor had recently completed. Then he turned to France, where he spent the last pennies of his little hoard, swung back to England—and then home.

Horace Greeley had said bluntly, when he and Taylor talked about writing up his tour in letter form for the *Tribune*, that he wanted "no descriptive nonsense. Of that I am damned sick." If Taylor found that he could not, and would not, obey Greeley's dictum entirely, he nevertheless kept it in mind. Accordingly, the descriptive passages in *Views A-Foot* are held within bounds. The narrative does not stop while the author indulges his love for picturesque composition. As a matter of fact, Taylor's ability to combine description with anecdote accounted for a good deal of the book's popularity.

Furthermore, since this was the book of a poor young man,

stately prose would have been off key. Taylor sees all the sights but sees them from below. His status and his nationality come out in other ways. Early in the book, for instance, just before the visit to Abbotsford, he writes about journeying to Ayr for the Burns festival. He becomes sarcastic about the fact that admission costs fifteen shillings, a sum that once would have barred Burns himself from such a function. Shortly afterward, while passing through Newcastle, he happens to see a group of striking miners who sing a plaintive ballad on their wrongs. "It made my blood boil," says Taylor, "to hear those tones, wrung from the heart of poverty by the hand of tyranny."

American readers responded warmly to Taylor's book as they would never have to that of, say, a well-to-do Philadelphia banker. They responded to his basic democracy, as manifested most by his interest in the underdog but also revealed in many a humanitarian aside during his tour. They responded, further, to the evident contrast between his young American uprightness and the deca-dence of the Old World. When he noticed that Burns's homestead had become a sordid tavern, his readers waxed indignant with him. When he knitted his brows at European vice, they too grew dis-turbed and shocked. And—most important in Taylor's own judgment—they responded to what he himself later characterized as "that spirit of boyish confidence and enthusiasm, to which alone I must attribute the success of the work."

Besides these factors in the book's success, one more, of a dif-ferent kind, can be detected. It was the implied challenge to the reader to see Europe on as little money as possible. When Taylor opened a chapter on Germany with "I have lately been comput-ing how much my travels have cost me up to the present time, and how long I can remain abroad to continue the pilgrimage," many a reader probably leaned forward to figure it out with him. In this way *Views A-Foot* proved to be a how-to-do-it book, for it demonstrated how to see Europe cheaply. Taylor soon saw the value of this function of the book; a year after its initial publica-tion he tacked on a chapter of advice to impecunious would-be tourists.

A decade separated the handsome lad who tramped through

Europe from the bearded celebrity who took ship for the Near East to gather material for *The Lands of the Saracen*. By this time Taylor had come to love native costume, and we have several pictures of him in Arab dress. In one of them he looks away from the reader, his heavy-lidded eyes brooding under his turban, his nostrils arched, his dashing beard and mustachioes a-curl. His hand lies on his scimitar, ready to draw if need be. This is the Bayard Taylor who made ladies swoon when he lectured. This is, in fact, a kind of matinee idol though without any repellent glossiness or prettiness.

The tour that *The Lands of the Saracen* was based on covered Syria, Palestine, Lebanon, Turkey, Malta, Sicily, and Spain. Though the chapters on Turkey turned out to be the richest and best, the whole book when compared with *Views A-Foot* shows both a substantial change and a great advance. It is an older, surer, sophisticated traveler writing now. With maturity has come a genuine skill in the management of scene as well as the ability to relish the spicy appeals to sense. The humanitarian young Victorian has been submerged in the worldly artist. The boyish enthusiasm has been transmuted into a gusto for exotic experience.

Evidences of increased deftness in writing can be found everywhere in the pages of the book. The descriptive pieces continue to move instead of standing still—perhaps Taylor remembered Greeley's advice—but move with added grace. There are many other good points too. The sentences, though inclined to be long, are reasonably well knit. If Taylor's grasp of English syntax is not that of Thoreau, it has nevertheless improved. The verbs are often powerful and vivid. The vocabulary is frequently rich but seldom heavy.

Here, for instance, is Taylor painting a nighttime scene. He is watching for the arrival by boat of the Turkish Sultan, who intends to pray ceremonially at a mosque across the water from where Taylor stands:

> A long barge, propelled by sixteen oars, glides around the dark corner of Tophaneh, and shoots into the clear, brilliant space in front of the mosque. It is not

lighted, and passes with great swiftness towards the brilliant landing-place. There are several persons seated under a canopy in the stern, and we are trying to decide which is the Sultan, when a second boat, driven by twenty-four oarsmen, comes into sight. The men rise up at each stroke, and the long, sharp craft flies over the surface of the water, rather than forces its way through it. A gilded crown surmounts the long, curved prow, and a light though superb canopy covers the stern. Under this, we catch a glimpse of the Sultan and Grand Vizier, as they appear for an instant like black silhouettes against the burst of light on shore.

This paragraph moves in swift surges, driven by its active, immediate verbs. The phrases, often separated by commas, are short. The vocabulary is not ornate, yet it contributes to the Eastern atmosphere. The management of light and shade—the chiaroscuro, the visual imagery—reveals the hand of a conscious artist. Equally important, the scene is well contrived dramatically. When the first boat scuds out, we expect the Sultan to be in it. But before we can identify him, another and more magnificent boat has skimmed into view; and this is the one he occupies. Much as we want to see him, we glimpse him only for a moment. Then he vanishes, into the mosque. The paragraph rises swiftly to its climax and then drops.

The adroitness of Taylor's writing contributed of course to its popularity. It is a safe guess, however, that the average reader felt rather than comprehended Taylor's art; he was far more interested in what Taylor was saying than in how he managed to say it so effectively.

For what he was offering the reader of *The Lands of the Saracen* was an abundance of escape. True, this volume did not have the dancing girls in person to symbolize the fact. So far as Taylor's work was concerned they had already appeared, it happened, with their bodies curving "like a snake from the hips to the shoulders," in his preceding book, *A Journey to Central Africa*, along with a section entitled "A Sensuous Life Defended." But *The Lands of the Saracen* had no need of them. It contained the two most remarkable set pieces of their sensory kind in all Taylor's travel books.

One is the chapter "The Visions of Hasheesh." The other is "A Dissertation on Bathing and Bodies." Taylor purposely put them next to each other at the end of the first quarter of the book.

He had already taken hasheesh once and described his sensations in *A Journey to Central Africa*. Yet this had been a superficial experience. His insatiable curiosity (he confessed it frankly) impelled him to take it again, this time in a much heavier dose. Because he had eaten supper first, it was slow in affecting him. But then it began.

"The walls of my frame were burst outward and tumbled into ruin. . . . I felt that I existed throughout a vast extent of space. . . . Within the concave that held my brain were the fathomless deeps of blue; clouds floated there, and the winds of heaven rolled them together, and there shone the orb of the sun."

The exultation increased.

> Before me—for a thousand leagues, as it seemed—stretched a vista of rainbows, whose colors gleamed with the splendor of gems—arches of living amethyst, sapphire, emerald, topaz, and ruby. By thousands and tens of thousands, they flew past me, as my dazzling barge sped down the magnificent arcade; yet the vista still stretched as far as ever before me. I revelled in a sensuous elysium, which was perfect, because no sense was left ungratified. But beyond all, my mind was filled with a boundless feeling of triumph. My journey was that of a conqueror—not of a conqueror who subdues his race, either by Love or by Will, for I forgot that Man existed—but one victorious over the grandest as well as the subtlest forces of Nature. The spirits of Light, Color, Odor, Sound, and Motion were my slaves; and, having these, I was master of the universe.

That was the ecstatic climax. Then the drug started to stimulate him too much. He became "a mass of transparent jelly, and a confectioner poured me into a twisted mold. I threw my chair aside, and writhed and tortured myself for some time to force my loose substance into the mold." The torment grew till he could bear it no longer. "I threw myself on my bed, with the excited blood still roaring wildly in my ears, my heart throbbing with a force that seemed to be rapidly wearing away my life, my throat dry as a potsherd, and my stiffened tongue cleaving to the roof of my mouth—resisting no longer, but awaiting my fate with the apathy of despair."

In a stupor for several days and nights, he finally recovered consciousness enough to go to a nearby bath. It restored some of his alertness. A brown Syrian polished his limbs; another attendant gave him a glass of tingling sherbet; and he started to feel like himself again.

Thus the chapter ended. But the note of the bath had been introduced, and in the next chapter it was amply developed. The two chapters are as different as the proverbial day and night. In contrast to the violent, aching, almost insane sensations of "The Visions of Hasheesh," those of the "Dissertation" lave the traveler in seas of mellowness, flowing through his almost etherealized body and giving it a sense of perfect well-being.

There is nothing that approaches the "Dissertation" in American writing of the 'forties and 'fifties. As a poet Taylor created little but commonplace rhymes. As an essayist, as a man of letters, he seldom rose above mediocrity. But the chapter on bathing and bodies, though marred for Americans in one or two places by poor taste, is a tour de force, a minor triumph. It exalts the body, and particularly the male body, as did nothing else of the time.

"Come with me," he proposes, "and I will show you the mysteries of the perfect bath." From the bright bazaar we go into the elaborate building that houses the public baths of Damascus. Taylor describes the first rites of the ceremony; and then the attendant —only a dark shape in the mist—

> leads us into an inner hall, with a steaming tank in the center. Here he slips us off the brink, and we collapse over head and ears in the fiery fluid. Once—twice—we dip into the delicious heat, and then are led into a marble

alcove, and seated flat upon the floor. The attendant
stands behind us, and now we perceive that his hands
are encased in dark hair-gloves. He pounces upon an
arm, which he rubs until, like a serpent, we slough the
worn-out skin, and resume our infantile smoothness
and fairness. No man can be called clean until he has
bathed in the East. Let him walk directly from his accustomed bath and self-friction with towels, to the
Hammam el-Khyateën, and the attendant will exclaim,
as he shakes out his hair-gloves, "O Frank! it is a long
time since you have bathed."

Next come the successive basins of hot and cold water, and
after that the soaping. The attendant brings in a wooden bowl, a
piece of soap, and a bunch of palm fibers.

He squats down beside the bowl, and speedily creates
a mass of snowy lather, which grows up to a pyramid
and topples over the edge. Seizing us by the crown-tuft
of hair upon our shaven head, he plants the foamy
bunch of fibers full in our face. The world vanishes;
sight, hearing, smell, taste (unless we open our mouth),
and breathing are cut off; we have become nebulous.
Although our eyes are shut, we seem to see a blank
whiteness; and, feeling nothing but a soft fleeciness, we
doubt whether we be not the Olympian cloud which
visited Io. But the cloud clears away before strangula-
tion begins, and the velvety mass descends upon the
body. Twice we are thus "slushed" from head to foot,
and made more slippery than the anointed wrestlers of
the Greek games.

Then the basins again, and the bath nears its end. One more hot
plunge, one more rest, and then "the course of passive gymnastics,
which excites so much alarm and resistance in the ignorant
Franks." "Give yourself with a blind submission into the arms of
the brown Fate," Taylor advises, "and he will lead you to new
chambers of delight." We enter those chambers, it turns out, by

234

allowing the boy to crack all our joints. But that is only the beginning. At the end, "the slight languor left from the bath is gone, and an airy, delicate exhilaration, befitting the winged Mercury, takes its place."

Afterward we lie in transcendent repose, having drunk a "*finfan* of foamy coffee, followed by a glass of sherbet cooled with the snows of Lebanon." We puff lazily on a narghileh, drowse a bit in "a bed of rosy clouds, flooded with the radiance of some unseen sun," and awake reborn, to return into the sunny streets of Damascus. "But as we go homewards, we involuntarily look down to see whether we are really treading upon the earth, wondering, perhaps, that we should be content to do so, when it would be so easy to soar above the house-tops."

Granted, this is not a prose of mandarin elegance or of classical refinement. But in its epicurean tasting of physical sensation, in its yielding utterly to innocuous physical delight, the "Dissertation" is matchless. Doubtless many an American male gazed in the distance after reading it, and drew on his cigar with a certain discontent. Many an American female too probably closed the chapter with a slight blush, and thereafter looked at her husband a bit more speculatively than before.

At any rate, the travel books of Taylor, of Melville, of Dana and their fellows satisfied an American need, or, more strictly, a complex of needs. The number of travel books multiplied throughout the twenty years preceding the war. A few of the best sellers of our period would even stay in print after the new century began. There would be twentieth-century editions of *Two Years before the Mast*, *Views A-Foot*, and *The Lands of the Saracen*. And *Typee* and *Omoo*, riding on the billows of Melville's modern vogue, would ultimately come out in full scholarly as well as popular form.

16

The Stirring Past

With pride in his heart and a glitter in his eye the ante-bellum American surveyed his country's past. Though that past was relatively short, he felt it to be glorious. This was a nation that had never lost a war and had always been right; and, he affirmed, its chronicles proved it.

In their most popular form these chronicles were of three sorts, and the audience for each of the three considerably overlapped. The first was the textbook on American history. Ordinarily, because we are dealing with adult rather than juvenile culture, we have not considered schoolbooks. But the most widely adopted work on American history for children was also probably the most popular among adults. It would be unrealistic, in consequence, to ignore the writing of Mrs. Emma Willard. A square-jawed feminist and educator, she saw her *History of the United States*, first printed in 1828, go through new editions steadily. By 1860, printings of it and several subsidiary works from her pen had reached 400,000 copies.

Since schoolchildren were to be much of her audience, the

marks of the classroom on the *History* are heavy. In her preface to the 1842 edition Mrs. Willard announced herself a great believer in what today are termed visual aids, and the book itself is arranged with a chartlike clarity. The frontispiece is a tree of American history with branches fanning out from 1492 to 1842; the book is divided into periods to correspond with the various branches; and the margins are crowded with dates and summaries. Yet all this is only a means to an end. The end, according to the preface, is "improvement in individual and national virtue." In her book, Mrs. Willard says proudly, will be found "no examples of profligate females" nor "of bold and criminal ambition." Because the American past has been distinguished by its unparalleled goodness, it offers the reader an unparalleled number of lessons in virtue. Not that the nation has been completely innocent, she adds hastily—"doubtless, there were bad men in America"—but our record is relatively, if not absolutely, unstained. Compared with selfish France or wicked England, those "old and wily nations, the character of America is that of youthful simplicity, of maiden purity; and her future statesman will say, as he reads the story, my country was the most virtuous among the nations."

Yet the eagle screamed more loudly in the preface than in the textbook itself. In describing the disasters for us which marked the military history of the War of 1812, Mrs. Willard did not flinch. She obviously had no relish for chronicling our abortive invasions of Canada, for instance, and she must have sighed in relief when she got to our naval victories; but in dealing with our defeats she did not omit misleadingly nor compress drastically. Similarly, in describing the Seminole War, which was still unfinished when she wrote, she could not quite bring herself to paint Osceola and his defrauded tribesmen as unmitigated savages. And in her *Last Leaves of American History: Comprising Histories of the Mexican War and California,* published in 1849 as a supplement to her major work, she inched her way further toward modern standards of scholarship; for now she often gave more than one side of a story and also analyzed the accuracy of certain of her sources.

But if Mrs. Willard made some progress toward historical truth, the same could not be said of the leading practitioner of the second sort of chronicle, folk biography. From the first time Mason Locke Weems sat down to write a chapter until the last, he displayed a magnificent contempt for accuracy. From the title page, with its erroneous announcement that Weems had been the rector of Mount Vernon parish, to the deathbed scene, his *Washington* dealt with fancy as much as fact. The little book was really a work of piety, building up an image of a mythical hero which greatly satisfied the simple reader. It reached the vast audience of the childlike as well as of the children. It was a eulogy; it was a homily filled with anecdotes and fables such as those of the cherry tree, the cabbage seeds, and the apples; it was a fireside tale. It was not history as presently defined, but its tremendous popularity— close to twenty editions even before the Parson's death in 1825— makes it impossible to ignore in any account of the role of history in American culture.

The Reverend Jared Sparks, editor, historian, and president of Harvard, represents the third kind of chronicler, the writer of scholarly history. His most popular venture into historical writing was likewise a biography. When Mott published *Golden Multitudes* in 1947, he estimated that about five hundred lives of Washington had been printed so far. Two reached Mott's over-all bestseller list, Mason Weems's and Jared Sparks's. Issued just before the 'forties opened, Sparks's went through twenty-four editions during the decade. He made it precisely the book to appeal to the enlightened general reader. By the generous standards of the time, its historiography proved sound enough; moreover, its style and mode of presentation were the product of considerable literary skill.

Much of his book he wrote from primary sources. By offering the inheritor of the Washington manuscripts, Justice Bushrod Washington, a share in the anticipated profits, Sparks not only was permitted to see those papers, he was able to keep them for ten years. In addition, he saw the private papers of other Revolutionary leaders. Besides using manuscripts he either searched personally through relevant public records, both in the United States and overseas, or else commissioned others to examine them. Lastly, a few of the men who knew Washington were still alive, and Sparks got further information from them.

When it came to selecting from all these different sources, he tried (he said in his preface) to bring out the facts that best exhibited "in their true light the character, actions, and opinions of Washington." He added, rather ambiguously, that he had introduced no comments of his own except those needed for "just proportions in the parts and a unity in the whole."

In the actual writing, his touchstone was indeed whether or not an event revealed the kind of man Washington was. Great events in which the General had played a part Sparks was constrained to describe anyway, but he also described many minor ones when they threw light on his subject. He said, for instance, in Chapter VII, "One incident illustrative of [the General's] character should be here mentioned," and then he recounted it. Sparks's own comments always appeared favorable to Washington but that was to be expected. He moralized much less than his contemporaries, however. And even to today's readers, this *Washington* lacks the pious tone and oily emotionalism characteristic of most such ante-bellum productions. The piety, unpalatable now, was demanded then; so was the strongly patriotic point of view.

Not the least of reasons for the book's popularity were the narrative technique and the style. The story line remained clear in spite of some rather abrupt transitions and the background material was introduced with proper deftness. Color and flavor were sacrificed for an elegant eighteenth-century lucidity. Yet it was not too elegant; the syntax was unobtrusive and not overpoweringly formal; the vocabulary was the common literate one of the day. Here is a sample of Sparks's style:

> No part of the President's duties gave him more anxiety than that of distributing the offices in his gift. Applications innumerable flowed in upon him even before he left Mount Vernon, many of them from his personal friends, and others supported by the recom-

mendations of his friends; nor did they cease as long as any vacancies remained. He early prescribed to himself a rule, however, from which he never swerved, which was to give no pledges or encouragement to any applicant. He answered them all civilly, but avowed his determination to suspend a decision till the time of making the appointments should arrive, and then, without favor or bias, to select such individuals as in his judgment were best qualified to execute with faithfulness and ability the trust reposed in them.

Although the entire book is written, as in this paragraph, at one remove from life, mid-century readers did not find it dull. This was the proper mode for describing America's greatest hero. Notwithstanding, the paragraph also throws light on the popularity of Parson Weems's tale with its eye for human interest and its pages full of lively little anecdotes. Sparks's biography moves with dignity while Weems's bounces briskly along. And Mrs. Willard's work occupies a middle ground between the two.

The reading public grew strikingly, we can recall, as the 1850's set in. The fields of European and Latin American history, in particular, provided several successful books of interest. Although United States history continued to be the most popular subject, it was by a much smaller margin than before; and the books on foreign fields caused a considerable stir.

A group of professional historians, among them three scholars of genuine brilliance, William Hickling Prescott, John Lothrop Motley, and Francis Parkman, were writing during the decade. Prescott had already made a reputation through his distinguished publications in the 'forties. Motley caught the public's attention with the appearance in 1856 of *The Rise of the Dutch Republic;* before that he had been known only as the author of a pair of negligible novels. Parkman, publishing his first books in little editions of seven hundred copies or so, would not win a generally favorable reception till after the Civil War. Here Prescott alone will concern us, since he alone was popular during our period.

Besides these men two other, and diverse, historians deserve to be noted. One was George Bancroft, already winning fame for his multivolumed history of the United States. Nowadays his belief in progress seems increasingly naïve, and his confidence that the Almighty had our nation under His special guidance finds no favor with objective historians. A century ago, however, these attitudes of Bancroft's strengthened his appeal to readers and helped build up the sale of his books. The other man was a foreigner, Thomas Carlyle, who, in his guise of literary man turned historian, likewise gained a great public reputation though on a different basis. His *French Revolution* quickly became an American success because it was filled with movement, color, and the vividness of strong personalities. In addition, subscribing as he did to the "great man" theory of history, Carlyle made the approach to his work easy for the public to understand and enjoy. His natural form was biography, and his *Cromwell*, although never so popular as *The French Revolution*, received considerable attention in this country during the decade. But Prescott, historian of Spain and the Spanish conquests in the New World, was both the best and the best known of his kind.

The Spanish Empire at its peak became his great subject. Already half blind by the time he graduated from Harvard, he never stopped suffering from poor eyesight. The history that he drove himself to write could be produced only through the help of hired secretaries and the "noctograph," a machine that guided his hand as he set down his sentences. However, his wealth and social connections allowed him more than mechanical assistance. They gave him access to collections of manuscripts both here and abroad which less affluent or less energetic scholars had previously ignored. His choice of the Spanish Empire as a subject was particularly influenced by the enthusiasm for Spain and its literature possessed by his good friend George Ticknor, the first Smith Professor of French and Spanish at Harvard. Ticknor led Prescott to learn Spanish instead of the German he had originally thought of studying; and the Spanish language proved the key, as one might expect, to the rich primary sources for Prescott's great books.

Readers in the mid-nineteenth century recognized Prescott as the writer of three widely esteemed major works. The first was the *History of the Reign of Ferdinand and Isabella, the Catholic*, dated 1838; the second, the *History of the Conquest of Mexico* (1843); the third, the *History of the Conquest of Peru*, printed in 1847. The *History of the Reign of Philip the Second, King of Spain* made its appearance during the mid-'fifties, but it failed to compare in popularity with the three previous works chiefly because of intrinsic weaknesses not found in these earlier books.

The first book was, by the very nature of its subject, the hardest to write. Prescott's problem was to sum up a nation in a reign. His approach was topical, the main topics being the military, political, religious, cultural, and biographical history of the Spain of Columbus' time. The major difficulty was to find a unifying force in the history. This difficulty Prescott was unable to overcome in *Ferdinand and Isabella*. However, the admiration for nationalism developed by his own Federalist background and the belief in human progress which permeated the American air helped Prescott by carrying over into his study of Spain and giving it a consistency in point of view, at any rate, which had some of the effects of unity in it.

But if Prescott could not achieve unity—and it may be that it is not necessarily advisable to achieve it for any reason except a belletristic one—he was able to gain incidental benefits from that fact. He wrote a history that was unusually flexible in the kinds of factors it considered. "There is a constant interplay," two twentieth-century scholars have noted, "between environmental and race factors, traditions, international stresses, military technology, and personalities." The portraits of personalities, moreover, do have the unity of a formalized pattern. At the beginning is apt to be a list of the character's traits as seen by Prescott; then come "a comparison of his ethics with the accepted code of the age, a review of his accomplishments, and perhaps a contrast with a similar figure in another era or country." Queen Isabella, for instance, is set off against Queen Elizabeth of England.

If *Ferdinand and Isabella* fared well, *The Conquest of Mexico* fared even better. By the end of the 'fifties, printings of the first work, here and in England, had reached well over 17,000 copies and printings of the second (which easily overcame its late start by selling nearly 7,000 copies in its initial year) had reached well over 20,000.

The Mexican work is Prescott's finest achievement. Unlike *Ferdinand and Isabella* it emerged as an organic whole. Unity of action (the epic story of the subduing of a large exotic nation by a few white soldiers and their brave allies) is buttressed by unity of person (the conquest is under the dramatic leadership of one man).

The Conquest of Mexico opens with a vivid panorama of Aztec civilization. In his lucid, polished style Prescott depicts the culture of the country. By no means content with a chronicle of the Aztecs' wars, he describes their politics, their class system, their theology with its grimly increasing human sacrifices, their science with its notable achievements in astronomy in particular, their agriculture, their commerce, and their domestic life. This first section ends with a splendid picture of the Golden Age of the Aztecs.

Prescott divides his history into seven sections or "books," and in the second he turns to the Spain of Charles V and describes the emergence of its colonial empire. Against that background he takes up the early life of his key character, Cortes. The rest of Book II—its title is "Discovery of Mexico"—carries Cortes' story through his voyage to the New World, his stay in Cuba, and his expedition into Mexico. Book III, filled with description of the Mexican scenery and people, traces the stratagems by which Cortes hoped to defeat Montezuma and his nation, the principal one being through the use of such native enemies of the Aztecs as the Tlascalans. Book IV describes the gathering storm of opposition to Cortes' plans; Book V describes the fury of the Aztec assault against the Spanish invaders. Book VI, "Siege and Surrender of Mexico," is the climax of this great historical work; it shows Cortes revitalizing his army and its allies and then capturing the Mexican capital. Once the bloody siege is over, the whole Aztec Empire crumbles. With this the epic story really ends; and yet it is a testimony to Prescott's literary skill that he can proceed to

243

add one more book (although a short one) to the history without giving an effect of anticlimax. The last book traces the subsequent career of Cortes, ending with his death in Spain twenty-five years after the conquest of Mexico. Enough interest in the further adventures of the vigorous soldier remains so that the reader is not tempted to put the volume aside. Nevertheless, the main story—and the main appeal—lies in the exotic, haughty Aztecs and their subjugation.

The Conquest of Peru was published in 1847; by the end of the next decade nearly 17,000 copies had been printed in this country and England. It too became a popular book but it ranks below *The Conquest of Mexico* in practically every respect. It does not have the same narrative drive, the same richness of texture, nor the same unity of conception. In his preface Prescott maintained that unity was preserved through focusing on the ultimate outcome, the permanent establishment of the supremacy of the Spanish crown; but the reader easily loses sight of this in the multitude of petty battles and intrigues.

Prescott again begins with a survey of the country's culture, Book I being devoted to the Inca civilization. Book II is on the discovery of Peru, Book III on the initial conquest of the country, Book IV on the bitter wars the Spanish conquerors fought among themselves for a division of spoils, and the last book describes the return of a measure of order and tranquillity to the terrorized land.

Regardless of their difference in degree, all three histories set a high standard. Many reasons for their popularity suggest themselves. The first lies in the subject of each book. The history of Ferdinand and Isabella was connected with the United States by a cord of patriotic interest. The queen, in particular, had an admirable niche in American folk history. The histories of Mexico and Peru possessed the romantic appeal of all accounts of exotic civilizations; and, since the Aztecs and the Incas had flourished in our own Western Hemisphere, they were of great interest to us. Nearly every detail that Prescott set down (and he set down many) must have been new to his audience, and yet because the civilization of the two empires was so advanced, the significance of the details could be easily perceived by the nineteenth-century man.

The organization of the three histories likewise proved admirable. Prescott kept control of his material, and the result was to the advantage of all readers. The simpler ones may not have grasped what made Prescott's history so firm and clear in its outlines, but the more cultivated could appreciate the grand design of each work.

Prescott's style was clear and polished but not so polished that it attracted attention to itself. His sentences were perhaps long for today's taste but by no means out of the ordinary a century ago. Though their rhythms were not literary, they had the unobtrusive smoothness that came from his careful method of composition. And things happened in those sentences—his eye was always moving. Alert for both action and description, he joined the two in a kind of writing that still holds the reader's interest.

Finally, his historiography was unexceptionable to his contemporaries. The basic attitudes were those of the majority of citizens: a belief in the validity of the Protestant Christian ethic, a tendency to make moral judgments (the Aztecs, for instance, deserved to fall because of their religious cruelty), a belief in the idea of progress, and a conviction that historical events often pointed a useful moral. Today such attitudes obtrude themselves. At that time they seldom repelled even the thoughtful reader, for in Prescott they are more often implicit than explicit. In this way he escaped the criticism of the most intellectual members of his audience. But the attitudes were there.

Here, from *The Conquest of Mexico*, is a passage that exemplifies the impressive kind of history he composed. The Spaniards, under Cortes, are on the march:

> On their route they passed through some deserted villages, in which were Indian temples, where they found censers, and other sacred utensils, and manuscripts of the *agave* fiber, containing the picture-writing, in which, probably, their religious ceremonies were

recorded. They now beheld, also, the hideous spectacle, with which they became afterwards familiar, of the mutilated corpses of victims who had been sacrificed to the accursed deities of the land. The Spaniards turned with loathing and indignation from a display of butchery, which formed so dismal a contrast to the fair scenes of nature by which they were surrounded.

They held their course along the banks of the river, towards its source, when they were met by twelve Indians, sent by the cacique of Cempoalla to show them the way to his residence. At night they bivouacked in an open meadow, where they were well supplied with provisions by their new friends. They left the stream on the following morning, and, striking northerly across the country, came upon a wide expanse of luxuriant plains and woodland, glowing in all the splendor of tropical vegetation. The branches of the stately trees were gayly festooned with clustering vines of the dark-purple grape, variegated convolvuli, and other flowering parasites of the most brilliant dyes. The undergrowth of prickly aloe, matted with wild rose and honeysuckle, made in many places an almost impervious thicket. Amid this wilderness of sweet-smelling buds and blossoms, fluttered numerous birds of the parrot tribe, and clouds of butterflies, whose gaudy colors, nowhere so gorgeous as in the *tierra caliente*, rivalled those of the vegetable creation; while birds of exquisite song, the scarlet cardinal, and the marvellous mocking-bird, that comprehends in his own notes the whole music of a forest, filled the air with delicious melody.

Yet it would be false to see the 1850's as a decade when everyone was paging eagerly through Prescott. There was, in fact, a historian who began publishing in the late 'forties and outsold all competitors in the 'fifties. This was Joel Headley. Though now utterly forgotten because he was a popularizer rather than an original scholar, he ranked first in public favor in his day. *Napoleon and His Marshals*, published in 1846, became his best-known book, with strong competition from *Washington and His Generals*, which he issued the next year.

His personal history was unusual. Breaking down in the course of his duties as minister of a small congregation in Stockbridge, Massachusetts, Headley went abroad to get well. He spent the summer of 1842 in Italy and sent travel letters back to America. Appearing in New York newspapers, they attracted enough response to justify their re-creation in book form and came out in 1844 under the title of *Italy and the Italians*. Completely abandoning the ministry, Headley found journalism more and more attractive. He showed a surprising capacity for it, and in the year of *Napoleon and His Marshals* he was appointed associate editor of Horace Greeley's New York *Tribune*.

By the end of his life, Headley had written more than thirty volumes of journalistic prose, of which his facile history was the most prominent part. Allibone's *Dictionary* notes that as early as 1853 the sale of his books had gone over the 200,000 mark. By the time the Civil War began, *Napoleon* had reached its fiftieth edition.

Its attractions are easy to see. Simple in vocabulary, commonplace in imagery, and clear in construction, it could be read with interest by a ten-year-old as well as by his father. This, for example, is a passage from Headley's description of the Battle of Eckmühl in which Marshal Davout distinguished himself.

> Banners were silently fluttering in the breeze; and in the openings of the woods, glittered bayonets and helmets, for the Archduke Charles was there with his army, waiting for the approach of the [French] enemy. Napoleon gazed long and anxiously on the scene, and then issued his orders for the attack. Davout came fiercely down on the left, while Lannes, with two divisions of the corps, assailed the village in front. In a moment all was uproar and confusion. The roar of artillery, the rolling fire of the infantry, and the heavy

shock of cavalry, made that village tremble as if on the breast of a volcano. In a few minutes the shouts of Davout's columns were heard over the noise of battle, as they drove the enemy before them. His success and that of Lannes together, had so completely turned the Archduke's left, that he was compelled to order a retreat. The streets of Eckmühl were piled with dead, and the green meadows ploughed up by the artillery, were red with flowing blood.

The attitudes underlying Headley's book were equally easy for the general public to appreciate. Only in his writing with sympathy about war was he going counter to any distinguishable American opinion—and even here it was a minority opinion, for the proportion of people against war was at this time undoubtedly small though vocal. James Russell Lowell could say in *The Biglow Papers*, "Ez fer war, I call it murder"; but he would be expressing the feeling of the few rather than of the many. At any rate, in his preface Headley tactfully excuses himself, on several grounds, for glorifying war. If he is arousing a thirst for glory in his young readers, it is a glory based on the struggle—even in the infidel French Revolution—for the principle of freedom, which Americans hold dear. "In the second place," he continues, "we need not fear the effect of stimulating too much the love of glory in this age of dollars and cents." And in the third place, "the struggles and triumphs of genius" should always be recorded, no matter what the field.

The other attitudes manifest in Headley's work must have found a still wider response among the general public. One of the most appealing was his assumption that Napoleonic France could be equated with the America of the Revolutionary War. He dwells on the fact that both encountered in England their bitterest enemy; both showed that she could at least for a time be defeated. Allied to the Anglophobia is another important attitude, contempt for aristocracy. Headley has Bonaparte discover for himself "the truth taught in every physical or moral revolution, that the great effective molding characters of our race always spring from the middle and lower classes." The simple love of physical courage and its attendant traits is the third important attitude to be found. With such views Headley's work recalled readers to an earlier, less money-minded day.

The final contribution to Headley's popularity stemmed from his biographical method. It was quite simple. The focus was on the chief and most characteristic trait of the subject, with the subordinate traits being clearly set in relation to it. The incidents were chosen to bring out that chief trait and, secondarily, the related ones. As Headley says in writing of Marshal Lannes, "One cannot follow him through all his after career, but must select out those particulars in which he exhibited his most striking qualities."

The traits are described and characterized tellingly. Headley never refrains from a judgment but at the same time seldom gives the impression of being a biased judge; this is true because he points out weaknesses as well as strengths in each of the marshals he portrays. Lannes may be daring beyond belief yet when confronted with the need, in the Egyptian campaign, "to bear up against the solitude and silence of the desert," he pettishly dashes his plumed hat to the sand and tramples on it. Nonetheless, Headley retains the sympathy of the reader for his subjects, and does so the better for not seeming to be a perpetual apologist for them.

That Americans wanted to read about themselves alone is of course incorrect, as the last few pages show. French and Spanish history, in particular, provided subjects of great interest. Yet in every case the specific subject had to have American affiliations or parallels, it seemed, before large numbers of people would read about it. And in the field of American history, and American biography too, the public again proved selective. It patently appreciated only the books that conformed to its image of America. The mass of Americans read, it may be hazarded, not for truth so much as for confirmation.

17
The Rampant Press

       Politics—bawling, lusty, partisan politics—was the staple of news. The press was frankly political. In 1850, the mid-point of our period, only 5 per cent of the papers called themselves independent. Every faction bought as many newspapers as it could and frequently rewarded the editors for their support with patronage and political favors. Often, no doubt, those editors were sincere enough and would have supported the party of their choice without being paid in one fashion or another. But regardless of sincerity or the lack of it, the partisan press, as Mott has pointed out in his history of American journalism, dominated the newspaper world in the decades before the Civil War.

    Americans of all varieties showed interest in politics and argued it with a zest greater than today's. In the presidential elections of the 'forties and 'fifties an estimated 80 per cent of all eligible voters went to the polls, as compared with the 60 per cent of a century later. The newspapers reflected this interest and probably helped, in their crowded columns, to increase it. In Mott's judgment the three great continuing news stories of the period were national politics, the Mexican War (which was at least partly political), and the gold rush. Only the gold rush failed to provide much grist for the political mill. Among the leading news breaks in the political story were of course the six presidential campaigns, with the trouncing of Martin Van Buren by "Tippecanoe and Tyler Too" in 1840 and of Frémont and dull Millard Fillmore by Buchanan in 1856 probably attracting most attention.

With this ready emphasis on partisan politics the newspapers should have had a strong influence on the voting public. The surprising thing is that they did not—or rather, to put it more accurately, they had less than one would expect. The majority of the newspapers were Whig but the majority of the presidential campaigns were won by Democrats. Admittedly, other factors helped to elect the Democrats and consequently blunt the edge of this paradox. Yet most of the voters, more often than not, showed themselves at odds with most of the newpapers.

There were, inevitably, some voters who did not read newspapers as there were many nonvoters, mainly women, who did. On the whole, however, the readership of the press grew decade by decade if not year by year. The number of papers rose rapidly enough to keep step with the increase in our country's population. In 1840 there were an estimated 138 dailies; in 1850, 254; and in 1860, 372. Similarly, in 1840 a count showed 1,266 weeklies; in 1850, 2,048; and in 1860, 2,971. On a state-wide scale the story is the same. Illinois is a case in point. Its newspapers have been thoroughly studied by Franklin Scott. Though he notes that census statistics are misleading because they include campaign sheets and newspapers of even the shortest life, it is nonetheless clear that Illinois had, as of 1840, three dailies and 38 weekly papers. By 1850 there were eight dailies and by 1860 no fewer than 23. The number of weeklies rose similarly, to 88 in 1850 and to 239 in 1860.

Although the political press managed to stay on top during the entire twenty years before the war, two energetic newcomers of different kinds emerged to compete with it on the East Coast, and particularly in New York. The first, clad in loud and usually sinful scarlet, was the penny daily, the paper of the new masses. Literacy of a sort, thanks to the spread of public education, was now a characteristic of the crowd. Furthermore, a series of striking advances in the printing industry, including the improvement of the flat-bed press and the appearance of the Hoe rotary press, was cutting the cost of printing newspapers to where anyone could buy them. The penny papers, led by James Gordon Bennett's New York *Herald*, founded in 1835, and Ben Day's New York *Sun*, founded a little earlier, soon determined what their grubby readers wanted and gave it to them with relish. Robbery, riot, and rape was the recipe. Police-court reporting appeared, at first tentatively and thereafter with all the assurance that public favor bestows. In its handling of the notorious Jewett-Robinson murder case the penny press promptly demonstrated the extremes to which it would go. Ellen Jewett was a young New York prostitute whom somebody slaughtered with a hatchet in her room in 1836. A rather dashing clerk named Dick Robinson was accused, tried, and acquitted; and the penny papers savored every minute of the trial.

In one respect the penny press gradually moved in a more praiseworthy direction. It began to develop a social conscience, announcing itself—at least at intervals—the champion of its underprivileged readers. This caused its policy to lean toward the Democratic instead of the Whig platform, for despite its tolerance of slavery the Democratic party remained the party of men with pennies rather than dollars.

The second newcomer was the reputable metropolitan daily. Its highest development could be found in two great New York papers, Horace Greeley's *Tribune*, founded in 1841, and Henry Raymond's *Times*, founded a decade later. Both devoted a good deal of space to political matters but also did much more. They covered civic events; they printed a certain amount of cultural material, ranging from book notices to synopses of lyceum lectures; they reported human interest stories; and they ran superior editorials. They cost two cents and the difference in price was significant.

Those are the chief generalizations to be made about the press of the time. For a bill of particulars, plus a few exceptions, we might look at a representative of the many small-town partisan weeklies, of the respected metropolitan dailies, and of the penny papers—all for a certain day. Suppose we turn to the issue of Wednesday, September 11, 1850 of the Pittsfield, Illinois, *Union*, the New York *Tribune*, and the New York *Herald*.

"Devoted to Politics, Literature, and General Intelligence" says the banner of the *Union*. Politics receives the most space, with two columns on the first page, five out of six on the second, and two on the fourth and last page dedicated to it. The *Union*'s editorial policy was then stoutly Democratic, its pages studded with statements such as: "Here we have, from a Whig source, an acknowledgement of the monstrous corruption and villainy which has been carried on by Whiggery since its attainment of power." Though national politics, including the Wilmot Proviso, fill a good many paragraphs, the coming state-wide elections share top billing. The virtues of the Honorable John Moore, Democratic candidate for state treasurer, are splendidly revealed in an exchange of complimentary correspondence, occupying over a column, between him and the Democratic state central committee. The opposition slate gets the back of the *Union*'s hand.

Literature is represented in three short tales, with a moral in at least one. In this one an anonymous lady from Brooklyn has her story told mainly as an occasion for some obvious religious reflections. "How important and how consolatory is true religion," the account exclaims. Another, colored with clumsy humor, is entitled "A Gentle Reproof" and tells of a wife who, never able to please her husband with her cooking, finally startles him by serving up a large bullfrog. The last is an anecdote about how a 'cute farmer named Hays won a horse race with his ox.

Under "General Intelligence" comes a miscellany of commercial news and other information (mostly clipped from other periodicals), and the advertisements, including a lengthy one from the Sligo Book Store and Paper Warehouse, along with the usual notices from merchants. And of course there are the medical notices. Though occupying two whole columns, these in the *Union* are relatively restrained in tone. A substantial one from Loudon & Co. lists its Indian Expectorant, Oriental Hair Tonic, Alterative Sarsaparilla, Carminative Balsam, Tonic Vermifuge, Indian Sanative Pills, Female Elixir, Fever and Ague Pills, Certain Cure for Piles, Circassian Hair Dye, and—as a climax—All Healing Salve.

Greeley's eight-page, six-column *Tribune* for September 11 contains much less news than its size would suggest, for nearly half of the space is allotted to advertising. A certain amount of international news, mainly from England and France, makes its appearance, with most space being given to the recent death of Louis Philippe. There is also a long and timely letter on "The Present Conditions and Rulers" of France. News from Washington seems quite well covered; New York State and New York City politics are likewise reported.

The interest in social reform which Greeley consistently showed results in such items as "Labor's Progress in New England," "The Socialist Banquet at Hoboken," and "The Sphere of Woman." Culture receives a little less than its due in this issue. A half-column book review, a book notice, and a list of book-trade announcements (paid, however) take care of the field of letters. The other arts are evidenced only in advertisements or "cards" about coming concerts, plays, operas, and lectures. With one exception. Throughout the entire paper the signs of a signal cultural event, the concert to be given that night by Jenny Lind, can be found. The *Tribune* even devotes several inches to reporting on the rehearsal. Though tickets are supposed to cost $3, one scalper offers to sell a pair for $40. The merchant trade also pays its shrewd tribute to her fame by advertising such vendibles as Jenny Lind gloves, walking canes, and opera cloaks.

The ethical level of this and other issues of the *Tribune* is relatively high; but that is by no means true of the third of our periodicals, Bennett's *Herald*. It contained only four pages, half the number in the *Tribune*, but that was enough to give its public what it wished. Yet some matter was innocuous. The front page for September 11 has news exclusively, part of it—including the death of Louis Philippe—being foreign, but most is domestic.

Politics in Washington ranks first in the domestic news through-out the paper; then come court decisions, and after that a scatter-ing of items, of which three particularly illustrate Bennett's ideas about his readers' tastes. The first is "Police Intelligence," the sec-ond news about disasters, and the rather surprising third a kind of rudimentary society news headed "Movements of Distin-guished People."

The reformer's radicalism of the *Tribune* is absent. Bennett mentions the Socialist convention at Hoboken simply to call it "that nest of disorganizers and anarchists." But there is a bow to culture. Jenny Lind appears on several pages. Her rehearsal is described, her voice lavishly praised, and her concert well adver-tised. There is also half a column of theatrical and musical news, along with paid announcements of the events reported.

In the *Herald*, as in the *Tribune*, something over half of the space went to advertising. Most of it turned out to be staid enough even in the *Herald*. Medical advertising, however, readily lent it-self to sensationalizing; and of all the criticism Bennett received, some of the bitterest came because of the leeway he allowed the medical profession in his pages. Besides the usual patent medicine "cards" he ran a full complement of advertisements by sex quacks of the crudest kind. In this issue their notices cover half a column. There are no bounds to their claims or to their criticism of their rivals. Venereal disease, sterility, and abortion they guarantee to take care of overnight. And the unblushing testimonials they cite to prove their skill are remarkable. "You cured me in one day of an old gonorrhea—D. M. Corbyn" is only an instance.

Halfway between the newspaper and the magazine of the 'forties, the "mammoth weekly" reared its bulk. It had started small but soon became a big book, in newspaper form, grown so on the appetite for sentimental fiction. In the 'fifties it was re-placed by the "story weekly," which was both much smaller and better edited; but it too thrived on the same kind of fiction.

The roots of the mammoth weekly go down into the 1830's. During that decade the Philadelphia *Saturday Courier* illustrated the typical progress from a journal rather like the average newspaper to a full-blown purveyor of purplish prose. In the early 'thirties its political and other news dwindled while its melodramatic stories swelled. By the end of the decade the *Courier* bragged that it had 32,000 subscribers, some of them living far from Philadelphia, and that it was "the Largest and Cheapest journal in the world." It benefited from the same spread of literacy as the newspapers, and from the same improvements in printing. New York and Boston tried to imitate and then outdo the *Courier*'s success. *Brother Jonathan*, launched in New York by Park Benjamin, appeared with even larger pages. And Boston unexpectedly produced the *Universal Yankee Nation*—"the largest paper in all creation." Ultimately its aggressive publishers put out a "Double Double Yankee Nation," which had sixteen pages of ten columns each. This was enough to provide the red-eyed reader with 8,540 square inches of print every week.

These weeklies filled their thousands of inches with all the tearful narratives they could, plus a sprinkling of poetry, anecdote, and curiosa. Much of their material they pirated from English publications or adapted brazenly from their own competitors. The choice of materials, however, was often amateurish. The editors of the 'thirties lacked the genius for suiting popular taste which was to distinguish several of their successors. Then too, the kind of fiction which the public was to read greedily in the two decades before the war did not appear until the editors searched for it.

In 1841 a change began to take place and the mammoth weekly, for all its size, soon felt the sting of competition. A family by the name of Williams in Boston started an appealing story newspaper they called *Uncle Sam*. Its format showed some taste, and its contents were headed by the fiction of Joseph Holt Ingraham. This was the early Ingraham of the bloody story, the racy romance, and the insinuating situation. This was the man who could dash off a tale a week and told Longfellow in 1846 that he had composed twenty novels in the previous twelve months.

By the end of the 'forties the rather naïvely edited weekly that the *Yankee Nation* typified found it had to face not only an *Uncle Sam* but also a rejuvenated *Saturday Evening Post*. In a Philadelphian named Henry Peterson the *Post* had gained a new, alert editor, who made it his job to print effective sentimental fiction if he had to stimulate it himself. He sought out Mrs. Southworth, then an unknown, and promptly printed a serial by her, *The Deserted Wife*. He continued to publish her melodramatic, tearful fiction as long as he could get it, and the *Post's* circulation rose from a number so small that it was kept a secret to an astounding 90,000. Peterson attracted several other sentimental novelists, among them Caroline Lee Hentz, to supplement Mrs. Southworth. They helped send circulation up. The paper's business methods, however, proved far less shrewd than its editorial ones; after a time the simple failure to collect subscription money pushed the *Post* off its peak.

Sensitive to public taste as Peterson was, he could never compare with Robert Bonner, the genius of the story weekly, who ventured into the field in 1851. Then twenty-seven, Bonner had entered this country as an Irish immigrant. He served his apprenticeship as a printer in Hartford and thereafter moved to New York, where he quickly made a reputation as the fastest compositor to be found. Soon he began writing items of New York news, which he sold to country papers. He made enough money to buy a little sheet called the *Merchants' Ledger*, and it was this that he converted (as the *New York Ledger*) within the space of a few years into the nation's most popular weekly. For his selections, both prose and poetry, he stole from the English of course. But he also began to pay American writers generous sums. Mrs. Sigourney sang regularly in his pages, and each time Bonner sent her $10 by return mail. Through the same sort of liberality he won Mrs. Southworth from the *Post*, starting in 1853, to an exclusive contract. She stayed with him till her death, and her widespread reputation helped lift the *Ledger* to the top. In 1855 he successfully wooed that tart-tongued female, Fanny Fern. First known merely for two mediocre novels, she now established her reputation through brisk, clever little essays and sketches. For her salt of wit Bonner paid Fanny $100 per column, a price that caused gasping among his competitors. But he clearly gained rather than lost by it. She too continued to write for him throughout her long career. By paying generously for what he regarded as the best, and by paying from the start, he enabled the *Ledger* to announce a circulation of 80,000 copies a week by 1856. And this was a figure that would double and redouble; four years later the *Ledger* would be able to boast of reaching close to the 400,000 mark; an annual subscription would cost $2; and Bonner would be a millionaire.

For a decade before Bonner the story-weekly field had been strongly competitive, and it remained so. But he clearly had the edge. He displayed, in addition to his free-spending talent for attracting authors, a pioneering aptitude for advertising. He bought space in his competitors' pages to repeat a single sentence for two or three solid columns. He printed the opening install-ments of *Ledger* serials in other papers, paid for them at space rates, and then cut them off so that their readers would be forced to buy the *Ledger* to finish the story. Once, in 1858, he bought a whole issue of Bennett's *Herald* for advertising purposes. Though this cost him $2,000 it was worth it. Bonner was the Barnum of the story weekly.

But he proved to be a militantly moral Barnum who never al-lowed his love for a huge circulation to make him a scandalmon-ger. For him James Gordon Bennett and his journalistic kind held no appeal; he kept his fiction pious enough to please a Queen Vic-toria. Yet it was, in its day, seldom thought dull. In the issue of March 6, 1858, for instance, the leading serial is Mrs. Southworth's sensational but chaste *The Bride of an Evening;* it is illustrated with a horrendous engraving of a female ghost entitled "The Spectre's Admonition." Then there are a brace of short stories by Sylvanus Cobb, Jr.; a moral tale by T. S. Arthur, "Algernon the Merchant"; an installment of an anonymous serial; some syrupy fiction by Georgianna Herbert and Emerson Bennett; several homilies, of which "Guard against Vulgar Language" is one; a few stanzas of inspirational doggerel; and—the only dash of spice in the concoction—a "Fresh Fern Leaf" from Fanny Fern.

The American newspaper was a workman, sweaty, busy, and shirt-sleeved; the American magazine was a gentleman, serious, sentimental, and sedate. He made less noise, but he attracted less attention. This is not to deny that the magazine prospered hand-somely before the 'forties opened. A good many observers noted its popularity, but it was a popularity that did not continue un-diminished.

The census of 1840 counted 227 periodicals, a figure that Mott in his history of magazines rightly considers too low; the real fig-ure probably came closer to 500. The census of 1850 offered a set of unusually confusing statistics, which allow us, nevertheless, to guess that the number of magazines had climbed to between six and seven hundred. The census of 1860, on the other hand, re-vealed a definite decline: if we omit transient political magazines, the number of regular ones sank to about 575. The depression of 1857 had hit subscription lists a substantial blow. Then, as now, magazines were regarded as luxuries rather than necessities and so literature suffered. The most popular periodicals, however, kept their feet, with one or two exceptions; and throughout the 'fifties one lusty newcomer managed to grow even larger and to exert increasing influence on magazine journalism.

This newcomer was the product of the most aggressively popu-lar publishing house in the United States, Harper & Brothers. *Harper's New Monthly Magazine* appeared in 1850, with as its initial editor the same Henry Raymond who was shortly to start the *New York Times*. Harpers, to quote Mott's history of American magazines, "immediately and profoundly [affected] the whole course of development of the American general magazine." The firm's prime purpose, at the outset, was to reach through its magazine an even wider American public with its piratings than it had been able to through its books alone. The owners were frank: "The magazine will transfer to its pages as rapidly as they may be issued all the continuous tales of Dickens, Bulwer, . . . and other distinguished contributors to British periodicals."

The publishers kept their unctuous promise, consistently ap-propriating new serials by the most popular of England's novelists. Despite the fact that the United States could boast its share of noted literary men—Emerson, Melville, Lowell, and Hawthorne among them—it had not a single novelist who combined the mass

259

appeal of a Dickens or Bulwer with their obvious literary skill. Notwithstanding, native writing managed to make its way into *Harper's* bit by bit.

The most pronounced native success in the early years proved to be J. S. C. Abbott's *History of Napoleon Bonaparte*. This interminable serial, winding its way through Volumes III to X of *Harper's*, catered to the romantic interest in the same figure who had served Joel Headley so well in *Napoleon and His Marshals*. The story was attractively illustrated with woodcuts.

Mott felt that four things were responsible for the sensational growth of *Harper's Magazine:* the pirated British serials, the emotional *Napoleon* by Abbott, the relatively large number of illustrations, and an assortment of minor but lively features of which the "Editor's Easy Chair" was a delightful example. Circulation reached 50,000 by the end of a half year and 200,000 by the time the Civil War began. Such success invited imitation, enforced it in fact, but *Harper's* continued to tower above all the other $3 magazines.

The number for January 1855 bears typical testimony to the attractions that *Harper's* held out. Even now many of the pages can be read with pleasure. The lead article is a surprisingly sympathetic yet scholarly sketch of the life of Andrew Jackson. Pictures are inserted throughout; they lighten the make-up and portray Jackson, then nine years dead, in some of the many interesting moments of his life. Next comes the second-last installment of Abbott's *Napoleon*, well designed to arouse grief for the expiring emperor and indignation at the way the British treated him during his last days. Abbott, peering into the future, ends by assuring the reader, "Through all coming ages, travelers from all lands will, with religious awe, visit the tomb of Napoleon. The voice of obloquy is fast dying away, and will soon be hushed forever."

A different kind of piece follows the *Napoleon*. It is a travel essay—that alone would make it popular. Moreover, its subject is the Holy Land, a sure-fire appeal to the religious strain so evident in American culture before the war. An anecdote entitled "Captain Obstinate" appears next, to be succeeded by a long, moralistic piece of historical writing headed "Personal Memoirs of the House of Romanoff." The Romanoffs are made out to be monsters. The author cites enough chapter and verse to be convincing and to make the lessons stick. A short story follows, and before the final page of the January number is reached there are two more, plus a brief essay. But these are trivial and serve merely to set off the major work of fiction in the issue, the current installment of Thackeray's *The Newcomes*.

The special departments occur near the end of the magazine. The first is a concise, objective "Monthly Record of Current Events." Then come the "Editor's Table," which this month served up an editorial on the present prospects of America; the "Editor's Easy Chair," which was to prove the most famous of *Harper's* features; and the "Editor's Drawer," which contained a medley of heavy jokes, polite witticisms, and doggerel. The last half-dozen pages have book notices, two genre illustrations, and "Fashions for January."

Here in the magazine's 143 pages was something for every literate American, a sound token of the acumen of the publishers, and of Fletcher Harper in particular. Half again as large as most other general magazines, *Harper's* offered the public an ample feast.

Among magazines the general monthlies, leaderless in the 'forties but dominated in the 'fifties by *Harper's*, exerted the widest influence on American culture. Next in importance came a variety of special-interest magazines so numerous and diverse as to defy concise description. The two leading sorts, however, can be discerned: the magazine for women and the religious journal. The outstanding periodical for women remained *Godey's Lady's Book*. Already foremost when the 'forties opened, it managed to accelerate its success to such an extent that by 1860 it could claim a circulation of 150,000. In the aggregate the religious journals also bulked large. Nearly all of them, however, were sponsored by a particular denomination and consequently their readership was confined to its members. Because there were simply not enough Methodists or Episcopalians, Baptists or Roman Catholics to subscribe, no one religious journal achieved the mass circulation of either the notable general magazines or the magazines for women. A few nondenominational religious journals supplemented the sectarian ones but their influence failed to extend far.

The rest of the special-interest journals varied enormously. There seemed to be a particular magazine for every kind of person: for farmers, for merchants, for doctors, for New Yorkers, for insurance salesmen, for invalids, for railroad men, for teachers, for musicians, for squatters, for billiard players, for coach makers, and for many other sorts and conditions of men. Out of this welter we might select one journal to represent, however inadequately, all the rest. Perhaps the best one to choose in order to balance our picture would be a magazine for Southerners. None represented with more vigor what Tocqueville termed this "ardent and irascible group" than did *De Bow's Review*. But before we turn to that hard-bitten periodical we should glance at *Godey's* for contrast.

To open its pages is to find oneself in a world befrilled and furbelowed far beyond the fashions of today. This was the age of the elaborate, especially for the ladies. The January 1855 number (to pick that date again) prints patterns for needlework to go on collars, on cuffs, on the four corners of pocket handkerchiefs, and even on children's drawers. The styles spread across the engraved plates show a wealth of feminine detail. And the daintiness extends to more than the fashions; the fiction, the lavender-scented verse, and the homilies seem to be needleworked as well.

On the other hand, plump Louis Godey and Mrs. Sarah J. Hale, the able co-editors of the magazine, ran a wide enough assortment of material so that *Godey's* could at least be skimmed by all the rest of the family too. Like most of the women's editors of today, this duo really aimed at producing a "home" magazine. January's lead article, consequently, could—and did—appeal to both sexes. It is "The Monarch of the Mountains," a romantic illustrated travelogue on Mt. Blanc. Husbands and wives could both gain too by reading the short story after it, subtitled "A Sketch of Southern Life," which contrasts the happy existence of young Mrs. Bertram with that of poor Mrs. Powell. Because she has borne six children in quick succession, Mrs. Bertram has been spending the last several years in the nursery. "But"—the author assures us —"she does not look in the least worn or harassed." It would have been tragic for her to marry Powell, however, as she nearly did; for that glib rascal is now a drunkard whose wife must sew for her meager living.

After another morsel of fiction a charade follows. This one, illustrated with comic silhouettes, gives directions for acting out "Fireworks." The charade was perhaps as popular a parlor amusement as is our latest card game, and even the children could take part. Among the nonfiction is an article on hair, another on flower stands, a lesson in drawing, the opening chapters of a life of Cortes for children, a cluster of twittering poems ("Lilian, sweetest of maidens, stood Just on the verge of womanhood"), and a dozen more pages on frills and fashions.

The departments, less extensive than *Harper's*, are gathered in their usual place at the end of the number. They include recipes ("Receipts"), the "Editors' Table," book notices, and a potpourri, "Godey's Arm-Chair." A little humor is added for taste. In point: "We once saw the celebrated Fowler, the Phrenologist, knocked back a little. He was feeling the bumps on the head of our late friend, R. Penn Smith. 'You have the organ of credulity very large, Mr. Smith.' 'There is no doubt of that,' said Smith, 'or I should not be here under your hands.' "

A suitably ardent and irascible young Carolinian, James De Bow, issued the first number of his *Commercial Review of the South and West* in January 1846. Its motto was "Commerce Is King," and it supported the interests of the merchants, planters, and manufacturers of the South (it proved to have little concern for the West) with devotion. In the first years it avowed an aversion to politics and a modest interest in literature, but time easily changed De Bow's mind; and literature received only casual attention whereas politics gradually permeated almost every page. By 1851 he was a strong secessionist, differing from his fiery friends only in advocating commercial war against the North as well as political disunion. Throughout the decade before Sumter,

De Bow's became a manual of Southern arguments against the North. Commercial and agricultural data continued to appear but not only for their intrinsic usefulness; they were also employed to buttress the secessionist propaganda the editor gathered. It ultimately became, according to Mott, the most popular of Southern journals in spite of an annual subscription rate of $5 instead of the customary $3. Before the 'fifties got under way, its course proved a precarious one but once into that decade *De Bow's* fared well.

The issue for January 1855, the same date as that for the magazines discussed earlier, illustrates its undeniably successful formula. This number runs to 144 pages of single-column type. The arrangement of the contents is helter-skelter, with articles, statistics, and brief notices dropped indiscriminately into five major departments: "Literary and Miscellaneous" (very little literature), "Agriculture and Farming," "Home and Foreign Com-. merce," "Mining, Manufactures, and Internal Improvements," and "Education."

The leading "literary" article describes the Chinese, not unsympathetically. It is followed by a review-article headed "The African Slave Trade," whose thesis is that "the Negro has closer affinities with the brute in all his instincts than any other of the human race. Left to himself . . . we behold the animal in all his pristine characteristics—lazy, debauched, incapable as an idiot of self-government or forethought, cruel and treacherous as an ape." The succeeding article, on Alabama, displays more objectivity. That state earns praise for its growing population and its agriculture but receives criticism for its blind neglect of manufacturing and education. The department formally devoted to agriculture includes a substantial amount of practical advice and government data, along with an occasional item such as "Ought Our Slaves Be Taught to Read?" ("Is there any great moral reason why we should incur the tremendous risk of having our wives and children slaughtered in consequence of our slaves being taught to read incendiary publications?") Incidentally, this item De Bow reprinted from the *Southern Presbyterian*.

"Home and Foreign Commerce" and "Mining, Manufactures, and Internal Improvements" cast a similarly wide net. De Bow obviously knew his way around both in his competitors' columns and in the already manifold government publications. He had been appointed superintendent of the census by President Franklin Pierce two years before and was making the most of his position. Also, he had broadened his reading and study so that the magazine provided an increasingly large amount of information and ammunition for Southern commercial interests.

The final section, on education, opens with an account of South Carolina's school system. This article, like the more general one on Alabama, mixes praise with judicious blame. De Bow obviously believed that although Southern illiteracy could be excused, there was no reason for allowing it to continue—the more so because of the fierce competition of a fairly literate North.

De Bow, Godey, Fletcher Harper, Bonner, Bennett, Greeley— they seem a motley group. But there can be no doubt that they and their fellow editors managed to make a considerable impression upon mid-nineteenth-century American culture. Their vices and virtues were various; but dullness, their subscribers testified, was seldom among them.

Part Five

EPILOGUE

18
A Trio for Columbia

    ❨❩ "I regard it as impossible for any individual accurately to describe a great nation," the Scottish phrenologist George Combe said frankly in the introduction to his book on the United States. The same could be said for any attempt to sum up its culture. The foreign travelers of Combe's time were wise. They seldom tried to summarize what they had written about us; when they ended their tour of this country they were apt simply to set down the date and place of their departure. "I left for England from Boston on the 8th," they might note; and that was that.

Yet even if we cannot summarize the particular culture we have been examining, we might say a few words—as we did about the American character in "An Aside to the Reader"—which would make its essence a little clearer. To do this, suppose we consider three themes that run through much of that culture, the themes of Love, Death, and Success.

    ❨❩ *Love*
    For the typical male partner in an ante-bellum romance we might select John Humphreys. He makes his appear-

ance, it may be recalled, in Susan Warner's *The Wide, Wide World*, where from the start the heroine, little Ellen Montgomery, idolizes him. The first time they meet he stands before her so handsome, keen-eyed, and grave that she springs into his sister Alice's arms and begins to weep. Because Ellen proves impetuous and flighty, he readily adopts the part of an older brother toward her. It is not long before he finds it necessary to scold her, with her own good in mind, for the slightest misdeed. She reacts as she ought. " 'I am very sorry,' said poor Ellen, from whose eyes the tears began to drop again,—'I am very wrong.' "

Throughout the book he remains her masterful guide. Near the end, when she has gone to live in Scotland with her aristocratic relatives, he displays equal assurance in dealing with them. After he has faced down the arrogant Lady Keith, he is taken to see his now maidenly Ellen. Into *his* arms she goes this time, "in an agony of joy." And of course she weeps. A little later he looks at her thoughtfully. " 'You are grown, Ellie,' said John,—'you are not the child I left you.' " He enfolds her again and kisses her brow and lips. Then with proper Victorian devotion, he breathes a few words of prayer above her head!

Next he goes to meet her uncle, who also proves to be much impressed by John's polite but "utter coolness." John speaks "with his usual perfect ease," and her uncle is constrained to introduce him to his family and show a measure of hospitality. As the book concludes, the hint is clear that some day she and John will be joined in a highly sanctified marriage.

Such a hero, far different from today's, naturally called for an equally different heroine. First of all, it should be pointed out that standing primly behind the ante-bellum conception of her was the Victorian belief that handsome is as handsome does. Certainly the dream girl of an ante-bellum essay or the heroine of a sentimental sketch had no hump on her nose nor did she squint. On the other hand, a touch of plainness—being conducive to humility—was not considered a great handicap. After all, as more than one hero carefully announced, he wanted virtue more than beauty in a wife. Of course with proper management he might get both. In her novel *Meadow Brook* Mary Jane Holmes devised a widely admired variation, which allowed the hero to eat his cake and have it too. She opened the story with the elfin heroine, Rosa Lee, convinced that she was an unattractive child. "I threw myself upon the ground, and burying my face in the tall grass, wept bitterly, wishing I had never been born, or, being born, that the ban of ugliness were not upon me." The passing of some years does not change her mind about her appearance. When she applies for a tutoring job in the South, she thinks she fills one of its prime specifications, homeliness. She is astonished when her prospective employer, a Southern gentlewoman with a flirtatious brother, says stiffly, " 'However plain you might have been in childhood, you are not so now. Neither do I understand how with those eyes, that hair and brow, you can think yourself ugly.' " A hundred pages later, those same eyes, blond hair, and sunny smile have helped to captivate the hero; but Rosa still feels plain—and acts with corresponding modesty.

There is probably no better way to see the mid-Victorian quality of such a heroine than by putting Fayaway next to her. This bewitching nymph in Melville's *Typee* possesses all the rich warmth that the Rosa Lees lacked. She is true flesh and blood. Melville describes her with a lingering detail seldom devoted to a Northern maiden. "Her free pliant figure was the very perfection of female grace and beauty. Her complexion was a rich and mantling olive, and when watching the glow upon her cheeks I could almost swear that beneath the transparent medium there lurked the blushes of a faint vermilion. The face of this girl was a rounded oval, and each feature as perfectly formed as the heart or imagination of man could desire. Her full lips, when parted with a smile, disclosed teeth of a dazzling whiteness. . . . Her hair of the deepest brown, parted irregularly in the middle, flowed in natural ringlets over her shoulders, and whenever she chanced to stoop, fell over and hid from view her lovely bosom." Her hands were delicate, her feet diminutive, and her skin "inconceivably smooth and soft." And her dress, says Melville, was normally "the summer garb of Eden."

Married love—as evidenced in ante-bellum culture—grew naturally from the earlier relationship between man and maid, between hero and heroine. Now that he had won his bride the man became if anything more dominating, more aggressive than before. He held the center of the domestic stage. The final tableau in *The Drunkard* is an excellent illustration. There in the middle of the stage Edward, the husband, sits while his child kneels to him and his wife stands leaning on his chair. Or as the Reverend J. N. Danforth put it in *The Token of Friendship* for 1844, "Home is the palace of the husband and the father. He is the monarch of that little empire, wearing a crown that is the gift of Heaven." In engravings of the time the wife's wide eyes dwell submissively on him and he looks nobly up to heaven or out in the distance. In the manuals for the female sex such as Mrs. L. G. Abell's *Woman in Her Various Relations* we find page after page of variegated advice, but the advice to face up to an overbearing husband is never included. Coöperation and submission are the keynotes: a *"calm, quiet home should ever be secured,"* says Mrs. Abell with emphasis.

In this ante-bellum period no wife dominates her husband if he shows any manliness at all. Only when he proves weak does his wife assert herself—and then the author usually pictures her as a scold. That this nearly universal male dominion actually existed is untrue. The ante-bellum woman doubtless had all the resourcefulness of woman today; the point is that the scope she could give it was much smaller. She consistently occupied an inferior position legally, socially, economically—and hence culturally.

On the other hand, the wife as mother became the favorite sentimental symbol in the family circle. Hers was the ever-flowing font of love. "Mother, Thou'rt Faithful to Me" sang Stephen Foster, and everyone joined him in the chorus. Print after print shows her surrounded by her children, in a veritable atmosphere of love. One H. J. W. composed a poem for *The Home Annual* of 1855 which expressed his feelings in words so banal that a million others could easily have used them too.

> I bless thee, mother, for thy care
>   Born with my earliest breath,
> For faith which sanctified thy prayer,

And love that knows not death.
I bless thee for each kindly word
   When health adorned my brow,
For every tone of pity heard
   When sickness bade me bow.

In describing mother love, ante-bellum culture could indulge its feelings to the full. It almost always showed itself ill at ease in describing conjugal affection, mainly because of sexual taboos, but it felt no constraint about dwelling on the fondness of mother and child. Many a sentimental scene or passage was created, from the genre painter Lily Spencer's "This Little Pig Went to Market" to Mrs. Sigourney's sugary lyric "Eve." Such love even found its way into sculpture. In Rocchi's "Maternal Affection," for example, which the Cosmopolitan Art Association raffled off in 1860 along with the Spencer picture, mother and child gaze at each other with great devotion.

When we come, lastly, to love for the elderly of both sexes, we find a significant distinction. To put it perhaps too simply, old men were reverenced; old women were loved. The archetype of the old wise man, especially as it developed in the exceedingly popular sentimental novels, received respect, even veneration, but not love. The archetype of the earth mother, on the other hand, often earned affection for grandmothers as well as for mothers themselves. Grannies were usually portrayed as gentle and wise; though they might put on an elderly irascibility, at heart they were kind. And what they had to say embodied the maternal intuition of the folk.

❧ Death

The family circle stood for the sort of love that our culture approved of without reserve. When that circle was broken by death, the whole culture mourned. The dead or dying mother always remained one of the deeply appealing subjects to the artist, the novelist, the poet. "What is home without a mother?" asked another popular song of the mid-'fifties and the sorrowful answer was clear. *Ernest Linwood*, a novel of the time by Caroline Hentz, has a representative deathbed scene. The mother of Gabriella, the heroine, lies dying and Gabriella cries to her in desperation, "Leave me not alone in the world, so cold, so dark, so dreary,—oh, leave me not alone!" Her mother answers, with "her heart fluttering . . . like a dying bird," " 'Oh, my Gabriella, my child, my poor smitten lamb!' " The scene continues harrowingly and comes to its climax when the mother, who has known her share of sorrow, says, "And now, before my spirit wings its upward flight, receive my dying injunction. If you live to years of womanhood, and your heart awakens to love,—as, alas, for woman's destiny it will,—then read my life and sad experience, and be warned by my example." Yet when Gabriella looks at her mother's face after death she sees that "beauty and youth had come back to her reposing features, and peace and rapture too. A smile, such as no living lips ever wore, lingered round her mouth and softened its mute expression. She was happy. God had given his beloved rest."

The death of a child could be portrayed with equal emotion. The three most appealing scenes during the twenty years before the war were those picturing the death of Nell in *The Old Curiosity Shop*, of Paul in *Dombey and Son*, and of Eva in *Uncle Tom's Cabin*. Each became so famous that it entered our cultural heritage.

Sanction for death as a subject could easily be found in the works of both the popular and the great. For by an irony of literary history Mrs. Sigourney, death's shrillest devotee, was collecting a full seventy of her poems—every one about death—in *The Weeping Willow* at the same time that Edgar Allan Poe was arguing in "The Philosophy of Composition" that "The death . . . of a beautiful woman is, unquestionably, the most poetical topic in the world."

❧ Success

But it would be misleading to close a book about American culture on the note of death. It may be, as a matter of fact, that the very interest in death was a luxury that the country felt it could afford because of its own robust life. For then the

United States impressed everyone by its vigor and constant growth. Today we carefully turn our backs on death and look the older as we do so.

Success, when defined by ante-bellum mores, meant the dominating of life. Success, physical and spiritual, mental and moral, could consistently be achieved. Thus argued the culture, at any rate, and it could point to many a statistic—from the increase in the national income to the swelling of church membership—to prove it right. The literature of success was immense, we know. In its overt form, as the manual of personal improvement, it appeared in many guises and in a multitude of copies. The gospel it preached was one of free will and industry. If the reader wished, he could almost certainly gain success through hard work. As Alcott put it in *The Young Man's Guide*, the one thing "absolutely necessary to those who expect to raise themselves in the world" was "a constant, unwearied application to the main pursuit." Other things were helpful, certainly, and Alcott cited them; they included frugality, caution, temperance, and of course honesty. But the emphasis was on industry.

In token of the fact that success was more than a matter of material things, *The Young Man's Guide* includes chapters on the formation of character (this comes first in the book, in fact), improvement of the mind, and social and moral improvement.

The American ideal of success also manifested itself in less overt ways, both in literature and in the arts.

Success in the novel meant for the hero the winning of the heroine, capturing her with his stalwart attractions. For the heroine it meant the prospect of a happy, usually submissive marriage. Young love might be thwarted, on either side, early in the story but seldom if ever at the end; the number of novels that concluded tragically must have been minute. Along with the success of physical courtship almost always went material success: a prospering business, an unexpected bequest, and the like. And over and above that, a triumph of ethical and religious values. In *Ernest Linwood* it chances to come after marriage but is no less emphatic because of that. As Ernest says ardently to Gabriella, "My faith has hitherto been a cold abstraction; now it is a living, vital flame, burning with steady and increasing light." And so complete was the triumph of good in the typical American novel that evil was often dismissed rather casually at the finish of the book, having already suffered from the recoil of its own malicious actions. The sense of sin, and the preoccupation with it, that characterized Hawthorne is to be found in no widely popular novelist of our two decades. Good is, in effect, so successful that it can afford to be generous toward evil.

Success proved as important in poetry as in fiction, but in a different way. Less space was spent on actually describing success; more was spent on urging the reader onward to it. Legions of inspirational poems must have been based on the belief that the reader could actually be inspired to succeed. Though in the lyric this success would normally not be material, it would still be success. The most famous verses by Longfellow, even though they came at times out of his deepest sorrow, are inspirational in this sense. "Life is real! Life is earnest! And the grave is not its goal," he exhorts his host of readers. In a more sublimated form the theme of success made a frequent appearance in the travel literature. Dauntless men wrote their accounts of how they had explored the jungles of Africa, scaled slippery crags, or crossed the treacherous ice floe. In the arts the theme of success was, as one might expect, still further sublimated. Yet it could be sensed in the opulent summer foliage of the landscape paintings, the handsome Gothic or Tuscan houses (more elaborate than need be), the monumental public buildings, the heroic sculpture. Conversely, little or no evidence appeared of an artistic interest in the seamy side of life. The closest that American painting came to a Hogarth, for example, was in the canvases of Bingham; and he stood out as a rarity. American music was never sordid, American drama seldom mean. American culture in general was positive, open, optimistic.

A Note on the Sources

☙❧ Because this is a study of adult culture, books for children and young people have not been appraised, nor have the schoolbooks except when they had an extensive general sale among adults.

Besides the two general categories of books mentioned in "An Aside to the Reader" three individual works should be cited because in their various ways they have to do with part or all of the period to be discussed. None is recent. The first, Meade Minnigerode's *The Fabulous Forties* (1924), can be classed as social history. Though subtitled *A Presentation of Private Life* it makes a number of lively forays into things as public as political campaigns. Fred Lewis Pattee's *The Feminine Fifties* (1940) is a charming, discursive study of the literature, popular as well as classical, of that decade. E. Douglas Branch's *The Sentimental Years* (1934) surveys the period from 1836 to 1860. In its broad sweep his book covers literature, the fine arts, reform, religion, and several other elements in ante-bellum life. It represents a more substantial effort in scope and scholarship than either of the other volumes, and still has much to offer the reader even though over twenty years of research have passed since its publication. The only important weakness of *The Sentimental Years* lies in its scanty interpretation of the data it gives.

The Anatomy of American Popular Culture is, however, based largely on a study of primary sources. In the chapters about art, for instance, the concentration has been on the actual painting, the statue itself; in printed works it has been on the particular book, pamphlet, or magazine. Their provenience is given in the text. Consequently, in the notes that follow here, only the more obscure or unexpected primary sources are cited; the remaining citations are of secondary works.

In "An Aside to the Reader" I take the view that a culture can mature. I realize that I am going contrary to the usual view of the cultural anthropologist, who does not ordinarily deal in historical developments. Translated into his terms what I am saying is that in the two decades before the Civil War a culture emerged which was the first strongly to resemble our present one. To turn to specifics: Bethune's appraisal of the progress of art in America came from an essay of his which was the concluding one in a series, by various prominent writers, collected and printed by G. P. Putnam in *The Home Book of the Picturesque* (1852).

In chapter 1, on the drama, the material about Harry Watkins comes from Maude and Otis Skinner, *One Man in His Time: the Adventures of H. Watkins, Strolling Player, 1845–1863. From His Journal* (1938). The chief source for data on Anna Cora Mowatt is her *Autobiography of an Actress* (1854). For Bird it is *The Life and Dramatic Works of Robert Montgomery Bird* (1919) by Clement E. Foust; and for Forrest, W. R. Alger, *Life of Edwin Forrest* (1877).

In chapter 2, on music, the emphasis has had to be placed, even more than usual, on contemporary accounts. For there is not, to date, any good history of music in America. John Tasker Howard, *Our American Music* (1954) is routine and synoptic, with over-much stress on the classics; whereas Gilbert Chase, *America's Music* (1955) concentrates too much on popular and folk music. Nevertheless, I have drawn a few times on both authors. The quotation from Lowell Mason about democratizing song is from his *Song in Worship* (1878). Some information on Foster comes from John Tasker Howard, *Stephen Foster: America's Troubadour* (1953). George Ferris' description of Ole Bull is from his *The Great Violinists and Pianists* (1881). The quotation on Bull from the *Herald* is in the issue of November 26, 1843. More modern data on Bull are from Mortimer Smith, *The Life of Ole Bull* (1943). Rosenberg's account of Jenny Lind is from *Jenny Lind in America* (1851). Much of the remaining material about Foster, Bull, and Jenny Lind comes from newspaper items.

In chapter 3, on architecture, the impressions of Francis Grund about the condition of the workers are in his *The Americans in Their Moral, Social, and Political Relations* (1837). Jarves' quotation about Grecian architecture comes from his *The Art-Idea: Sculpture, Painting, and Architecture in America* (1864), a basic book for the background of this chapter. For the domestic architecture itself the basic book is Downing's *The Architecture of Country Houses* (1850). The quotation from Owen on Gothic comes from his *Hints on Public Architecture* (1849).

In chapter 4, on house furnishings, I have formulated my "ideal type" (in the sociologist's sense) of the American parlor chiefly from the pictures and descriptions in Downing, *The Architecture of Country Houses* and Mrs. J. W. Thorne, *American Rooms in Miniature* (1940); and from seeing the latest parlors in the Winterthur Museum's re-creation of American interiors.

In chapter 5, on painting in the 1840's, the main sources are the files of the *Transactions* of the American Art-Union for 1844–1849 and the *Bulletin* of the same society for 1848–1851. Incidental information about the Cosmopolitan Art Association comes from the files of its *Journal* for 1856–1860. The quotation from C. E. Baker, "The American Art-Union" is in M. B. Cowdrey, *American Academy of Fine Arts and American Art-Union* (1953). The quotation about a good engraving is from George W. Bethune, *The Prospects of Art in the United States* (1840). The material on Asher Durand is from John Durand, *The Life and Times of A. B. Durand* (1894); some material on Mount is from Bartlett Cowdrey and Hermann Warner Williams, *William Sidney Mount* (1944); and some material on Bingham is from Albert Christ-Janer, *George Caleb Bingham of Missouri* (1940).

In chapter 6, on painting in the 1850's, the main source is the files of the *Cosmopolitan Art Journal* (1856–1860) and supplements, with their historical as well as current accounts of art news. Wolfgang Born's estimate of Sonntag is from *American Landscape Painting* (1948); the remarks about Durrie by Oliver Larkin are from his useful and far-ranging *Art and Life in America* (1949). The analysis of Currier & Ives is based on Harry Peters, *Currier & Ives* (1929).

In chapter 7, on sculpture, the best source of information on Greenough is still the *Letters . . . to His Brother* (1887), edited by Francis Boott Greenough. Hone's opinion of Greenough's statue is quoted from his *Diary* (1927). Jefferson on sculpture comes from *The Writings* (1904), vol. xiv. The material about Powers and the "Greek Slave" comes mainly from Henry Tuckerman, *Book of the Artists* (1867) and Anon., *Powers' Statue of the Greek Slave* (1847). The files of the *Cosmopolitan Art Journal*, especially for 1857 to 1859, have the data on the Cosmopolitan Art Association's interest in sculpture. Statements about the sculpturing by John Rogers are based on Mr. and Mrs. Chetwood Smith, *Rogers Groups* (1934). Matter on folk art is mostly from Jean Lipman, *American Folk Art* (1948).

In the Interchapter, 8, the typically vague comment about how many of the books by Mrs. Mary Jane Holmes were sold comes from J. C. Derby, *Fifty Years among Authors, Books and Publishers* (1884). Much more specific is the kind of information in Orville Roorbach, *List of Booksellers in the United States and the Canadas* (1859). Among present-day scholars W. S. Tryon and William Charvat have, between them, dominated the field. Much of the information in the latter part of the Interchapter comes from: W. S. Tryon, "Book Distribution in Mid-Nineteenth Century America," *Papers of the Bibliographical Society of America* (1947); "Ticknor and Fields' Publications in the Old Northwest, 1840–1860," *Mississippi Valley Historical Review* (1947–48); "The Publications of Ticknor and Fields in the South, 1840–1865," *Journal of Southern History* (1948); and William Charvat, "James T. Fields and the Beginnings of Book Promotion, 1840–1855," *Huntington Library Quarterly* (1944–45). Tryon and Charvat jointly published *The Cost*

Books of Ticknor and Fields and Their Predecessors (1949). Other information aside from that about Ticknor & Fields is derived from S. A. Allibone, *Critical Dictionary of English Literature and British and American Authors* (1858 and 1870), which is extremely rich in figures and estimates; and a series of articles in the *Boston Post* by "Nor'wester," running from October 25 to December 31, 1859, answering the question—with statistics—about "Who Reads an American Book." The Summary of Trends at the end of the Interchapter is based on the census reports.

In chapter 9, on manuals of all kinds, the variety of volumes cited in the opening pages is from Orville Roorbach, *Bibliotheca Americana;* and the titles and authors of the books are given in his form. "The Pic-Nic" and the other sketches by Timothy Arthur which are mentioned are collected in his *Sketches of Life and Character* (1849). *Representative Men of Connecticut* was compiled anonymously by W. F. Moore and printed in 1894.

In chapter 10, on religious works, the *Brief History* of the American Tract Society which is cited appeared in 1855. The anecdote about Susan Warner is in Anna Warner, *Susan Warner* (1909). The story about Ingraham comes from the *Life of Henry Wadsworth Longfellow* (1886), edited by Samuel Longfellow.

In chapter 11, on the popular novels of the 1840's, Hawthorne's angry comment on women writers comes from the *Letters of Hawthorne to William D. Ticknor* (1910). Information on Dickens and his American publishers comes mainly from Frank Luther Mott, *Golden Multitudes* (1947) and W. G. Wilkins, *First and Early American Editions of the Works of Charles Dickens* (1910). The quotation from Longfellow on Dickens is in the *Life of Henry Wadsworth Longfellow.* Information about Lippard from Randall's *Life* (1855) is supplemented by another contemporary source, J. B. Elliott's biographical sketch at the end of Lippard's *Thomas Paine: Author-Soldier of the American Revolution.*

In chapter 12, on the popular novels of the 1850's, most of the information on Jung's archetypes comes from the essay "Mind and the Earth" in his *Contributions to Analytical Psychology* (1928). Other information on archetypes is scattered throughout his writings. Mrs. Hentz, *The Planter's Northern Bride* actually came out in 1851 while *Uncle Tom's Cabin* was being written, but its greatest popularity developed after the appearance of *Uncle Tom* in 1852. The autobiographical material on Susan Warner is drawn from Anna Warner, *Susan Warner.* Most of the secondary material on Mrs. Southworth is from Regis Boyle, *Mrs. E. D. E. N. Southworth, Novelist* (1939); that on Mrs. Stowe is from Forrest Wilson, *Crusader in Crinoline* (1941).

In chapter 13, on poetry, John B. Harcourt's Brown University dissertation, "Themes of American Verse, 1840-1849" (1952) has furnished background information about the kinds of poems produced. Its limitation has been that it fails to make a systematic study of how often the various popular themes were employed. Gordon Haight's book on Mrs. Sigourney came out in 1930. For the facts on Longfellow's great popularity as a poet we are again indebted to Professors Tryon and Charvat. The main sources in print are: Charvat, "Longfellow's Income from His Writings, 1840–1852," *Papers of the Bibliographical Society of America* (1944); Tryon's study of Tennyson's and Longfellow's sales in "Nationalism and International Copyright," *American Literature* (1952); and Tryon and Charvat, *The Cost Books of Ticknor and Fields and Their Predecessors.* The most important unpublished item is Longfellow's account book, now in the Harvard Library. Longfellow's notes on the popularity of *Hiawatha* are in the biography by Samuel Longfellow.

In chapter 14, on the informal essay, I have fictionalized the sketch of Calvin Marsh to make him in general a representative reader of the period. The estimate of sales of a million for *Reveries of a Bachelor* is from Branch, *The Sentimental Years.* For the explication of the opening paragraph of Emerson's "Self-Reliance" I am indebted to Dr. Francis Adams. The high praise of Tuckerman given by the *Southern Quarterly Review* is quoted in Allibone; the commendation by Washington Irving is from *The Life and Letters of Washington Irving* (1857). Background information on "Ik Marvel" is from W. H. Dunn, *The Life of Donald G. Mitchell* (1922).

In chapter 15, on travel books, the background information on Bayard Taylor comes from R. C. Beatty, *Bayard Taylor* (1936).

In chapter 16, on historical writing, considerable information on Prescott is from the introduction by William Charvat and Michael Kraus to their *William Hickling Prescott: Representative Selections* (1943).

In chapter 17, on the periodical press, the bulk of the figures are from census reports. They are supplemented by figures in Frederic Hudson, *Journalism in the United States* (1873) and Franklin Scott, *Newspapers and Periodicals of Illinois* (1910). In *Villains Galore* (1954) Mary Noel has recited the lively history of both the mammoth weekly and its successor, the story weekly; and the account of them in this chapter is based on her book. Background data on American magazines comes from Mott, *A History of American Magazines,* a classic work whose first volume appeared in 1930 and fourth volume in 1957.

In the Epilogue, 18, the quotation from George Combe is found in his *Notes on the United States* (1841); the one by the Reverend Mr. Danforth on home is given in Minnigerode, *The Fabulous Forties.* The picture by Mrs. Spencer and the sculpture by Rocchi are reproduced in the *Cosmopolitan Art Journal* (1859) and its Supplement.

Acknowledgments

ll To the Guggenheim Foundation and the Newberry Library I am grateful for the fellowships that let me do the actual writing of this book. Most of my research was done at the Library of Congress. It is literally the best library in the world, and without its facilities I could not have attempted the kind of cultural history I did. It would be unfair of me to single out individuals for praise on the Study Room staff or among the reference librarians of the Jefferson Room. However, I imposed most of all on the helpfulness of Mr. Elbert Mitchell and Mr. Stewart Dickson. For aid in the siting of my research at the Library of Congress I am grateful to Congressman John Henderson and his administrative assistant, Mr. L. V. Monzel.

My debt to my university, the University of Maryland, is large. In particular, Professor Charles Murphy, head of the Department of English, Dean Leon Smith of the College of Arts and Sciences, and Dean Ronald Bamford of the Graduate School evidenced their support. During three of the years I was working on the book, Mr. Harrison Meserole acted as my research assistant. He was most helpful and the book owes much to his ability and industry. He was succeeded by Mr. Irving Lowens as the job neared its end. For emergency aid in typing the correspondence that my research entailed, I was able to call on Mrs. Alda Brincefield and Mrs. John Coulter of the English Department. Very frequently there is no substitute for one's own college library. On such occasions I could always depend on the University of Maryland library in College Park. The director, Mr. Howard Rovelstad, and Miss Betty Baehr were my mainstays.

ACKNOWLEDGMENTS

My acknowledgments for illustrations are given in the text but I wish here to thank the various institutions that let me illustrate my book from their collections. For the preparation of the index I am indebted to Mr. Michael Wace. For good counsel I am indebted, in this study as in others, to Dr. Louis Wright and Professor Leon Howard. And to my wife I owe the most.

C. B.
London

Index

Abbott, J. S. C., 260

Abolitionists: and proslavery influence of Stephen Foster's songs, 27–28; and *Uncle Tom's Cabin*, 185–186; and the poets, 196

Alcott, William, 124–127, 152

Alger, W. R.: on Edwin Forrest, 16, 17

Allibone, S. A., 23, 114–115, 199

American Art-Union, 60, 61, 67–76 *passim;* founded, 61–62; method of working, 62–63; services to artists, 63–64, to public, 64–65; managers' code, 65–66; and Emanuel Leutze's work, 76; and antebellum painting, 77–78; decline of membership, 78; lottery illegal, 78; ceases functioning but influence continues, 79

American Bible Society: aims, 142; sales of Bibles, 142–143; difficulties of, 143–144; and slavery, 144

American Tract Society: output, 132–133; aims, 133; methods of distributing tracts, 134–136; types of publication, 136–137; *A Call to the Unconverted*, 137–138; sales of tracts, 139, their appeal, 139–140; and the Bible, 141

Apollo Association. *See* American Art-Union

Architecture, 38; Greek Revival and Gothic, 40–41; of public buildings, 41–44; of houses in Greek Revival style, 44–45, in Gothic style, 45–47, in Italian style, 47–49

Architecture of Country Houses, The (Downing), 46–47, 48, 56

Arthur, T. S., 120–124

Bailey, Dr. Gamaliel, 184

Baker, C. E.: on the American Art-Union, 60–61, 65–66

Baker, Charles, 64

Bancroft, George, 241

Baratta, Eumone, 100–101

Barnum, P. T., 33, 35, 36

Beauties of Modern Architecture, The (Lafever), 40

Beecher, Henry Ward, 125

Belletti, Sig. Giovanni, 34

Benedict, Julius, 34

Bethune, George W.: on art, x, 66

Bible, the: its sales and influence, 140–142; and the American Bible Society, 142–145

Biblical novels, 145–148

Bibliotheca Americana (Roorbach), 119–120

Bingham, George Caleb, 64, 73–75

Bird, Dr. R. M.: *The Gladiator*, 6–7, 13–16

Bonner, Robert: publishes *New York Ledger*, 257–258

Books: manuals, ethical and practical, 120–131; religious tracts, 132–133, 137–140; the Bible, 140–145; Biblical novels, 145–148; works of Dickens and Scott, 150–162; works of George Lippard, 162–168; domestic novels, 169–183; *Uncle Tom's Cabin*, 184–187; poetry, 190–200; essays, 205–218; travel, 221–235; history, 236–249. *See also* Publishing trade

Bookselling trade, 110, 111, 112

Boston Glee Book, The (Mason), 23–24

Bride of an Evening, The (Southworth), 6, 258

Brother Jonathan, 256

Brotherhood of the Union, 167–168

Building trade: wages in, 39–40

Buildings, public, architecture of: capitol at Nashville, 41–42; Smithsonian Institution, 42–44

Bull, Ole, 19, 30, 31; his tour of America, 31–32

Bulwer, Edward Lytton: *The Lady of Lyons*, 3, 6, 10–12

Call to the Unconverted, A (Baxter), 137–138

Carey, Mathew, 154, 155

Carey & Hart, 194

Carmina Sacra (Mason), 22

Channing, E. T.: on *Two Years before the Mast*, 225

Charvat, William, 113, 114, 198

Chickering, Jonas, 21

Church, Frederic, 64

Circulation and Character of the Volumes of the American Tract Society, 136–137

Cole, Thomas, 69–71

Colportage, 134–135

Commercial Review of the South. See *De Bow's Review*

Conquest of Mexico, The (Prescott), 242–244, 245–246

Cooper, James Fenimore, 203

Copyright: and the pirating of English novels, 153–154

Cosmopolitan Art Association, 60, 61, 87, 88; established, 80; reasons for success, 80–81; publishes *Art Journal*, 81–82; membership statistics, 82–83; ceases functioning, 83; its "critical platform," 83; choice of pictures, 84–86; and sculpture, 100–103

"County Election" (Bingham), 74

Critical Dictionary of English Literature and British and American Authors (Allibone), 114–115

Cummins, Maria, 177, 179

Currier, Nathaniel, 89, 90

Currier & Ives, 87, 88–91

Curse of Clifton, The (Southworth), 182–183

Curtis, George William: and Emerson, 216; *Nile Notes of a Howadji*, 216–217; *The Potiphar Papers*, 217; *Prue and I*, 217–218

Dana, Richard Henry, Jr.: *Two Years before the Mast*, 221–222, 223, 224–225

Deas, Charles, 63

De Bow, James, 263–265

De Bow's Review, 262, 263–265

Derby, C. L., 80

Dickens, Charles, 149, 150; his American publishers, 154–156; reasons for his popularity, 156–160; the South's attitude toward, 160–162

Downing, Andrew Jackson, 43; his

design for Gothic house, 46–47; on the Italian style, 48–49; follows English fashion, 50; on furnishings, 56, 57, 58

Drama. *See* Theatre

Dream Life (Marvell), 213–214

Drunkard, The (Smith), 6, 7–10, 272

Durand, Asher, 68–69

Durrie, George, 88–89

Emerson, Ralph Waldo: his gradual success, 205; his ideas, 206–208

Ernest Linwood (Hentz), 273–274, 275–276

Essays: Washington Irving's, 202–203; Emerson's, 205–208; Tuckerman's, 208–211; Mitchell's, 211–214; Fanny Fern's, 214–216; Curtis', 216–218

Evans, G. G., 113

Faed, John (Scottish painter), 84, 85

"Farmers Nooning" (Mount), 72

Fashion (Mowatt), 6, 12–13

Fern, Fanny. *See* Willis, Sara Payson

Fern Leaves from Fanny's Port-Folio (Fern), 214, 216

Ferris, George: on Ole Bull, 31

Fields, James T., 113–114. *See also* Ticknor & Fields

Forrest, Edwin: and English theatre, 13; in *The Gladiator*, 14–16; in Shakespeare, 17–18

Foster, Stephen, 19; his popular songs, 24–25; their popularity analyzed, 25–26; his antipuritanism, 26–27; his view of the South, 26–28; and the "softer emotions," 28–29

Furnishings: in the parlor, 51–57; of the cottager, 56, 57; of the rich man, 57; decline in the symbols of nationalism, 58–59; as sign of acquisitiveness, 59

"George Washington" (Greenough), 92–94, 95

Germania Society, 30

Gladiator, The (Bird), 6–7, 13–16

Godey's Lady's Book, 261, 262–263

Gothic architecture, 40, 43, 45–47; and Smithsonian Institution, 42–43, 43–44

Gothic novel, 164

Gould, Nathaniel: on sacred music, 22

Goupil, Vibert & Co., 61, 63, 78

Greek Revival architecture, 40, 43, 44–45

"Greek Slave, The" (Powers), 81, 92–93, 96–99, 100

Greeley, Horace, 39, 228, 247, 252

Greenough, Horatio, 93–94, 95

Griswold, Rufus, 190, 191, 196

Hallelujah, The (Mason), 23

Harper & Brothers, 132, 155–156, 221; and *Harper's New Monthly Magazine*, 259–261

Harper's New Monthly Magazine, 259–261

Headley, Joel: his popularity, 247, 248–249

Hemans, Mrs. Felicia: her popularity, 189; Mrs. Sigourney's essay on, 190–191; nature of her appeal, 191; and "deserted bride" and "dying child" themes, 192; most famous poems, 193

Hentz, Caroline Lee, 177; her novels, 178–179, 273–274

Herald (New York), 252, 254–255

Herring, John, 85

Hiawatha (Longfellow): sales, 198–199

History of Napoleon Bonaparte (Abbott), 260

History of the Reign of Ferdinand and Isabella, the Catholic (Prescott), 242

History of the United States (Willard), 236–237

Hoffman, Richard, 34

Holmes, Mary Jane, 177; and *Meadow Brook*, 179–181

Hone, Philip: on Greenough's Washington statue, 94

House I Live in, The (Alcott), 124–125

Houses: cost of, 38, 40; methods of building, 39; Greek Revival style, 44–45; Gothic style, 45–47; Italian style, 47–49; furnishings, 51–59

Illustrated Poems (Sigourney), 194–196

Ingraham, Joseph Holt, 145–148, 256

International Art-Union, 61

Irving, Washington: reasons for his popularity, 202–203; on Tuckerman, 208

Italian style architecture, 47–49

Ivanhoe (Scott), 151

Jarves, James Jackson: on architecture, 42; on painting, 64, 68, 76–77

Jefferson, Thomas: on statues, 95

Jewett, John, 185

"Jolly Flatboatmen, The" (Bingham), 73

Jung, C. G.: his psychology and the domestic novel, 171–172, 176–177; and poetry, 189

Kellogg, Miner, 97

Kensett, John, 64, 67–68

Kirkland, Mrs. Caroline: on "The Greek Slave," 97

Knill, Rev. Richard, 140

Lady of Lyons, The (Bulwer), 3, 6, 10–12

Lamplighter, The (Cummins), 179

Lands of the Saracen, The (Taylor), 230–232; on taking hasheesh, 232–233; on the Damascus baths, 233–235

"Landscape" (Durand), 68–69

Larkin, Oliver: on George Durrie, 89

Last Leaves of American History (Willard), 237

Leutze, Emanuel, 63, 75–76

Life on the Mississippi (Twain): quoted, 45, 52–55

Lind, Jenny, 19; arrives in New York, 32–33; first concert, 33–34; on tour, 35; her character, 35–36; mentioned, 254, 255

Lippard, George, 149; his popularity, 162; early writings, 163; his appearance, 164; *The Quaker City*, 164–167; his radicalism, 167–168

Loesser, Arthur: on pianos, 20, 21

Longfellow, Henry Wadsworth, 189; contents of *Poems*, 197–198; method of publishing, 198; sales of his books, 198–200

Macready, William, 16, 18

Magazines, 115; statistics, 116, 259; *Harper's New Monthly Magazine*, 259–261; *Godey's Lady's Book*, 261, 262–263; *De Bow's Review*, 262, 263–265

Marsh, Calvin W., 201–202

Marvell, Ik. *See* Mitchell, Donald

Mason, Lowell, 19–20; his religious hymns, 22–23; his secular music, 23–24

Meadow Brook (Holmes), 179–181, 270–271

Melodeons, popularity of, 21

Melville, Herman: *Typee:* his experiences in the South Seas, 225–227

Mills, Clark, 96

Mitchell, Donald (Ik Marvell), 211; *The Lorgnette*, 212; *Reveries of a Bachelor*, 202, 212–213; *Dream Life*, 213–214

Modern Psalmist, The (Mason), 23

Mount, William Sidney, 72–73, 74

Mowatt, Anna Cora: *Fashion*, 6, 12–13

Music, popular, 19–37; ownership of pianos, 20–21, of melodeons, 21; and rise of evangelicalism, 21–23; Mason's *Boston Glee Book*, 23–24; Stephen Foster's songs, 24–29; European music, 29–31; Ole Bull's concerts, 31–32; Jenny Lind's concerts, 32–36; other popular music and the singing-school movement, 36–37

Nashville, capitol at, 41–42

National Academy of Design, 79, 87, 88

National Psalmist, The (Mason), 23

Nationalism, *xii–xiii*; lack of, in architecture, 49–50; in furnishings, 58–59; in painting, 65–66, 83–84; in *History of the United States*, 236; and George Bancroft's books, 241

Nature's Nobleman, the Mechanic (Watkins), 5

New York Ledger, 257–258

New York Religious Tract Society, 133

Newspapers, 116; and politics, 250–251; increase in numbers, 251; the penny press, 252; the *Tribune* and the *Times*, 252; Pittsfield (Ill.) *Union*, 253–254; mammoth weeklies, 255–258

Nile Notes of a Howadji (Curtis), 216–217

Novels: Biblical, 145–148; Scott's, 150–154; Dickens', 154–162; Lippard's, 162–168; domestic, and the role of the unconscious, 169–172; *The Wide, Wide World*, 172–177; Mrs. Hentz's, 178–179; Maria Cummins', 179; Mary Jane Holmes', 179–181; Mrs. Southworth's, 181–183; *Uncle Tom's Cabin*, 184–187

One Man in His Time (Watkins), 4

Optimist, The (Tuckerman), 209–211

Owen, Robert Dale, 43

"Oxbow, The" (Cole), 70

Painting, 63–64; John Kensett's work, 67–68; Asher Durand's work, 68–69; Thomas Cole's work, 69–71; William Mount's work, 72–73; George Bingham's work, 73–75; and the American Art-Union, 77–78; and the Cosmopolitan Art Association, 85–86; Mrs. Spencer's work, 86–87; Sonntag's work, 87–88; George Durrie's work, 88–89; and Currier & Ives, 88–91. *See also* American Art-Union; Cosmopolitan Art Association

INDEX

Patriotism: and G. Washington, *xii*, 239. *See also* Nationalism

Peterson, Henry, 256–257

Peterson, T. B., & Brothers, 132, 156

Pianos, popularity of, 21

Pilgrim's Progress (Bunyan), 138

Pioneer Patriot, The (Watkins), 6

Pirating of English books, 153–154, 155

Planter's Northern Bride, The (Hentz), 178–179

Poems (Longfellow), 197–198

Poetry: its popularity, 188; sentimentality, 188–189; Mrs. Hemans' work, 190–193; Mrs. Sigourney's work, 193–197; Longfellow's work, 197–200

Politics: and newspapers, 250–251

Porter, Ebenezer, 133

Potiphar Papers, The (Curtis), 217

"Power of Music, The" (Mount), 72–73

Powers, Hiram: and "The Greek Slave," 96–99

Practical House Carpenter, The (Benjamin), 40

Prescott, W. H., 240, 241; *History of the Reign of Ferdinand and Isabella*, 242; *Conquest of Mexico*, 242–244; *Conquest of Peru*, 244; his style and historiography, 245

Press, the. *See* Newspapers; Magazines

Prince of the House of David, The (Ingraham), 145–147

Prue and I (Curtis), 217–218

Publishing trade: increasing business, 110; difficulties of distribution, 110–111; selling to booksellers, 112–113; publicity, 113–114; sources of statistics, 114–115. *See also* Magazines; Books

Quaker City, The (Lippard), 163, 164–167

Queechy (Wetherell), 177

"Quench Not the Spirit" (religious tract), 139–140

Quill, Charles: on houses, 44

Reading, increase of, 109–110

Religion, *xiii–xiv*; and music, 21–23, 26; and books, 132–148; and *Uncle Tom's Cabin*, 186–187; and magazines, 261–262. *See also* American Tract Society; American Bible Society

Renwick, James, Jr., 42, 43

Reveries of a Bachelor (Marvell), 202, 212–213

Rogers, John, 103–104

Roorbach, Orville, 119–120, 222

Rosenberg, Charles: on Jenny Lind, 32–33

Saturday Evening Post, 256–257

"Saturday Night" (Faed), 84

Schroedter, Adolf (Düsseldorf painter), 85

Scott, Sir Walter, 149, 150–151; reasons for his popularity, 151–154

Sculpture, 92, 105; Greenough's "George Washington," 92–94; democratic and aristocratic traditions, 94–95; Clark Mills's statue of Jackson, 96; Powers' "The Greek Slave," 96–99; influence of American Art-Union and Cosmopolitan Art Association, 99–100; Cosmopolitan's choice of sculptures, 100–103; folk sculpture, 105

290

"Self-Reliance" (Emerson), 207, 208

"Shake Hands?" (Spencer), 86–87

"Shakespeare and His Friends" (Faed), 84, 85

Shakespeare's plays, popularity of, 7

"Shape note" system, 36

Sigourney, Mrs. Lydia Huntley: her popularity, 189; her essay on Mrs. Hemans, 190–191; a bad poet, 193; method of publishing, 193–194; *Illustrated Poems:* the Historical and Religious Formulas, 194–196; her work a-political, 196–197

Singing-school movement, 37

Sketch Book, The (Irving), 202, 203

"Slave Auction, The" (Rogers), 103–104

Slavery: and Stephen Foster's songs, 27–28; and the American Tract Society, 137; and the American Bible Society, 144; and Dickens, 160; and *The Planter's Northern Bride*, 178–179; and *Uncle Tom's Cabin*, 185–187. See also Abolitionists

Smith, William Henry: *The Drunkard*, 6, 7–10

Smithsonian Institution: architecture of, 42–43, 43–44

Solomon, Abraham, 85

Sonntag, William (American painter), 87–88

South, the: in Stephen Foster's songs, 26–28; architecture in, 41–42, 45; popularity of Scott's novels in, 152–153; and Dickens' works, 160–162

Southern Harmony and Musical Companion (Walker), 37

Southern Literary Messenger, 160–161

Southworth, Mrs. E. D. E. N., 6, 181–182, 257; her novels, 182–183

Sparks, Rev. Jared, 238; his *Washington*, 238–240

Spencer, Mrs. Lily, 86–87

Steinway, Henry, 21

Stowe, Harriet Beecher, 183–184; and *Uncle Tom's Cabin*, 184–187

Strickland, William, 41

Sun (New York), 252

Taylor, Bayard, 34; *Views A-Foot*, 228–229; *The Lands of the Saracen:* on taking hasheesh, on bathing, 230–235

Ten Nights in a Bar-Room (Arthur), 120, 121–123

Theatre, 3–18; competition from England, 13; naturalistic acting, 16; popularity of Shakespeare, 16–18

Thorwaldsen, Bertel, 102

Ticknor & Fields, 111–112, 113, 114, 132, 154, 197, 198

Times (New York), 252

Tracts. See American Tract Society

Transcendentalism, 205, 206

Travel books, 222–223; *Two Years before the Mast*, 221–222, 223, 224–225; *Typee*, 225–227, 271; Bayard Taylor's books, 228–235

Tribune (New York), 252, 254

Tryon, W. S., 111, 114, 198

Tuckerman, Henry, 208; essay on Mrs. Hemans, 190, 191; on Lamb, 204–205; opinions on his work, 208; *The Optimist*, 209–211

Twain, Mark: quoted, 45, 52–55, 152

Two Years before the Mast (Dana), 221–222, 223, 224–225

Typee (Melville), 225–227, 271

Uncle Sam, 256

Uncle Tom's Cabin (Stowe), 184–187

Union (Pittsfield, Ill.), 253–254

Universal Yankee Nation, 256

Views A-Foot, or Europe Seen with Knapsack and Staff (Taylor), 228–229

Wages of building workers, 39–40

Walker, William, 37

Warner, Susan (Elizabeth Wetherell), 136; and *The Wide, Wide World*, 172–177; and *Queechy*, 177

Washington (Sparks), 238–240

Washington (Weems), 238

Washington, George: as patriotic symbol, *xii;* biographies of, 238–240

"Washington, George" (Greenough), 92–94, 95

"Washington Crossing the Delaware" (Leutze), 75–76

Watkins, Harry: career, 3–5; as playwright, 5–6; in *The Drunkard*, 9; on Mrs. Mowatt, 12; mentioned, 13, 18

Waverley (Scott), 150–151

Weeklies, mammoth and story: their growth, 255–256; *Saturday Evening Post* and *New York Ledger*, 256–258

Weems, Mason Locke: *Washington*, 238

Wetherell, Elizabeth. *See* Warner, Susan

Wide, Wide World, The (Wetherell), 172–177, 269–270

Wilcox, Horace C., 127–130, 131

Willard, Mrs. Emma, 236; nationalism and her *History of the United States*, 237

Willis, Sara Payson ("Fanny Fern"): reasons for her success, 214–216; writes for *New York Ledger*, 257

Young Man's Guide, The (Alcott), 125–127, 275

"Youth" (Cole), 71